TERTULLIAN'S TREATISE
ON THE INCARNATION

BY THE SAME AUTHOR:

Tertullian's Treatise against Praxeas
Tertullian's Tract on The Prayer
St Augustine's Enchiridion

Q. SEPTIMII FLORENTIS TERTULLIANI
DE CARNE CHRISTI LIBER

TERTULLIAN'S TREATISE ON THE INCARNATION

The text edited with an Introduction, Translation and Commentary

by

ERNEST EVANS

D.D. Oxford, Hon. D.D. Glasgow
Vicar of Hellifield, and
Canon of Bradford

WIPF & STOCK · Eugene, Oregon

Wipf and Stock Publishers
199 W 8th Ave, Suite 3
Eugene, OR 97401

Tertullian's Treatise on the Incarnation
The Text edited with an Introduction,
Translation and Commentary
By Evans, Ernest
Copyright©1956 SPCK
ISBN 13: 978-1-4982-9767-7
Publication date 5/30/2016
Previously published by SPCK, 1956

CONTENTS

INTRODUCTION

De Carne Christi and its antecedents   *page* vii
The Argument   x
The Incarnation and the Resurrection   xviii
Marcion and Apelles   xxiv, xxxi
Manuscripts   xxxii
Note on *natura, conditio, condicio*   xxxv

LATIN TEXT AND ENGLISH VERSION   4

NOTES AND COMMENTARY   82

INDEX OF SCRIPTURAL REFERENCES   185

INDEX LOCORUM   188

INDEX VERBORUM LATINORUM   193

INTRODUCTION

DE CARNE CHRISTI AND ITS ANTECEDENTS

Tertullian's treatise *De Carne Christi* was intended, as its author several times remarks, to serve as *praestructio* or scaffolding for the further work *De Resurrectione Carnis*. It appears to have been written well within the first decade of the third century, and certainly before Tertullian became seriously influenced by Montanism. The date 206 will not be far out, though it may be somewhat too early, since we have to allow time since about 197 for the *Apologeticus*, the two books *Adversus Nationes* and the brilliant essay in 'natural religion' entitled *De Testimonio Animae naturaliter Christianae*, as well as for at least four dogmatic treatises, one of which, *Adversus Marcionem*, is of great length and underwent two revisions.

Bearing on the subject of the present treatise, we have in Tertullian's earliest work (*Apol.* 21) a statement of the doctrine of the Incarnation which subsequently required no alteration in point of fact, but only the rejection of a somewhat misleading term.

But I shall first explain *what* he is (*substantiam*) so as to make intelligible the *manner* of his birth (*nativitatis qualitas*).[1] I have already stated that it was by word and reason and power that God made this world and all that is in it. Among your philosophers also there is agreement to regard *logos*, i.e. speech and reason, as the artificer of the universe.... To that speech and reason, and moreover power, by which we have stated that God made all things, we also ascribe as proper substance spirit, which has in it speech as it pronounces and with it reason as it ordains and as its assistant power as it brings to pass. This spirit, we have been taught, was brought forth from God, and by that bringing forth was begotten, and therefore is named Son of God, and God, as a consequence of unity of substance. For God also is spirit. When a ray stretches forth from the sun, there is a portion from the whole: but the

[1] But *qualitas* also implies rank or dignity, and something of that kind is to be understood here.

sun must be in the ray, because the ray is the sun's ray, and because the substance is not divided but extended. There is spirit from spirit, and God from God, in the same way as there is light kindled from light. The original matter (*materiae matrix*) remains intact and undiminished however many offshoots you borrow of its quality. So also that which has come forth from God is God and Son of God, and both are one God. Thus spirit from spirit and God from God has made duality in counting, in sequence but not in quality, and has not come away from its original but come forth. Now this ray of God, as was always prophesied beforehand, having come down into a certain virgin and been fashioned as flesh in her womb, was born as man commingled with God. Flesh informed by spirit is suckled, grows up, becomes articulate, teaches, works miracles, and is Christ.

And again (ibid.):

Him therefore whom they had supposed a man for his humility, they must needs regard as a magician for his power, seeing that with a word he cast out devils from men... thus making it evident that he was the Word of God, that is, the Logos, that primordial first-begotten Word with power and reason for its escort and spirit for its basis, that same Logos who with a word both was making and had made all things.

This statement, committed to writing by Tertullian within a year or two of his conversion, is demonstrably derived from his predecessors in the faith. It is to be found in similar terms in Justin and in Irenaeus (whose works were known to him) and with no significant difference in his contemporaries Clement and Origen: Ignatius writes to the same effect, though in more allusive language. The expression *homo deo mixtus*, repeated at *De Carne Christi* 15 (and cf. ibid. 3 *deum in hominem conversum*), was afterwards (*Adv. Prax.* 27) withdrawn as misleading and *hominem indutus* (which had already occurred *De Carne Christi* 3) substituted for it: though it is evident from the context in each case that Tertullian's meaning is the same whichever expression he uses.

The series of dogmatic works (with the exception of *Adversus Praxean* and *De Anima*, which belong to the Montanist period) appears to have been systematically planned, for as far as their relative dates can be ascertained they follow a natural order of subject-matter. The earliest of them was *De Praescriptione Haereticorum* intended to prejudge the case against all heretics whatsoever (but with the gnostics particularly in view) on the plea that the novelty of their doctrines and the recent emergence of their sects prove their falsity: for the truth must lie with the churches which are in agreement with the apostolic sees of Christendom to which we have to assume that their founders committed the true faith: and further, the Scriptures themselves are the possession of these churches, and these alone (and not the heretics) have the right to appeal to them.

The five books *Against Marcion* were published separately as they were completed. The earlier books at least got into circulation in falsified or mutilated form, and had to be revised once and again by their author. In *De Carne Christi* 7 there is an explicit reference to the fourth book against Marcion, and throughout this book there are many reminiscences of the argument and the phraseology of the larger work. Hermogenes was a painter, resident apparently at Carthage, who attempted to explain the evil that is in the world by the theory that God made it out of some pre-existent matter which was intractable under his handling: the book *Adversus Hermogenem* controverts this excursion into Marcionism by one who was not himself a Marcionite.

The treatise *Against the Valentinians* is a translation of parts of the first book of Irenaeus *Against the Heresies*. Irenaeus had thought that part of the attraction of gnosticism was that it claimed to communicate to its adherents precious and secret knowledge: for it was their practice (for which they were severely criticized by the church writers) to baptize first and instruct afterwards. It was therefore reasonable to expect that if their secret doctrines could be discovered and published abroad, a great deal of their attraction would disappear. Irenaeus therefore begins his work by describing at length the tenets of the various gnostic sects, beginning with those of the Valentinians, who were the most influential of them. With the same end in view Tertullian turned into Latin the pertinent sections of his predecessor's work, adding little or nothing of his own: even the quips and sarcasms are copied along with the rest. Somewhat later than this the book called *Scorpiace* (i.e. remedy against scorpion-bites) is Tertullian's own argument against the gnostic pretension that believers are justified in denying Christ so as to escape persecution. It appears that readers of *De Carne Christi* are supposed to have read *Adversus Valentinianos* and to have a general knowledge of what the gnostic doctrines were.[1]

THE ARGUMENT

Like others of Tertullian's works, the present treatise, along with its sequel *De Resurrectione Carnis*, is cast in the form of a *suasoria*. As a form of academic exercise the *suasoria* was a speech purporting to be delivered in court against an adversary himself present and open to attack. Tertullian, however, is not indulging in any mere academic exercise: he is as serious as the great orators were, and the more so as the subject of his oration is of greater moment. In the present instance, perhaps in conscious imitation of Cicero, he presents his case in two speeches, the *actio prima*, concerning the reality of Christ's flesh, clearing the ground so that the *actio secunda* may prove the resurrection of the flesh of all mankind.

The rules governing the construction of the *suasoria* were based on the practice of the great orators and the doctrines of the rhetoricians,[2] though it is evident that the orators at least regarded them as general directions and not as imperative laws.[3] Generally speaking, a well constructed speech was supposed to fall into four or five parts:[4]

(*a*) The purpose of the *exordium* or *principium* was to conciliate the mind of the audience, an effect which, it was suggested, could frequently be obtained by attacks on the character, intelligence, or

---

[1] See Addendum on p. xliii.
[2] See Benedetto Riposati, *Studi sui 'Topica' di Cicerone* (Milan, 1947), especially the chapter *Partes Orationis*, pp. 264–284, where reference is made to Cicero and other Greek and Latin writers on rhetoric.
[3] Cf. Cicero, *De Oratore*, II. 19. 77–83 where Cicero (or Antonius) describes the rhetoricians' doctrine as *perridicula*—i.e. as common sense dressed up in unnecessarily fine language, defining rules on a subject in which accurate definition is impossible.
[4] Cicero, *Topica* 97; *De Inventione* I. 4. 19; I. 31. 143; II. 19. 79.

veracity of the opponents, *si eos aut in odium aut in invidiam aut in contemptionem adducemus*.¹

(*b*) The *narratio* was a statement of the question at issue, developing if necessary into *partitio*, the division of the subject under its several aspects.

(*c*) The *fides quae sequitur narrationem* comprised the proof of one's own case (*confirmatio*) and the refutation of the adversary's (*reprehensio*).

(*d*) Room is sometimes found for an *amplificatio*, in which *quae pro nobis essent amplificanda et augenda quaeque essent pro adversariis infirmanda atque frangenda*.

(*e*) The *peroratio* or *conclusio*.

This is the scheme here followed by Tertullian. The *exordium* (§ 1) consists of a brief statement of the case and of its practical importance, together with an attack on the intelligence of Marcion and Apelles, who are spoken of throughout as though present in court. The *narratio* (§§ 2–16) necessarily develops into *partitio*, for the claims of Marcion, Apelles, the Valentinians, and others have to be examined separately: and, as they have to be separately refuted, the *reprehensio* in each instance follows the statement of their case. The *amplificatio* (§§ 17–23) considers in detail the scriptural texts which bear on Christ's human descent and his nativity, rescuing them from false interpretations which have been put upon them, and showing that their only conceivable meaning is that Christ was possessed of truly human flesh derived from his mother, and through her from David, from Abraham, and from Adam. The *peroratio* (§§ 24–25) summarizes the scriptural evidence and suggests that the decision of the present question will serve as a leading case for the further claim that our natural human flesh will undoubtedly rise again, seeing that it is of the same quality as the flesh of Christ which has already risen.

The *narratio* and *partitio* (§§ 2–16) form a refutation of three sets of unsatisfactory answers to the questions briefly stated in the *exordium*—*caro Christi an fuerit et unde et quomodo fuerit*. As against Marcion, Tertullian sets out to prove that the flesh of Christ was

¹ Cicero, *De Inventione* I. 15. 20. Of this advice Tertullian, in the present work and elsewhere, makes only too abundant use.

real human flesh, and that the events of his life were real events, devoid of pretence or phantasy (§§ 2-5). As against Apelles, who was not at all points in agreement with his master, it is shown that Christ's flesh was born by a real human birth, of a mother known and acknowledged to be his mother (§§ 6-9). Against certain unnamed Valentinians and Alexander, Tertullian proves that Christ's flesh was neither 'soul made visible', nor was it of angelic origin or quality, nor composed of 'spirit', in the peculiar gnostic sense of that term (§§ 10-16).

Under this general scheme, the argument proceeds as follows:

Exordium (§ 1)

Those who deny that our flesh will rise again are forced by their own logic to deny that the flesh of Christ, who it is admitted did rise again, was truly human flesh. Thus it is our task to prove the verity of Christ's flesh as against Marcion who denied both flesh and nativity, against Apelles who admitted the flesh but denied the nativity, and against Valentinus who professedly admitted both but put an unnatural meaning upon them.

Narratio and partitio (§§ 2-16)

(a) Against Marcion (§§ 2-5). The annunciation to Mary, combined with the prophecy of Isaiah, and the Gospel narrative concerning the angelic host, the shepherds, the wise men and Herod, the circumcision, and the prophecies of Simeon and Anna—all of which Marcion has excised from his gospel—are plain evidence of Christ's nativity (§ 2). Denial of Christ's human birth can only be based upon the assumption that for God to be born is either impossible or unseemly. But with God nothing is impossible except what is not his will. The question what may or may not have been his will cannot be discussed as a matter of abstract theory, but only in the light of recorded fact: and the records prove that it was God's will to be born. Even if we disregard the nativity stories which Marcion has excised, we have to admit that the fact that Christ gave the impression of being human is a proof that he was human and had been born into that estate: for one thing that is impossible for God is that he should act deceitfully. Moreover, our adversaries have no reason to fear that God, in truly assuming manhood, should have ceased to be God. God cannot cease to be what he is: and we for our part have never alleged that God was in such sense made flesh as to cease for the future to be what he was before. When angels appeared in human shape they were still angels: and the Holy Spirit remained Holy Spirit when he descended in the bodily form of a dove (§3). Since, then, the assumption of human flesh is neither impossible for God nor imperils his deity, our adversaries are thrown back upon their remaining argument. They rehearse with perverse delight what they term the filth and nastiness of childbirth, stigmatizing it as unworthy of God. In so doing they show their distaste for humanity itself. But it was precisely this humanity that Christ loved, redeeming it at great cost, having chosen the foolish things of the world to confound the wise (§4). For that matter, what can be more foolish than the Passion of Christ? And this would have been an impossibility if he had not been truly man. Marcion in fact denies that Christ's Passion was more than appearance, and that his death was a real death: in so doing he provides excuses for those who put him to death. We, however, maintain that Christ is both spirit (for God is spirit) and flesh (for man is flesh), and that he is both of these not in pretence but in truth, since he himself is the Truth (§5).

(*b*) Against Apelles (§§6–9). Marcion's successors, differing in this respect from their master, admit the verity of Christ's flesh, though they deny that it was born. Yet how could it have been flesh, except it had been born? They reply that it could have been derived from the stars, or from the substances of the upper, the ideal, world, alleging the example of the angels who, without any process of birth, appeared in the flesh to the patriarchs and others. But those angels are not in parallel case with Christ; they assumed flesh without any intention of dying, and thus there was no need for them to be born. But Christ's intention was to die, and so it was essential that he should be born: whereas, on other occasions, in the theophanies, when God the Son presented himself in human flesh, it was not as yet his purpose to die, and consequently there was no need for him to be born. Moreover, there is no evidence that those angels did derive their flesh from any celestial substance: it is equally possible that they constructed for themselves flesh out of nothing. We know nothing for certain about this, for Scripture is silent on the matter. This however we do know, that if flesh is to experience death it must first have experienced nativity (§6). The text, 'Who is my mother, and who are my brethren?' is quoted by Apelles as though our Lord were denying that he had a mother or brethren. Actually the question was intended as a rebuke to his mother and his brethren, either because of their unbelief or because of their importunity in distracting him from his divine work. There is also in this text a parable of the synagogue in the mother who was estranged, and of the Jews in the brethren who did not believe (§7). When Apelles and his like suggest that Christ's flesh was composed of celestial elements they are inconsistent with their own principal theory, that the universe was created by a certain 'fiery prince of evil'. If that were true, the whole world would be the outcome of sin, and the celestial elements, being part of the world, would owe their existence to sin: so that, as between celestial and terrestrial, there would be nothing to choose in the matter of badness. Certainly the apostle writes, 'The second man is from heaven': but on reflexion it becomes evident that he is not suggesting that there was in Christ a different sort of celestial matter, but is contrasting the heavenly and spiritual (that is, the divine) substance of Christ, the second Adam, with the earthly substance of the flesh of the first Adam (§8). So far is it from being the case that Christ's flesh was of celestial quality, that it bore such definite evidences of its terrestrial origin as to conceal from common eyes the fact that he was the Son of God: and moreover, his Passion, with the indignities to which he was subjected, is sufficient proof that his flesh was not only human, but even uncomely (§9).

(c) Against certain unnamed theorists, and Valentinus and Alexander (§§10–16). There are some who affirm that Christ's flesh was made out of soul. We ask, to what purpose? If for the purpose of saving the soul (for these people regard the flesh as incapable of salvation) we ask whether they suppose it was impossible for him to have saved the soul except by first turning it into flesh. If such were the case, it was no soul of ours that he delivered: for our soul has not been turned into flesh (§ 10). Again they argue that God's reason for turning soul into flesh, and making it into a body, was that he was anxious to make soul visible to men. This is as much as to say that he turned soul into darkness for the purpose of causing it to shine. Moreover, even if it were necessary to display soul as body, it would have been much more fitting to display it in its own body (for soul, being a real thing, is body, of a kind), or (if soul be itself incorporeal) as some new kind of body, and not as a body already earmarked as that of something else, namely flesh. It was, however, Christ's will to live a human life: and this he could only do by assuming a soul of human fashion, not turning it into flesh but clothing it with flesh (§ 11). Further, what reason was there for making soul visible to itself? It was already sufficiently cognisant of itself. The reason why the Son of God came down and took to himself a soul was not that soul should obtain cognisance of itself in Christ, but that it should be made competent to know Christ in itself: for it was in danger of perishing, not through ignorance of itself (for it was not ignorant of itself) but through ignorance of the divine Word (§ 12). And further, if soul were turned into flesh so as to be shown to be soul, it would follow that flesh must be turned into soul so as to be shown to be flesh. In such a case neither of them would be itself, and each of them would be neither. If things are not what they are, and cease to be described by their own names, all rational thought becomes impossible. But the evidence of the Gospels, and of our Lord himself, is that he possessed both soul and flesh, and that each of them retained its own characteristics: nor is there anywhere any indication of the existence of such a combination as flesh-soul or soul-flesh (§ 13). A further suggestion —made to meet our objection that their theory would leave Christ without an effective soul—is that he also clothed himself with an angel. There can be no satisfactory reason for this. His reason for clothing himself with manhood was the redemption of mankind. There can have been no such reason for him to clothe himself with an angel, for he had received from the Father no commandment concerning the salvation of angels. Nor can it have been that he needed the angel as helper for a work he was competent to do of himself, and indeed there would have been no need for him to come in person if he were going to use an angel as his agent. Certainly, the scripture refers to him as the angel of great counsel: but here 'angel' means messenger, and indicates function, not nature. It is true that, as clothed with manhood, he has been made lower than the angels: yet he never speaks, as the prophet does, of 'the angel that spake in me'; and since he never says, 'Thus saith the Lord' but always 'But I say unto you', he shows himself greater than the prophets, even though, in the flesh, he has been made lower than the angels (§ 14).

Valentinus invented for Christ a kind of 'spiritual' flesh—flesh composed of the elements of his supposed transcendental ideal world. There can be no limit to conjectures, once we lay aside the testimony of the Scriptures, which say that Christ is man, and the Son of Man. It is objected, by one of Valentinus' faction, that if Christ's flesh was of earthly origin it must of necessity have been conceived 'by the will of a man'. There is no such need. Nor is there any force in their argument that flesh of earthly origin would make Christ lower than the angels: for we admit, and Christ himself admits, that as man he is lower than the angels. 'Why then, they ask, if Christ's flesh is like ours, does not ours also rise again immediately after death, like his?' Because it has to wait until he has put all enemies under his feet (§ 15). The same sectary brings as an argument in favour of his theory a statement he imputes to us, that Christ took upon him flesh of earthly origin so that he might bring to nought the flesh of sin. This is to misinterpret the apostle's meaning, which is not that he caused flesh to cease to be flesh, but that he brought to nought the sin that was in the flesh; for in taking upon him our flesh he made it his own and thus caused it to cease to be sinful (§ 16).

Amplificatio (§§ 17–23)

Leaving now this discussion of other men's baseless suggestions, we rest our case on the fact that it was from the Virgin that Christ took his flesh, and that it was flesh, of her substance, that he took from her. As the author of the new birth he must needs himself be born in a new manner. The new birth takes place when man is born in God: for God has been born in man, taking to himself flesh of the ancient seed without the operation or agency of the ancient seed: so that Mary's faith in the divine message undid the effect of Eve's faith in the serpent's deception (§ 17). It was neither proper nor feasible for the Son of God to be born of human seed: for in that case he would have been wholly a son of man and could not have been also the Son of God. But he himself, in such a saying as 'The spirit is willing but the flesh is weak', gives clear indication of both the one and the other of his two substances, the Spirit (for God is spirit) and the flesh (§ 18). When the evangelist says that Christ was not born 'of the will of the flesh', he does not mean to deny that he was born of the substance of the flesh: nor is that the significance of 'not of blood'. What he does deny is the actual material of human male seed, which it is admitted is the operative heat of the blood. But as concerning the mother's womb the circumstances are different: if he did not take to himself flesh from the womb, it was to no purpose that he ever entered the womb: the process would have been less complicated outside the womb (§ 19). Our adversaries make some attempt to play about with prepositions, substituting 'by a virgin' for 'of a virgin' and 'in the womb' for 'of the womb'. But both Matthew and Paul and John declare that Christ was born 'of' Mary; and Christ himself in the psalm says, 'Thou art he that didst rend me out of my mother's womb'—a strong expression which indicates that he actually adhered to his mother's body and at his birth brought with him some of her substance (§ 20). Moreover, what reason would there be for his being born of the Virgin unless that which the Virgin brought forth is something of her own? How is he the fruit of her womb, unless the fruit is hers whose the womb is? How is he the flower out of the root of Jesse, unless the flower springs 'out of' Mary? (§ 21). Again, how is Christ the seed of Abraham and of the loins of David, and how is he the second Adam, unless he is 'of' Mary who is descended through David and through Abraham from Adam? (§ 22). In the case of Christ there is a special appropriateness in the expression 'openeth the womb': for the virginity which remained intact at the conception became womanhood at the nativity—which is why the apostle says 'born of a woman' (§23).

Conclusio (§§24, 25)

In a number of texts of the prophets and apostles the Holy Spirit summarily condemns these and all other heretics who deny either the unity of God, or Christ's divine sonship, or the reality of his human flesh (§24). A decision on the plea here argued will establish a precedent in view of further discussion of the resurrection: for we have made it clear that the flesh of Christ which is risen again is flesh of our pattern, and consequently his resurrection has set the norm for ours (§25).

THE INCARNATION AND THE RESURRECTION

If the discourses of St Peter and St Paul, summarized in the Acts of the Apostles, are an authentic record of early apostolic preaching, it is evident that the main tenor of that preaching was that Jesus of Nazareth, who had (as the audience could easily recollect or ascertain) died upon the cross and been buried, had also upon the third day risen (or been raised) from the dead and had afterwards ascended into heaven: that his resurrection from the dead (which the audience apparently had no difficulty in accepting as a fact, on the testimony of the apostles that they had seen him and spoken to him) must be interpreted, in view of certain texts of the Scriptures, as proving that he was the expected Messiah: and that, this being so, it must be assumed, in view of the same or other texts of Scripture, that he would come again to fulfil the remaining Messianic function of judgement: and further, that only such as had meanwhile become reconciled to him by repentance and baptism would be recognized by him as his own at his coming, and would have nothing to fear of his displeasure.[1]

---

[1] The above is the substance of St Peter's speech on the day of Pentecost. If this is not an authentic record, it would be as well to admit the impossibility of our ever discovering what the early preaching was. There are no other records to which reference can be made. And, if the apostles said anything less than

The silence of this early preaching concerning any resurrection but that of Christ is not difficult to understand. The discourses were not addressed to believers, who might have needed further enlightenment or have been moved to ask questions, but in every case to those whom the apostles desired to convince: and, their primary purpose being to establish the Messiahship of Jesus and to convert the hearers to action in accordance with that belief, there was no need, and little opportunity, to go beyond the facts, their interpretation in the light of the Scriptures, and the exhortation to repentance and baptism. Moreover, the thought of the possible, or even probable, proximity of the second Advent with its 'times of refreshing' (Acts 3. 19), would have precluded any widespread concern about the future of the individual believer: it was not until later (1 Thess. 5. 13) that anxiety arose concerning those who before the Advent had fallen asleep. The Jewish mind was not accustomed to think of any future life there may be in terms of the immortality of the soul—which was a Greek conception—but in terms of the conservation or the redintegration of manhood in all its constituents. As soon as the apostles' converts were assured of their place within the Messianic kingdom, at once they would assume that they would be there in their completeness. Christian doctrine from the beginning is not of the immortality of the soul (if that concept had meant anything at all to the Jewish mind, it might have been taken for granted) but of the resurrection of the dead.

But almost at once, in 1 Corinthians 15, we find the germ of future objections. 'Flesh and blood cannot inherit the Kingdom of God': this is what the objectors said, and St Paul admits the fact[1] but denies the deductions they drew from it. To them 'flesh and blood' meant the material constituents of human bodies with

they are recorded as saying, they can have said nothing that it was worth any one's while to believe or to disbelieve, nothing upon which a 'good news' could have been built, and nothing to justify the authorities in trying to silence them.

[1] 1 Cor. 15. 50. τοῦτο δέ φημι means 'This I admit'. If the apostle had been making the statement on his own account he would probably have said τοῦτο δὲ λέγω.

all their inconveniences and disabilities. In these Gentile circles there has apparently been no thought of an earthly Messianic kingdom with its centre in Jerusalem: the kingdom of God is located in heaven, and these material things are unworthy of a place there. The objectors (even though they were Greeks) do not seem, so far as St Paul's words take us, to have substituted a theory of the immortality or the resuscitation of the soul: they were merely uncertain of the future of themselves and of those who had fallen asleep in Christ. Stated in those terms, the objection was unanswerable, as St Paul admits. But the Christian hope cannot be stated in those terms: so long as we view human nature only in terms of its disabilities we shall get nowhere: it must be considered in view of its possibilities. Which is what St Paul proceeds to do—or rather, he has already, in the preceding paragraph, shown how he is going to do it. The body, after its resurrection, will be a 'spiritual body'—which, as the context shows, cannot be taken to mean a body composed of spirit, for in that case the present 'natural body' would need to be composed of soul. Rather will it be the case that as the body now, while 'natural', is governed by the soul and thus is something much better than dead matter, so, after the resurrection and the transformation which Christ will effect at his coming, the body will be so under the control of spirit that its present disabilities will all disappear. St Paul might not have recognized our terms, but what he seems to mean is that while the substance of the body remains itself, there will be such a change of its quality that it will no longer be rightly described as 'flesh and blood', and will escape the opprobrium which is usually implied by that phrase.

St Paul's explanation seems to have removed any difficulties of this kind, at least for the time being: for it appears from Heb. 6. 2 that the resurrection of the dead and eternal judgement were among those doctrines which the second generation of Christian believers could be assumed to accept without question as 'first principles of Christ'. Some complication was introduced into the matter, even beyond those circles in which the Johannine Apocalypse was explicitly known, by its distinction (20. 4–6) between a first resurrection, of the martyrs alone, who will reign on earth with Christ for a thousand years, and the second and general resurrection to be followed by the judgement and the establishment of the new heaven and the new earth. This theme, which afterwards came to be looked upon with disfavour, is taken up throughout the second century not only by simple-minded persons such as Papias, but by writers also of unexceptionable credit such as Justin and Irenaeus. It was pressed with vigour by the Montanists (though it does not seem that Tertullian was very interested in it) and this may be one reason why succeeding generations tacitly allowed it to drop.

That difficulties were felt about the resurrection, even in circles professedly orthodox, is evident from the solution of them offered by Athenagoras. But for the most part, during the second century and later, those who denied the general resurrection were moved not by the *a posteriori* consideration of physical difficulties but by the *a priori* assumption that material things are evil in their origin, are unworthy of God's interest and attention, and are incapable of being made fit for the life to come. This at once affects, or is affected by, two further doctrines, of creation and of the incarnation, and it is these with which Tertullian has to deal in the series of treatises *Against Hermogenes*, *On the Flesh of Christ*, and *On the Resurrection of the Flesh*. There is also involved the doctrine of the Atonement, which in the long run, though they are not always explicit about it, is the test by which, in the view of the fathers, all doctrines stand or fall. And finally, there is involved the question of morals, particularly in that restricted sense in which in some quarters the seventh commandment (and all that it implies) was and is regarded as the primary (and almost the only) moral precept: for if the flesh is not of God's creation, if it was not really sanctified by the Incarnation, and if it can have no part in eternal life, then it is a thing of no account; and in that case it seems to be a matter of opinion whether it should be maltreated with excessive rigorism, or equally maltreated by allowing it unbridled licence—for each of these views found favour among the sectaries against whom controversial works are directed.

We have said that the doctrine of redemption, in its final effects as in its efficient cause, is inextricably bound up with the doctrine of creation, and that both these doctrines are equally bound up with the doctrine of the Incarnation. If it is the case that the created world is God's handiwork, there arises a general presumption that the elements of the world, purged (as necessary) of imperfections for which God cannot be held responsible, have a permanent value in the eyes of their Creator. If it is the case that at the Incarnation God the Son took upon him created human nature in its completeness, and after his resurrection carried it up into heaven, there again arises a presumption that what he has done in himself he will also do with us, and that at the consummation of all things it will be human nature in its completeness which will enjoy the full benefits of redemption. If, on the other hand, material things in general, and the human body in particular, either as what they are or as the best they are capable of becoming, are so smirched and degraded as to be unworthy of God's interest, or even more if they are smirched and degraded in their very origins, or if the nature of God himself is such that he is incapable of any interest in them, it would follow that the supposed incarnation of the divine Word or Son never really happened, that his human life and his redemptive act were a mere appearance, that the resurrection which the apostles preached amounted to no more than the disappearance from human view of what had been merely the phantasm of a body, and that the doctrine of redemption must be reduced to the status of a parable of what God would have done had he been competent (or had he thought it necessary) to do it.

Thus it was with reference to Christ's human nature, with reference to the truth of the Incarnation, that docetism first raised its superficially attractive head, and it was with the same reference again that it showed itself in the gnosticism and Marcionism of the second century, the Apollinarianism of the fourth, and the monophysitism (and its derivatives) of the fifth century and later, not to speak of its recurrence in certain parodies of Christianity in our own times. There is always (to give the misguided such credit as is due) a desire to be more zealous for God's honour than he is for his own. But the reference could not be held at that one point. The doctrine of creation was bound to be affected, as the theorists of the second century saw, for if the created world is unworthy of God, or incapable of being redeemed by him, neither can he be held responsible for its beginnings. And moreover, if Christ's assumption of human nature was mere pretence, or was incomplete in any particular, then the redemption of mankind has to be interpreted as equally a matter of human orientation or as equally incomplete. It is by the doctrine of the Atonement, in the first or the last resort, that Christian verity stands the test, and it is by their incompetence to meet that doctrine that all heresies fall.

It is then with good reason that Tertullian, having treated of the doctrine of creation in response to the theories of the Valentinians and Hermogenes, finds it advisable to clear up the doctrine of the Incarnation as a necessary prelude to the discussion of the resurrection of the dead. His method, here as elsewhere, is to discountenance all argument from preconceived theories. To his mind theology is not a deductive but an inductive science. Its function is not to draw theoretical conclusions from universal major premisses as to what God ought to be and to do, but to discover from the evidence of the Scriptures what in fact God is, and what he is recorded to have done and to have promised to do. Certainly there is an initial prejudice in favour of the traditional faith of the apostolic churches. Tertullian is even prepared to claim that the mere statement of this faith might reasonably be regarded as sufficient to discountenance all forms of heresy. But he will not insist on that. He is ready, *ex abundanti*, to examine the records in each several case, using the apostolic faith (as he uses the thoughts, and sometimes the words, of his predecessors in this field) not as a major premiss to govern all discussion but as an unobtrusive norm or canon (*regula*) by which to ensure the validity of his own interpretation of the facts recorded.

On the subjects discussed in this treatise and its companion the scriptural data are: (1) That our Lord Jesus Christ is evidently declared, both in fact and word, to be both God and Man; (2) That since the beginning of Christianity the apostolic preaching and the faith of the Church have been that having truly died upon the cross for our redemption he rose again from the dead and afterwards ascended into heaven; (3) That the apostles themselves, with our Lord's own words to guide them, taught that as Christ rose again from the dead, so he will also raise us up again at his coming; and (4) That in the older record of God's revelation it is stated (on the authority of the Holy Spirit) that God is the sole and only creator of the world, and that since the beginning he has been preparing by his guidance of events and by the word of prophecy for the redemptive act which Christ was to perform and is still to complete; and that it has been abundantly proved that there is no part of his creation which is beyond the range of his grace and power. These facts are beyond question: but they are a consistent whole and not a series of isolated data. Tertullian holds the faith in a wide and inclusive grasp, while prepared, if need be, to examine it in detail so as to prove its consistency with itself and with the documents which vouch for it. He will do this, as he repeatedly says, *ex abundanti*, at the same time as he examines the theories of his adversaries and shows that they are inconsistent both with themselves and with the records from which they also claim, as it suits their purpose, to derive some degree of support.

The adversaries in view in the present work are Marcion, his one-time disciple Apelles, and the Valentinians. A brief account of Marcion and Apelles follows: to give a satisfactory account of the Valentinian system would entail the transcribing of the whole of Tertullian's treatise against them, or of the first book of Irenaeus against the Heresies, which all subsequent writers on the subject drew upon. Sufficient for the understanding of Tertullian's criticisms will be found in the notes on the text (pages 87, 128, 146, and 165).

MARCION

It is perhaps unfortunate that our information about Marcion and his tenets comes almost exclusively from his adversaries; but it by no means follows that the statements they make are false.[1] Cer-

---

[1] This account of Marcion and his doctrines is drawn up almost entirely from data supplied by Tertullian. Much has been written on the subject since the publication of the *Dictionary of Christian Biography*: but George Salmon's article there is still valuable as giving most of the available references, along with a far from unsympathetic assessment of Marcion himself. It is also a brilliant piece of writing.

tainly we may discount Tertullian's sarcasms on his Pontic origin, for he came from Sinope, not (as Tertullian suggests) from the Crimea: we may refuse also any suggestion (which indeed Tertullian does not make) that he was insincere. We may perhaps, but with some hesitation, accept the statement that when he first appeared in Rome[1] his faith was that of the Church—with hesitation because a developed doctrine such as his is not the work of a day, or even of a few months. In Tertullian's day a letter was extant which was referred to as evidence of his original orthodoxy. But when and for what purpose was it written?[2] Hardly, as is suggested, for the satisfaction of the Roman Church at his reception into it: neither then nor now are churches accustomed to demand written professions of faith from laymen, or even clerics, unless they are already suspect. It is true, but not for our purpose important, that in the first fervour of faith he made the Roman Church a present of 200,000 sesterces, which were returned to him when he was expelled from the Church. In the same context[3] we are told that he was twice expelled from the Church, and the unlikely statement is made that when he sought to be restored a third time he was promised acceptance on condition that he brought back with him all whom he had led astray—a condition manifestly impossible of fulfilment—but that he died before he could manage this. He had in fact, in less than a generation, succeeded in founding not a mere local sect but a worldwide society with an organization copied from (perhaps in some respects in advance of) that of the Church, a society strong enough

[1] The date is somewhat uncertain. About 130 would not be far out. Dr Salmon wrote (in the article referred to) that 'the beginning of Marcionism was so early that the church writers of the end of the second century, who are our best authorities, do not seem themselves able to tell with certainty the story of its commencement'. But it was already a menace when Justin wrote his *Apology*: *Apol.* I. 26, 58 and perhaps *Dial.* 35.

[2] *Adv. Marc.* I. 1, *primam eius fidem nobiscum fuisse etc.* Another letter is referred to, *De Carne Christi* 2, *rescindendo quod retro credidisti, sicut et ipse confiteris in quadam epistula et tui non negant et nostri probant.*

[3] *De Praescr.* 30, *Postmodum Marcion paenitentiam confessus, cum condicioni datae sibi occurrit, ita pacem recepturus si ceteros quos perditioni erudisset ecclesiae restitueret, morte praeventus est.*

to survive, even if on a reduced footing, for several centuries. He must therefore have been a man of strong convictions and impressive personality, as well as of some business ability, all of which seems inconsistent with frequent wandering into the Church and out.

It is not easy to determine at what point his doctrine started, or which was its central tenet. He rejected the Old Testament as being, though a true historical record, the work of an inferior god: but of antisemitism there is no suggestion. Many ancient heretics were deeply concerned about the origin of evil. Marcion had things to say about this, attributing it (as did others) to the intractability of matter and the incompetence of the creator. Tertullian mentions this,[1] and suggests also the influence of secular philosophy:[2] but neither of these appears to be central. Tertullian also remarks that Marcion's primary error, an error which he was the first to make, was in his doctrine of God: 'Doubts about the Son were more common than doubts about the Father, until Marcion inferred, in addition to the Creator, another god whose sole attribute was goodness.'[3] And it is the case that he postulated two gods, 'of unequal rank, the one a judge, stern and warlike, the other mild, placid, only kind, and supremely good'.[4] The creation of the world and the whole course of history recorded in the Old Testament, along with the Christ there prophesied, whom the Jews are still expecting, he ascribed to the former: to the latter he ascribed the saving of the world through the Christ whom Christians believe. And here perhaps we come to the heart of the matter.

According to Marcion, Christ appeared, unheralded and unexpected, the representative of a god hitherto unknown, an

---

[1] *Adv. Marc.* I. 2, *languens enim (quod et nunc multi, et maxime haeretici) circa mali quaestionem, unde malum*, etc.
[2] *De Praescr.* 7, *Ea est enim materia sapientiae saecularis, temeraria interpres divinae naturae et dispositionis*, etc.
[3] *De Praescr.* 34, *Facilius de filio quam de patre haesitabatur donec Marcion praeter creatorem alium deum solius bonitatis induceret.*
[4] *Adv. Marc.* I. 6, *Marcionem dispares deos constituere, alterum iudicem ferum bellipotentem, alterum mitem placidum et tantummodo bonum atque optimum.*

intruder into a world not his own, with the function of delivering men from the power of their creator. He appeared in a phantasm of a body, and it is the soul only which he will save, the flesh being incapable of salvation. His mission was to reveal that unknown god, and involved the repudiation of all that was past: so much so, that the righteous men of the Old Testament, the servants of the creator, have no part in this new redemption, which is however extended to such as Cain and others who by rebellion against the creator showed themselves capable of being transferred to his rival and superior.[1]

There is one apparent inconsistency in Marcion's reconstruction. Naturally, as the Christ who appeared by Jordan had but a phantasm of a body, there can have been no nativity, no childhood, and no growth to manhood: the early chapters of St Luke, which narrate such things, have to go, and all other references to earthly relationships have either to be removed or explained away. One might have expected the passion to be similarly excised. But this Marcion did not do,[2] though he was bound to interpret it docetically. And this perhaps is the key to the matter. The passion was too important, too deeply entrenched in Christian thought and devotion, for anyone to omit it: and it seems as if, in Marcion's view, Christ himself was so important that he must be placed in isolation from all earthly relationships, unconnected with anything that had ever gone before, independent even of the God who made the world. The name of Christ is always attractive: the exaltation of Christ has always an appeal. It might have been a matter for marvel if a new theory of the creation of the world, coupled with a repudiation of the prophets and a series of *antitheses* in which one scripture was set against another, had proved so attractive as to become the basis of a world-wide society in half a generation: but that the exaltation of the name of Christ, however wrongheaded in manner and consequence, should have

---

[1] *Adv. Marc.* I–III, *passim.*
[2] *De Carne Christi* 5, *Sunt plane et alia tam stulta, quae pertinent ad contumelias et passiones dei: aut prudentiam dicant deum crucifixum. aufer hoc quoque, Marcion.* Evidently he had not done so: the passion narrative was retained in his mutilated gospel.

had this effect is not at all surprising. And it is consistent with this that Marcionites, almost alone of the heretics of that day, did not refuse martyrdom, and that not even Tertullian has any strictures he can make upon the morals either of Marcion or of his followers.

It may have been some such considerations as these, or possibly it was exclusive and unintelligent concentration upon what are still euphemistically referred to as 'Bible difficulties', which suggested to Marcion that separation of the Old Testament and the New which came to be regarded as his special characteristic.[1] The denial of the divine authority of the Old Testament inevitably entailed a good deal of editing of the New. All those texts had to be removed in which our Lord speaks of himself, or is spoken of by the apostles, as fulfilling the Law and the Prophets, as well as all those others in which the Old Testament is quoted with approval or in support of Christian teaching. Seizing upon a certain text of Galatians (which some moderns have used for the same purpose, with even less excuse) Marcion postulated a fundamental disagreement between the rest of the apostles and St Paul, affirming that while the others became apostates to Judaism, Paul alone became an authentic apostle of Christ. Hence Marcion's New Testament consisted of the Gospel according to St Luke which (largely on the evidence of the Acts, which Marcion rejected) is known to be of Pauline origin, and ten epistles of St Paul[2]—though even here there had to be some editing, for the Nativity stories of St Luke were unacceptable, as were the last two chapters of Romans, and other isolated texts which were either removed or rewritten.[3]

The Old Testament was not rejected by Marcion as being un-

---

[1] *Adv. Marc.* I. 19, *Separatio legis et evangelii proprium et principale opus est Marcionis.*

[2] Excluding the Pastorals and (of course) Hebrews. The Pastorals were afterwards accepted by Marcion's disciples.

[3] Tertullian's fourth and fifth books against Marcion examine these documents text by text with intent to show that Marcion is proved mistaken even on evidence accepted by himself. Hence we can ascertain with fair accuracy what Marcion's text was.

true but as being non-Christian. It was still regarded as an authentic record of human history and as the work of the servants of the God who made the world. Hence Marcion was compelled to invent another god, the father of his Christ, and another Christ (the one promised in the Old Testament) who was still to come to save the Jews only by giving them political supremacy.[1] Marcion's Christ appeared suddenly and unannounced by the banks of Jordan[2] in the fifteenth year of Tiberius Caesar to reveal to mankind the existence of a superior god hitherto unknown and unsuspected, who would deliver them from the inflictions imposed upon them by their Creator. This Christ possessed but a phantasm of a body, for of course it was impossible for him to make use of the works of the Creator—though, as Tertullian points out, Marcion himself did not consistently follow out this principle, for he still used the Creator's water for baptizing and the Creator's bread and water for the eucharist, as well as the Creator's land to kneel upon. Docetism, however, is of the essence of this system,[3] extending in a sense even to the Passion, for Marcion's Christ possessed no body which could suffer, though he did (apparently) suffer in himself from the indignities to which the Creator's servants subjected him. Marcion adopted from St Paul (Eph. 4. 9) the doctrine of the descent into hell—a non-corporeal descent, of course—so that the gospel was preached even to the dead, with the result that the good men of the Old Testament (Noah, Abraham, and others), being satisfied with their own God, rejected this newcomer, whereas the bad men (Cain, the men of Sodom, and so forth), being already in rebellion against their own

---

[1] *Adv. Marc.* I. 19, *cum ea separatio legis et evangelii ipsa sit quae alium deum evangelii insinuaverit adversus deum legis.* It is to be observed that Tertullian consistently speaks of the Creator as the true God, and of Marcion's *deus snperior* as no god at all. He will not even address the latter by the proper vocative *deus*, but (as if the word were a proper noun, the name of an idol) as *dee* (*Adv. Marc.* I. 29).

[2] Or, according to another version, 'came down' to Capurnaum (Luke 4. 31), all reference to Nazareth being omitted.

[3] *De Carne Christi* I, τῷ δοκεῖν, which evidently is not part of Tertullian's refutation, but was a principle insisted upon by Marcion himself.

God, received the gospel and were saved. The resurrection appearances of this Christ were also docetic, though no more so than his previous appearances: eventually the phantasm of a body disappeared into the nothingness from whence it came. It follows from this—*immo praecedebat*—that the salvation of mankind is of the soul only: or, as it is sometimes more accurately put, of the spirit—for the soul is the breath of life breathed into Adam by the Creator, whereas the spirit was secretly breathed in by the 'superior god' without the knowledge of anyone but himself.

Marcion's doctrines were apparently for the most part disseminated by word of mouth. He had composed a book entitled *Antitheses*: we have no precise knowledge of its contents, but it may well have consisted of series of opposing texts calculated to illustrate the opposition of the Old Testament to the New. It seems as if the strongest weapon of the Marcionites was exposition of the Scriptures in the sense of their own views. Tertullian's answer to them, the five books *Against Marcion*, is a brilliant presentation of the case for the other side. These may owe something to a book which Irenaeus at least intended to write (whether he did or not, is uncertain); but most of them are evidently pure Tertullian, always at his most forcible, sometimes at his best, and only occasionally at his worst. If anyone were ever persuaded by argument, this work might have had that effect: there is no reason for supposing that it did not check the growth of the sect. Neither Marcion nor Tertullian could have been expected to know of the modern doctrine of progressive revelation. Both of them were aware (at least from St Paul, Galatians 4. 21–26, which Marcion had not excised, though he had altered it a little[1]) of the allegorical method. Tertullian uses it, but only sparingly, and never transgressing the bounds of good sense: Marcion apparently used it, not to resolve the difficulties of the Old Testament, but to impugn the historicity of inconvenient passages in the Gospel.

It has been asked whether Marcion is to be counted as one of the gnostics. He was apparently acquainted at one time with

---

[1] *Adv. Marc.* v. 4, *Marcionem novissimam Abrahae mentionem dereliquisse, nulla magis auferenda, etsi ex parte convertit.*

INTRODUCTION   xxxi

Valentinus[1] but borrows none of his speculations. His doctrine of the hitherto unknown god is broadly different from the essentially unknown god of the gnostic schools. He is a docetist, but in a different sense from theirs. His Creator is not a misguided demigod, but a real God whom he misrepresents. But, most of all, his gospel is not one of salvation by knowledge but of salvation by faith, albeit in a merely phantasmal Christ, and this alone would set him apart from them all.

APELLES

Concerning Apelles not so much is known.[2] He was a disciple of Marcion, but left (or was expelled from) the Marcionite society. The suggestion of incontinence as the reason for his expulsion may rest on a misconception: in any case it is one so commonly preferred by ancient controversial writers against their adversaries that it may be safely disregarded.[3] Apelles apparently, having been associated with Marcion in Rome, withdrew to Alexandria, where he developed his doctrine, a modified Marcionism, which (according to Tertullian) admitted that Christ possessed true human flesh but continued to deny the nativity.[4] At some period, apparently late in his career, he attached himself to a clairvoyant girl named Philumena who claimed (or was reputed) to be possessed by an 'angel', who communicated to her revelations (φανερώσεις) which were written down and read in public by Apelles. Apelles' own book was entitled συλλογισμοί, 'reasonings'—though the word itself suggests that Apelles may have

[1] *De Carne Christi* 1.
[2] The facts are collected and discussed in the article by Dr Hort in *D.C.B.*
[3] *De Praesc.* 30, *Si et Apellis stemma retractandum est, tam non vetus et ipse quam Marcion institutor et praeformator eius, sed lapsus in feminam desertor continentiae Marcionensis ab oculis sanctissimi magistri Alexandriam secessit. inde post annos regressus non melior, nisi tantum quia iam non Marcionites, in alteram feminam impegit, illam virginem Philumenen quam supra edidimus* (§6)...*cuius energemate circumventus quae ab ea didicit Phaneroses scripsit.*
[4] *Adv. Marc.* III. 11, *Nam et Philumene illa magis persuasit Apelli ceterisque desertoribus Marcionis ex fide quidem Christum circumtulisse carnem, nullius tamen nativitatis, utpote de elementis eam mutuatum.*

attempted to resolve some of the ἀντιθέσεις proposed by Marcion. We last hear of him as resident at Rome, very old and quiet, and disliking controversy, in the last decade of the second century.

Tertullian had written a treatise against the Apelleasts, which has not survived. He refers to a theory of theirs that flesh was constructed for seduced souls by a certain 'fiery prince of evil'.[1] This has a gnostic sound and would indicate that Apelles held a theory of creation nearer to that of Basilides or Valentinus than was Marcion's theory as elsewhere described by Tertullian, though not unlike the Marcionite mythology described by Esnig.[2] There seems a possibility that this mythology was that of the later Marcionites, inherited not from Marcion but from Apelles: and again a possibility that the serpent-worshipping Marcionites converted by Theodoret and the serpent-worshipping Yezidis who (at least until about 1918) lived in the neighbourhood of Mosul had preserved a distorted version of that doctrine—as if one should say, 'This is the god who is capable of doing harm, and therefore the one who had better be kept in a good temper.' Apelles himself, whatever his theories, seems to have been a less formidable opponent than his master.

MANUSCRIPTS

For the information (as distinct from the opinions) recorded in this note the editor is indebted to the second volume of the second part of Tertullian's works by Aemilius Kroymann (mentioned below), and to the preface to Tertullian's works in *Corpus Christianorum* (1953), the writer of which is unnamed.

The text of *De Carne Christi* depends on the testimony of three groups of authorities, as follows:

I *Codex Agobardinus* [A], of the ninth century, now at Paris (B.N. fonds latin 1622), formerly the property of Agobard, Bishop of Lyons (816–840). This, in its now mutilated state,

---
[1] *De Carne Christi* 8 and *De Anima* 23 (quoted on page 122).
[2] For which see Salmon's article on Marcion in *D.C.B.*, pp. 821, 822, and the reference to Neumann's translation from the Armenian there given.

contains thirteen treatises of Tertullian. It seems to be the only representative of a larger collection of Tertullian's works compiled perhaps as early as the fifth century. No other extant manuscript seems to have been copied from this. Of the present treatise it contains only chapters 1–9 and part of 10.

II A group of manuscripts, apparently first- or second-hand copies of a codex (now lost) which was at Cluny in the eleventh century and itself seems to represent a collection of twenty-one treatises, made in Spain, perhaps under the direction of St Isidore, Bishop of Seville (600–636). Most extant manuscripts are of this group. Its most important representatives are

> Montepessulanus [M] (Montpellier H 54) of the eleventh century.
> Paterniacensis [P] (Schlettstadt 439), also of the eleventh century.
> Magliabechianus [F] (Florence conv. soppr. I. vi. 9) of the fifteenth century (1426).
> Magliabechianus [N] (Florence conv. soppr. I. vi. 10) of the fifteenth century.

These last two appear to be copies of two now lost manuscripts of the Cluny group, both of which were known to Beatus Rhenanus and were used by him in his first and third editions (1521, 1539).

III *Codex Trecensis* [T] (Troyes 523) formerly at Clairvaux, itself of the twelfth century and the only extant representative of a collection of five treatises made apparently in the fifth century, possibly (it is suggested) by Vincent of Lérins. This manuscript has only recently come to light, having been discovered by Dom Wilmart in 1916, though it or some of its kindred were known to Martin Mesnart (1545) who records some of its readings, and (it seems) to the copyists of the otherwise valueless manuscripts quoted by Oehler as Leidensis and Luxemburgensis.

The older editions were based for the most part on manuscripts of the Cluny group, which it was easy enough, when need arose, to check by reference to Agobardinus. The discovery of Trecensis complicated matters, throwing doubt on readings which might otherwise have been considered satisfactory: and it was natural enough that the greatest possible weight should be given to an authority newly come to light. Aemilius Kroymann, in the most recent edition [*C.S.E.L.* vol. LXX, 1942] observes with truth that it most frequently supports Agobardinus when it differs from the Cluny group: and this creates a presumption in favour of Trecensis against the others when Agobardinus fails. It is however obvious that at least two, and perhaps all three, of these sets of authorities have passed under an editorial hand, possibly the hand of the fifth-century scholars who collected the works: and the present editor (*quamvis nullius maxime loci homo*) is bound to confess that his own impression is that a very large number of the readings of Trecensis come from the hand of an editor who (with a good knowledge of Tertullian's style) wrote down what he thought the author was likely to have written in preference to what the evidence was that he did write. Among other things, having observed that Tertullian usually refers to God the Father as *deus* and to God the Son as *dominus*, the editor of Trecensis alters *deus* to *dominus* in several instances where it rightly and naturally is used of our Lord. He also, on occasion, seems to accommodate scriptural quotations to the text with which he was familiar.

The text here presented cannot in the nature of things claim to be definitive: possibly we never shall attain to a definitive text, though there remain very few places where doubt about the text involves any serious doubt about Tertullian's meaning. Let it be said here that in no serious case has the reading of Trecensis been rejected without careful consideration and for reasons which are given in the notes. The manuscript readings throughout the book are quoted (with this grateful acknowledgement) from Kroymann's *apparatus criticus*. Kroymann has suggested also a considerable number of readings of his own, some of which he has incorporated into his text: he has also proposed in a number of places a revised punctuation, where occasionally the same expedient had occurred to me independently. With many of Kroymann's new readings I have to my regret found myself unable to agree: my hope is that I have expressed my disagreement with that deference and courtesy which is due to a scholar who was already an expert on this subject while I was still a child.

NOTE ON 'NATURA', 'CONDITIO', 'CONDICIO'

In my edition of *Adversus Praxean* I discussed the meaning of *substantia* (pages 39–45) and *status* (pages 50–52), suggesting that the former is indicated by the existential verb, while the latter represents the copula in so far as it attaches attributes which are permanent, and constitute the *natura* of the object. I did not discuss the meaning of *natura*, because in that work Tertullian himself avoids using the word: that omission I propose now to rectify. In the same work (pages 201, 280) I referred to *conditio* and *condicio*, suggesting that they are often confused in the manuscripts and that the former means creation, while the latter means attributes in some sense dependent on the *status* of the object. I now think that, though there is some confusion in the manuscripts, this is not so common as I then supposed, and that Tertullian in any case used the words with care: and I shall suggest that *conditio* refers to the same set of facts as *status* and *natura* (that is, to attributes which pertain to an object as it is in itself), while *condicio* refers to attributes accruing to an object by virtue of its relation to things outside itself.

Natura

Adv. Hermog. 43. Nam de natura materiae quoties cadas accipe. supra dicis, Si autem esset materia natura mala non accepisset translationem in melius, nec deus aliquid compositionis accommodasset illi: in vacuum enim laborasset. finisti igitur duas sententias, nec materiam natura malam, nec naturam eius a deo potuisse converti, horum immemor postea inferens, At ubi accepit compositionem a deo et ornata est, cessavit a natura. Si in bonum reformata est, utique de malo reformata est, et si per compositionem dei cessavit a natura, ⟨a⟩ mali natura cessavit: ergo et mala fuit natura ante compositionem, et desinere potuit a natura post reformationem.

The last sentence is unintelligible in Oehler's text. The above punctuation is mine, as is the insertion of *a* before *mali*.

For observe how often you trip up regarding the nature of that pre-existent matter. First of all you say, 'But if matter had been by nature evil it would not have been capable of change for the better, nor could God have succeeded in giving shape to its formlessness: for his labour would have been in vain.' Here you lay down two propositions, that matter is not by nature evil, and that if it had been it would have been impossible for God to change its nature: and then, forgetting this, you conclude, 'But when it received at God's hands its form and ornament it relinquished its nature.' If the transformation which took place was into goodness, evidently it was a transformation out of evil: and if by God's handling of it it relinquished its nature, it was a nature of evil which it relinquished. Consequently, before God's handling of it it was by nature evil and there was no impossibility of its receding from its nature as a result of transformation.

Apparently *natura* here represents the Aristotelian φύσις both in its instrumental and in its attributive sense. We could hardly, in the present context, follow Aristotle in giving the word a genetic meaning,[1] for the pre-existent matter of which Hermogenes supposed that God had created the world is *ex hypothesi* without beginning and (until the creation) its *natura* was always what it was. The same observation will hold when we come to consider *natura dei*: *natura* is necessarily permanent. We may suppose then that the *natura* of an object is the asemblage of those qualities which it possesses by virtue of its being what it is: or, correcting ourselves slightly, we might suggest that if the *status* of an object is that assemblage of qualities which make it what it is, its *natura* will be those qualities which make it such as it is. So that, if it were to change its nature and acquire a different set of qualities, it would also change its status and become a different object and acquire a different name (as Tertullian says of *argilla* and *testa*, §13): it would also in the process become a different *substantia*, i.e. another thing altogether.

Secondly, we observe that attributes are only natural if they really belong, in the closest sense in which a person or thing is capable of having belongings.

---

[1] Aristotle, *Metaphysics*, Δ, 4, φύσις λέγεται ἕνα μὲν τρόπον ἡ τῶν φυομένων γένεσις, οἷον εἴ τις ἐπεκτείνας λέγοι τὸ υ, κτέ.

Adv. Marc. II. 6. Ut ergo bonum iam suum haberet homo emancipatum sibi a deo et fieret proprietas iam boni in homine et quodammodo natura, de institutione adscripta est illi quasi libripens emancipati a deo boni libertas et potestas arbitrii, quae efficeret bonum ut proprium iam sponte praestari ab homine.

Free paraphrase will here be more intelligible than translation. It was God's intention that man should be possessed of goodness: and this goodness (which must in any case be God's gift) must be not merely conferred upon man from without but must be his very own. The Roman law of conveyancing affords a parallel which is more or less (*quasi*) to the point. A property is transferred from one person to another (e.g. from a testator to his assigns) by the formality of *mancipatio*, there taking place a fictitious sale in the presence of five witnesses and of the *libripens* who holds the balance in which there is a pretence of weighing the price, in effect the mere token of a price which is not actually paid.[1] In the case of man and his goodness the donor is God, while the *libripens* is liberty and the power of free choice (which itself is God's gift *de institutione*, by virtue of creation): and in consequence man is capable of possessing and exercising as his own (*emancipatum sibi*) that goodness which is in its origin an attribute of God. Goodness thus becomes man's *proprietas et quodammodo natura*, he himself possesses it and is credited with it.

Adv. Marc. I. 22. Tertullian is arguing that if Marcion's god had really been God and had been good he would not have waited so long to redeem the world which, Marcion alleges, was created bad or at least imperfect.

For death already existed, and so did the sting of death, which is sin: so also did that malice of the creator, against which it was incumbent upon the goodness of that other god to come to the rescue. For thus it would have satisfied this first rule of divine goodness, proving itself a natural goodness by coming to the rescue immediately the need arose. For in God all attributes must needs be natural and congenital (*naturalia et ingenita*), for thus only will they be eternal, as God himself permanently is (*secundum statum ipsius*): otherwise they must be reckoned

---

[1] See the Dictionary of Greek and Roman Antiquities, s.v. *mancipium*, and Ramsay's *Roman Antiquities*, pages 302, 304.

contingent and extraneous, and consequently temporal, the opposite of eternal (*aeternitatis aliena*). Thus we must postulate in God a goodness that is perennial and ever-flowing, such as, being laid up in the treasuries of those natural attributes which are characteristically his (*in thesauris naturalium proprietatum reposita*) might be in existence previous to the causes and occasions of its exercise, so as to take up each one of these as it arose and (seeing it was there beforehand) might be neither too proud nor too remiss to deal with them. So then, my present question, why his goodness has not been in operation since the very beginning, is no less justified than my earlier question why he has not been revealing himself since the beginning: because of course it was by the exercise of his goodness that he ought to have been revealed, provided he existed at all. It is inconceivable that God should lack the power for any act, especially for the exercise of his natural attributes (*nedum naturalibus suis fungi*): for if these are restrained from having free course they cannot be natural. For neither has nature itself any leisure from itself (*et otium enim sui natura non novit*): by its activities it is known for what it is. Consequently there can be no suggestion that it was on his nature's account (*naturae nomine*) that he refused for a time to exercise his goodness: for nature is incapable of refusing itself (*natura enim se non potest nolle*), for it so conducts itself that if it refrains from action it ceases to be (*ut si cessaverit non sit*). But in the case of Marcion's god there has been a time when goodness has refrained from work: and it follows that that goodness was not natural which was for a time capable of refraining—for with natural attributes this is impossible. Also, as it cannot be natural, so must we conclude that it cannot be eternal: nor is it coeval with God, because it is not eternal as not being natural: and thus, in fact, it neither establishes its own perpetuity as regards the past nor vouches for it as regards the future.

I recapitulate. The goodness of God, like all his attributes (*naturalia*), is governed by the law of his eternity. It must needs be natural and congenital (*naturalis et ingenita*). The latter term (which does not here mean 'unbegotten') is hardly suitable for this context, but appears to be used because in general, in others than God, what is natural is *ingenitum*. The goodness of God must be eternal, *secundum statum ipsius*, and therefore *par deo*, coeval with God: it gives proof of its perpetuity in the past and promise of it for the future. Will it then follow that the *natura* of any person or object is *ingenita*, coeval with that person or object? With human goodness this may be the case; it is only because *libertas et potestas arbitrii* has failed to convey moral apprehension and possession of this natural gift that it has not become part of human *status*, has failed to give evidence of itself in the past, and cannot be sure of its future.

Conditio

I have suggested that *substantia*, *status*, and *natura* stand for the object itself as what it is in itself, in its essential being, and in its essential attributes. I further suggest that *conditio* will be found to refer to the same set of facts, but with the implied suggestion that a thing is what it is, is such as it is, and has those attributes which make it such as it is, because God made it so and it cannot be otherwise. This, it will seem, involves a certain necessary limitation, as in the two following examples:

Adv. Marc. I. 3, quantum humana conditio de deo definire potest.
Ibid. III. 6, humana conditio deceptui obnoxia.

But there are occasions when *conditio* refers to God, with whom there can be no question of creation, though perhaps of limitations imposed not by fact but by logic:

Adv. Marc. III. 6 (continued): non negans enim filium et spiritum et substantiam creatoris esse Christum eius, concedas necesse est eos qui patrem non agnoverint nec filium agnoscere posse per eiusdem substantiae conditionem, cuius si plenitudo intellecta non est, multo magis portio, certe qua plenitudinis consors.

There are of course numberless instances where *conditio* means 'creation', often as a verbal noun, and not infrequently as a concrete substantive: e.g. *Adv. Marc.* I. 15, *cum dixeris esse et illi* (i.e. Marcion's superior god) *conditionem suam et suum mundum et suum caelum*. An interesting example, which seems to combine both senses, comes from

Adv. Marc. II. 6: ceterum facile est offendentes statim in hominis ruinam antequam conditionem eius inspexerint, in auctorem referre quod accidit quia nec auctoris perspecta sit ratio.

Otherwise, it is easy to take immediate offence at man's ruin, through not having previously considered in what state he was created, and thus to discredit his Creator with what has occurred, because there has also been failure to appreciate what the Creator had in mind.

Here *hominis conditio* means man as God created him, but with special reference to those attributes with which he was created, particularly the possession of *libertas et potestas arbitrii*, the grant of which was a necessary consequence of the *bonitas et ratio dei*, God's goodness expressing itself both in fact and intention. *Conditio* means both the act of creation and 'that state in which he was created'—which gives us both *natura* and *status*.

Condicio

My suggestion is that *condicio*, when it refers to attributes, implies such of them as depend upon, or affect, external relationships. There seems to be frequently a retention, express or implied, of the original sense of contingency.

Adv. Marc. II. 5 (a Marcionite argument): Si enim et bonus, qui evenire tale quid nollet, et praescius, qui eventurum non ignoraret, et potens, qui depellere valeret, nullo modo evenisset quod sub his tribus condicionibus divinae maiestatis evenire non posset.

If the Creator had been at once good and prescient and powerful, the fall would never have taken place.

Here evidently the three *condiciones* are those stated in the three conditional clauses of the protasis. But they are more than that, for they are *condiciones divinae maiestatis*, attributes of God in relation to his creation: so shortly afterwards we have, *istas species . . . bonitatem et praescientiam et potentiam*.

Adv. Marc. II. 22, condicionalem idcirco et rationalem demonstravit recusationem eorum quae administranda praescripserat.

By saying 'your feasts', 'your solemn assemblies', God showed that his refusal to accept devotions which the Law prescribed was contingent upon Israelite misuse of them.

Also *Adv. Marc.* IV. 19, heretics 'condicionales et rationales (voces) simplicitatis condicione dissolvunt'—'statements made under special conditions and for specific reasons are misinterpreted under pretence of universalizing them'.

We now come to passages where the reference is to attributes, divine or human, which are contingent upon, or are exemplified in, relationship.

Adv. Marc. I. 7: ita ego non nomini dei, nec sono nec notae nominis huius, summum magnum in creatore defendo, sed ipsi substantiae cui nomen hoc contigit. hanc inveniens solam innatam infectam, solam aeternam et universitatis conditricem, non nomini sed statui, nec appellationi sed condicioni eius, summum magnum et adscribo et vindico.

Tertullian is arguing that the concept *summum magnum*, that than which nothing greater is conceivable, is applicable to the Creator alone, i.e. the true God, as distinguished from the supposititious good god invented by Marcion. It is true, he admits, that the term *deus* is a common noun, used not only for heathen gods but even in Scripture for men who are not gods at all. But this gives Marcion no right both to concede that the Creator is a god and to claim that there is also another god of a superior sort. We are not arguing about the word *deus*, either spoken or written, but about the *substantia*, the real entity, to which that term applies: and this entity is the only one which is known to be unbegotten and uncreated, alone is eternal and the creator of the universe, so that we lay claim to the concept *summum magnum* not for the name of that Entity but for his *status*, his attributes considered as his own, and not for his designation but for his *condicio*, his attributes considered in relation to all over which he is *summum magnum*.

So again *Adv. Marc.* I. 3, quae erit iam condicio ipsius summi magni? nempe ut nihil illi adaequetur, id est ut non sit aliud summum magnum.

Now of human relationships:

Adv. Marc. I. 24, alia est nostra condicio apud auctorem, apud iudicem, apud offensum principem generis.

Marcion claims to have been delivered by his good god from the power of the Creator: but the fact that he is still subject to disease and discomfort and to irritation from gnats and lice (all of which he blames the Creator for) shows that he has not been delivered but is still in bondage. We, however, approach the subject from another aspect, and stand in a different relation, not of bondage, to the Creator who is our maker and our judge, the begetter of our race, whom we have offended: that is to say, we suffer from the same things, but on different terms (*alia condicio*), because we know that redemption is a process in us, not a mere act of transference from one god to another.

Adv. Marc. II. 5: videamus et hominis condicionem, ne per illam potius evenerit quod per deum evenire non potuit. liberum et sui arbitrii et suae potestatis invenio hominem a deo institutum.

Here again there is contingency, though it is more remote. It was contingent upon man's attributes, and not on God's, that the fall took place. But man's attributes are not contingent: they are his through God's act of creation, by which, in relation to his Creator and to his environment he was made a free man and no slave, his own master (*sui arbitrii*) and not a minor *sub tutela*, and under his own control (*suae potestatis*) and not like a wife *in manu et potestate viri*.[1]

Adv. Marc. II. 9: denique cum manifeste scriptura dicat flasse deum in faciem hominis et factum hominem in animam vivam, non in spiritum vivificatorem, separavit eam a condicione factoris.

To be alive is an attribute of human soul: to be life-giving is an attribute of deity, a *condicio*, because it is an attribute in relationship with that to which life is given. So again:

Ibid.: ipsum quod anima vocitatus est flatus, vide etiam ne de afflatus condicione transierit in aliquam deminutiorem qualitatem: 'the fact that Scripture refers to the breathing (Genesis 2. 7) as "soul", may serve to indicate that the breathing (which we have already observed is a lesser thing than "spirit", which is divine) has passed on from the condition of being "breathed in", and has acquired a quality of even less dignity.'

Finally, a beautifully complicated sentence, which contains both *condicio* and *qualitas* and *proprietas*.

---

[1] I owe this interpretation to the Rev. Dr A. Ehrhardt.

De Anima 9: cum animae corpus asserimus propriae qualitatis et sui generis, iam haec condicio proprietatis de ceteris accidentibus corpulentiae praeiudicabit et haec adesse ei quam corpus ostendimus, sed et ipsa sui generis pro corporis proprietate: aut etsi non sint, hoc esse proprietatis, non adesse corpori animae quae corporibus ceteris adsint.

We assert that soul possesses body (as, by our Stoic metaphysic, do all existent things), but that this body is possessed of attributes which are peculiar to itself and are not shared by any other body. We further maintain that this condition of possessing characteristic attributes will create a presumption regarding those further non-essential attributes of corporeity, namely that soul possesses these (for we have proved that soul is a body) but that these also are *sui generis*, not shared by any other body, because soul's body is itself of a characteristic sort (*pro corporis proprietate*): or else, alternatively, if soul does not possess these, it is part of its characteristics that the body of soul does not possess those secondary qualities which other bodies do possess.

Evidently *proprietas* does not mean 'property' in any sense of the English word, but either that an object is itself and nothing else, or that it possesses attributes such as belong to it and to nothing else. *Condicio proprietatis* is somewhat difficult: but I suggest that it means that in relation to (or by contrast with) other bodies, the body of soul is of such a quality as to have these characteristics.

ADDENDUM TO PAGE X

From the Jung Codex of *The Gospel of Truth*, recently discovered in Egypt, and shortly to be published by Professor G. Quispel, it appears that the account of the origins and character of Valentinian gnosticism given by Irenaeus and copied by others is substantially correct. See Quispel, *Gnosis als Welt-Religion* (Zürich, 1951) and the translation by Dr F. L. Cross of three studies by Puech, Quispel, and van Unnik, *The Jung Codex* (London, 1955).

Q. SEPTIMII FLORENTIS TERTULLIANI
DE CARNE CHRISTI LIBER

SIGLA

A   Codex *Agobardinus Parisiensis* [B.N. 1622] saec. ix qui quidem post § 10 *sed animae nostrae* deficit.
T   Codex *Trecensis* [523] saec. xij.
M   Codex *Montepessulanus* [H 54] saec. xj.
P   Codex *Paterniacensis* [439] saec. xj.
N   Codex *Florentinus Magliabechianus* [conv. soppr. vj. 9] saec. xv.
F   Codex *Florentinus Magliabechianus* [conv. soppr. vj. 10] saec. xv.
R^1 Editio princeps Beati Rhenani quae Basiliae anno 1521 in lucem prodiit: qui Rhenanus et P usus est et Hirsaugiensibus quibusdam libris iam deperditis.
R^3 Editio tertia eiusdem Rhenani, Basiliae anno 1539 prolata.
R   Consensus duarum harum editionum.
B   Editio Martini Mesnartii, Lutetiae anno 1545 prolata: qui Mesnartius et A et T necnon alio iam deperdito libro videtur usus esse.
X   in hac nostra editione codd. MPNF et Rhenani editiones indicat si quando (ut persaepe fit) inter se consentiunt.

Gel.   Editio Sigismundi Gelenii, Basiliae, 1550.
Pam.   Editio Iacobi Pamelii, Antverpiae, 1579.
Iun.   Editio Francisci Iunii, Franckerae, 1597.
Rig.   Editio Nicolai Rigaltii, Lutetiae, 1534.
Urs.   Lectiones Fulvii Ursini a Rigaltio laudatae.
Oeh.   Editio Francisci Oehler, Lipsiae, 1854.
Kroy.   Editio Aemilii Kroymann, Vindobonae 1942 [*C.S.E.L.* vol. LXX], cui viro docto grato animo acceptum referimus quidquid in apparatu critico potuimus adnotare.

Q. SEPTIMII FLORENTIS TERTULLIANI
DE CARNE CHRISTI LIBER

1 Qui fidem resurrectionis ante istos Sadducaeorum propinquos sine controversia moratam ita student inquietare ut eam spem negent etiam ad carnem pertinere, merito Christi quoque carnem quaestionibus distrahunt, tanquam aut nullam omnino aut quoquo 5 modo aliam praeter humanam, ne si humanam constiterit fuisse praeiudicatum sit adversus illos eam resurgere omni modo, quae in Christo resurrexerit. igitur unde illi destruunt carnis vota, inde nobis erunt praestruenda. examinemus corporalem substantiam domini: de spiritali enim certum est. caro quaeritur: veritas et 10 qualitas eius retractatur, an fuerit et unde et cuiusmodi fuerit. renuntiatio eius dabit legem nostrae resurrectioni. Marcion ut carnem Christi negaret negavit etiam nativitatem, aut ut nativitatem negaret negavit et carnem, scilicet ne invicem sibi testimonium responderent nativitas et caro, quia nec nativitas sine 15 carne nec caro sine nativitate: quasi non eadem licentia haeretica et ipse potuisset aut admissa carne nativitatem negare ut Apelles discipulus et postea desertor ipsius, aut et carnem et nativitatem confessus aliter illas interpretari ut condiscipulus et condesertor eius Valentinus. sed et, qui carnem Christi putativam introduxit, 20 aeque potuit nativitatem quoque phantasma confingere, ut et conceptus et praegnatus et partus virginis, et ipsius exinde infantis

1: 2 moratam *X* morata *A* orta *TB^{mg}*.   ita *Rig*. ista *A*: *omittunt ceteri*.
4 distrahunt *TX* distruunt *A*.
7 Christo *AT* Christum *X*.
9 caro *AX* carnis *T²B*.
14 responderent *A* redderent *T*: *lectiones contaminant cett*.
18 confessus *AX vulgo* professus *T Kroy*.   illas *ATB^{mg}*· illis *X*.
20 nativitatem *A* nativitatis *TX*.

TERTULLIAN ON THE FLESH OF CHRIST

1 Those whose design it is so to disturb the faith of the resurrection as to deny that that hope extends even to the flesh—a faith which, until the emergence of these kinsmen of the Sadducces,[1] had remained exempt from controversy—with good reason tear asunder with inquisitions Christ's flesh as well as ours, alleging either that it existed not at all, or that in any case it was other than human: else, if it were admitted that it was human, this would constitute a leading case against them that flesh certainly does rise again, seeing it has risen again in Christ. We, in consequence, shall need to lay the foundations of the aspirations of the flesh at the point at which these dismantle them. We have to weigh up the corporal substance of the Lord: for concerning his spiritual substance there is no dispute. It is his flesh that is under inquisition. Its verity is under discussion, and its quality—whether it existed, and whence it came, and of what sort it was. A decision concerning it will lay down the law for our own resurrection.

Marcion, with the purpose of denying Christ's flesh, also denied his nativity: or else, with intent to deny his nativity, denied his flesh. Evidently his intention was that nativity and flesh should not give mutual testimony each to the other, inasmuch as there can be neither nativity without flesh nor flesh without nativity—as though he too could not by the same heretical licence either have admitted the flesh and denied the nativity, as did Apelles his pupil and subsequent renegade, or else, admitting both flesh and nativity, have put a different meaning upon them, as did his fellow-pupil and co-renegade Valentinus. And moreover, as he was the first to make the suggestion that Christ's flesh was putative, he could equally well have invented a phantasm of a nativity, so that the Virgin's conception and pregnancy and child-bearing, no less than the subsequent life of the Child himself, might have been held docetically: they would have

[1] Cf. Acts 23. 8.

ordo, τῷ δοκεῖν haberentur: eosdem oculos eosdemque sensus fefellissent quos carnis opinio elusit.

2 Plane nativitas a Gabriele adnuntiatur: quid illi cum angelo creatoris? et in virginis utero conceptus inducitur: quid illi cum [Esaia] propheta creatoris? odit moras, qui subito Christum de caelo deferebat. aufer hinc, inquit, molestos semper Caesaris
5 census et diversoria angusta et sordidos pannos et dura praesepia: viderit angelica multitudo deum suum noctibus honorans: servent potius pecora pastores, et magi ne fatigentur de longinquo: dono illis aurum suum: melior sit et Herodes ne Hieremias glorietur: sed nec circumcidatur infans, ne doleat, nec ad templum deferatur,
10 ne parentes suos oneret sumptu oblationis, nec in manus tradatur Simeoni, ne senem moriturum exinde contristet: taceat et anus illa, ne fascinet puerum. his opinor consiliis tot originalia instrumenta Christi delere, Marcion, ausus es, ne caro eius probaretur. ex quo, oro te: exhibe auctoritatem: si propheta es praenuntia
15 aliquid, si apostolus praedica publice, si apostolicus cum apostolis senti, si tantum Christianus es crede quod traditum est: si nihil istorum es, merito dixerim, morere. nam et mortuus es, qui non es Christianus, non credendo quod creditum Christianos facit: et eo magis mortuus es quo magis non es Christianus qui cum fuisses
20 excidisti rescindendo quod retro credidisti, sicut et ipse confiteris in quadam epistula et tui non negant et nostri probant. igitur rescindens quod credidisti iam non credens rescidisti: non tamen quia credere desisti recte rescidisti, atquin rescindendo quod

---

23 elusit *T Rig.* clusit *A* illusit *X*.
2: 2 utero *scribebam* uterum *AX* cum angelo creatoris et virginis utero *TB* (*manifesto errore*).
    3 propheta creatoris *scribebam* Esaia creatoris *X* (*forsan recte*) esset a propheta creatoris *A* essentia creatoris *TB*.
    6 deum *TMPNRB* dominum *AF*.
10 oblationis *TB* obligationis *AX*.
11 senex moriturus exinde contristetur *A*.
13 ausus es *AT* ausus est *XB*.
14 ex quo *Oeh.* ex qua *ATX* exhibe auctoritatem *A* auctoritate (*omisso* exhibe) *TX*.
18 creditum *ATFB^{mg.}* traditum *MPRB* om. *N*.

deceived the same eyes and the same minds as the supposition of flesh played tricks with.

2   Clearly it is nativity that Gabriel announces.[1] 'What,' says Marcion, 'have I to do with the Creator's angel?' And in a virgin's womb that conception is represented. 'What,' says he, 'have I to do with Isaiah, the Creator's prophet?'[2] He abhors delay. He was for bringing Christ unexpectedly down from heaven. 'Away,' he says, 'with Caesar's enrolments, always a nuisance, and with inns with no room:[3] away with dirty rags and hard mangers: let the angel host take the responsibility when it gives honour to its own God, and that by night: the shepherds had better watch over their flocks: no need for the wise men to be fetched along from afar: for all I care, they may keep their gold: also let Herod be a better man, lest Jeremiah have something to boast of;[4] and let not the Child be circumcised, lest he feel pain, nor brought to the temple, lest he burden his parents with the expense of an offering, nor put into the hands of Simeon, lest he make the old man sorry because he is soon to die: also let that old woman hold her tongue, lest she put the evil eye upon the boy.'[5] It is, I suppose, on these considerations, Marcion, that you have presumed to delete all those documents bearing on Christ's origins, to prevent his flesh being proved to be flesh. On whose authority, pray? Show your credentials. If you are a prophet, foretell something: if an apostle, preach publicly: if an apostolic man, agree with the apostles: if but an ordinary Christian, believe the traditional faith. If you are none of these—I have good reason for saying it—die. Nay, you are already dead, for you are not a Christian, seeing you do not believe that which, when believed, makes men Christians: and you are the more dead as you are the more not a Christian as having been one and having fallen away by annulling what you formerly believed, as you yourself claim in a certain epistle, and as your people do not deny, and ours prove. Therefore, when you annulled what you did believe, you annulled it as no longer believing it. Yet your having ceased to believe was no valid reason for annulling it: on the contrary, by

---

[1] Luke 1. 26–30.   [2] Isa. 7. 14.   [3] Luke 2. 1–14.
[4] Matt. 2. 1–18.   [5] Luke 2. 21–38.

credidisti probas ante quam rescinderes aliter fuisse: quod credidisti aliter, illud ita erat traditum. porro quod traditum erat id
erat verum, ut ab eis traditum quorum fuit tradere: ergo quod
erat traditum rescindens, quod erat verum rescidisti. nullo iure
fecisti. sed plenius eiusmodi praescriptionibus adversus omnes
haereses alibi iam usi sumus: post quas nunc ex abundanti retractamus, desiderantes rationem qua non putaveris natum esse
Christum.

3 Necesse est, quatenus hoc putas arbitrio tuo licuisse, ut aut
impossibilem aut inconvenientem deo existimaveris nativitatem.
sed deo nihil impossibile nisi quod non vult. an ergo voluerit
nasci (quia si voluit, et potuit et natus est) consideremus. ad compendium decurro. si enim nasci se deus noluisset, quacunque de
causa, nec hominem se videri praestitisset: nam quis, hominem
videns eum, negaret natum? ita quod noluisset esse nec videri
omnino voluisset. omnis rei displicentis etiam opinio reprobatur,
quia nihil interest utrum sit quid an non sit, si cum non sit esse
praesumitur: plane interest illud ut falsum non patiatur quod vere
non est. 'Sed satis erat illi, inquis, conscientia sua: viderint
homines si natum putabant quia hominem videbant.' quanto
ergo dignius, quo constantius, humanam sustinuisset existimationem vere natus, eandem existimationem etiam non natus subi-
turus cum iniuria conscientiae suae. quantum ad fiduciam reputas
ut non natus adversus conscientiam suam natum se existimari
sustineret? quid tanti fuit, edoce, quod sciens Christus quid esset
id se quod non erat exhiberet? non potes dicere, 'Ne si natus

  29 retractemus *A*.
3: 3 voluerit *libri* noluerit *Urs. Kroy.*
  5 voluisset *T* (*manifesto errore*).
  7 ita *AT* itaque *XB*.
  10 illud *om. A.*
  13 quo *AT* quantoque *XB*.
  15 quantum *A* quam tu *ceteri.*
  17 quod *AT* cum *XB*.

annulling what you did believe you prove that before you annulled it the case was different, and it was that different belief which was the traditional one. But what was traditional was true, as having been handed down by those who had the right to do so: and thus by annulling what was traditional you annulled what was true, and your act was illegal. But I have already in my book against all the heresies made fuller use of this kind of appeal to fundamental law. That I take for granted as I now of superfluity resume the discussion, demanding the reasons which led you to suppose that the birth of Christ never took place.

3 Inasmuch as you suppose this was within your competence to decide, it can only have been that your idea was that to God nativity is either impossible or unseemly. I answer, that to God nothing is impossible except what is against his will. So then we have to consider whether it was his will to be born: because, if it was, he both could be and was born. I betake myself to a short cut. If it had been God's will for himself not to be born—whatever his purpose might be—neither would he have permitted himself to have the appearance of being a man: for no one, seeing him a man, would refuse to admit that he had been born. Thus, what it had been his will not to be, it certainly would have been his will not to seem to be. Whenever any fact is objectionable, even the supposition of it is disapproved of: because it makes no matter whether a thing is or is not if, when it is not, there is a presumption that it is. But this certainly does matter, that God should not experience as a falsehood that which he is not in truth. 'But,' you say, 'his conscience was enough for him: it was men's fault if they thought him born because they saw him a man.' Well then, with how much more dignity, as well as consistency, would he have borne with men's estimate of him if really born, seeing that even though not born he would have had to bear with the same estimate, with wrong done to his own conscience besides. How much, think you, does it count towards our confidence in him, if while not born he did against his conscience put up with the repute of having been born? Tell me, what made it worth Christ's while, that when he knew what he was he should make himself visible as what he was not? Your answer cannot be,

fuisset et hominem vere induisset deus esse desisset, amittens quod
erat dum fit quod non erat': periculum enim status sui deo nullum
est. 'Sed ideo, inquis, nego deum in hominem vere conversum,
ita ut et nasceretur et carne corporaretur, quia qui sine fine est
etiam inconvertibilis sit necesse est: converti enim in aliud finis est
pristini: non competit ergo conversio cui non competit finis.'
plane natura convertibilium ea lege est ne permaneant in eo quod
convertitur in eis, et ita non permanendo pereant dum perdunt
convertendo quod fuerunt. sed nihil deo par est: natura eius ab
omnium rerum conditione distat. si ergo quae a deo distant, a
quibus et deus distat, cum convertuntur amittunt quod fuerunt,
ubi erit diversitas divinitatis a ceteris rebus nisi ut contrarium
obtineat, id est ut deus et in omnia converti possit et qualis est perseverare? alioquin par erit eorum quae conversa amittunt quod
fuerunt, quorum utique deus in omnibus par non est: sic nec in
exitu conversionis. angelos creatoris conversos in effigiem
humanam aliquando legisti et credidisti, et tantam corporis
gestasse veritatem ut et pedes eis laverit Abraham et manibus
ipsorum ereptus sit Sodomitis Loth, conluctatus quoque homini
angelus toto corporis pondere dimitti desideraverit, adeo detinebatur. quod ergo angelis inferioris dei licuit conversis in corpu-
lentiam humanam, ut angeli nihilominus permanerent, hoc tu
potentiori deo auferes, quasi non valuerit Christus eius vere
hominem indutus deus perseverare? aut numquid et angeli illi
phantasma carnis apparuerunt? sed non audebis hoc dicere: nam

20 fit *A* est *T* assumit *XB* (*om. P*).
23-4 converti enim...competit finis *om. TB*^{mg}.
24 conversio cui *XB* conversio eius cui *A Rig. Kroy.*
28 conditione *ATP* condicione *ceteri.*
28-9 a quibus et *T* et *om. AXB* aut a quibus *Urs.*
33 *ita pungebam* deus *om. A* deus ut *Kroy.*
38 adeo *AX* (a deo) ab eo a quo *TB.*
39 ergo *TXB* enim *A*   inferioris dei *A* inferioribus dei *T* inferioribus deo *XB.*
41 eius *om. XB.*
43 phantasmata *N Rig. Oeh.*

'Lest if he had been born and had really clothed himself with man he might have ceased to be God, losing what he was while becoming what he was not.' For God runs no risk of ceasing to be what he is. 'But,' you say, 'the reason why I deny that God was really and truly changed into man, in the sense of being both born and corporated in flesh, is that he who is without end must of necessity also be unchangeable: for to be changed into something else is an ending of what originally was: therefore change is inapplicable to one to whom ending is inapplicable.' I admit that the nature of things changeable is bound by that law which precludes them from abiding in that which in them suffers change—the law which causes them to be destroyed by not abiding, seeing that by process of change they destroy that which they once were. But nothing is on equal terms with God: his nature is far removed from the circumstances of all things whatsoever. If then things far removed from God, things from which God is far removed, do in the process of being changed lose that which they once were, where will be the difference between divinity and the rest of things except that the contrary obtains, namely that God can be changed into anything whatsoever, and yet continue such as he is? Otherwise he will be on equal terms with the things which, when changed, lose that which they once were—things with which he is not on equal terms, as in all respects so also in the outcome of change. You have read at one time, and believed it, that the Creator's angels were changed into human shape, and that the bodies they were clothed with were of such verity that Abraham washed their feet, and that by their hands Lot was snatched away from the men of Sodom,[1] and an angel also having wrestled with a man with the whole weight of his body desired to be let go, so fast was he held.[2] Well then, that which was permitted to the angels of the inferior God when changed into human corporeity, the faculty of none the less remaining angels—will you deny this to the more mighty God, as though his Christ had not the power, when truly clothed with manhood, of continuing to be God? Or did perhaps those angels too become visible as a phantasm of flesh? No, this you will not dare to say. For if in your

---

[1] Cf. Gen. 18; 19.   [2] Cf. Gen. 32. 24–26.

si sic apud te angeli creatoris sicut et Christus, eius dei erit Christus
45 cuius angeli tales qualis et Christus. si scripturas opinioni tuae
resistentes non de industria alias reiecisses alias corrupisses, con-
fudisset te in hac specie evangelium Iohannis praedicans spiritum
columbae corpore lapsum desedisse super dominum. qui spiritus
cum [hoc] esset, tam vere erat et columba quam et spiritus, nec
50 interfecerat substantiam propriam assumpta substantia extranea.
sed quaeris corpus columbae ubi sit, resumpto spiritu in caelum.
aeque et angelorum, eadem ratione interceptum est qua et editum
fuerat. si vidisses cum de nihilo proferebatur, scisses et cum in
nihilum subducebatur. si non fuit initium visibile, nec finis.
55 tamen corporis soliditas erat quoquo momento corpus videbatur:
non potest non fuisse quod scriptum est.

4 Igitur si neque ut impossibilem neque ut periculosam deo
repudias corporationem, superest ut quasi indignam reicias et
accuses. ab ipsa quidem exorsus odio habita nativitate perora,
age iam spurcitias genitalium in utero elementorum, humoris et
5 sanguinis foeda coagula, carnis ex eodem caeno alendae per novem
menses. describe uterum de die in diem insolescentem, gravem,
anxium, nec somno tutum, incertum libidinibus fastidii et gulae.
invehere iam et in ipsum mulieris enitentis pudorem, vel pro peri-
culo honorandum, vel pro natura religiosum. horres utique et
10 infantem cum suis impedimentis profusum, utique et oblitum.
dedignaris quod pannis dirigitur, quod unctionibus formatur,
quod blanditiis deridetur. hanc venerationem naturae, Marcion,
despuis, et quomodo natus es? odisti nascentem hominem, et

44 eius dei *AT* eiusdem substantiae *XB* eius dei substantiae *B^{mg}*.
45 cui angeli *T* (*forsan recte*).
48 sedisse *T* descendisse *F*.   49 hoc *om. TB^{mg}*.
52 aeque et *AT om.* et *XB*.
55 quoquo *A* quo *ceteri*.
4: 3 quidem *AX* iam *TB* (*forsan recte*)   odio habita *om. AX*.
  5 *quaero an* carnis sordes *scribendum sit*.
  6 in diem *TB om. ceteri*
  7 nec somno tutum *T Rig.* nec sono totum *A* nexum totum *XB*.
  9 horrendum *T* (*falso*).
  10–11 oblitum. dedignaris *scribebam* ablutum dedignaris *AT* oblitum.
    dedignaberis *XB*.

view the Creator's angels are as Christ is, Christ will belong to that God whose angels are such as Christ is. If you had not maliciously rejected some and corrupted others of the scriptures which oppose your views, the Gospel of John would in this matter have put you to rout when it proclaims that the Spirit in the body of a dove glided down and settled upon our Lord.[1] Though he was spirit he was no less truly dove than spirit, yet had not put to death his own proper substance by the assumption of a substance not his own. But, you ask, where is the body of the dove, now that the Spirit has been withdrawn into heaven? Just like the bodies of the angels, it was suppressed on the same terms on which it had also been produced. If you had seen it when it was being brought out of non-existence, you would have been aware also when it was being withdrawn into non-existence. As its beginning was not visible, neither was its ending. Yet it was a body, a body in three dimensions, at whatever moment it was visible as a body.[2] That which is written cannot possibly not have been so.

4 So then, if your repudiation of embodiment is due neither to the supposition that God would find it impossible nor to the fear that it would bring him into peril, it remains for you to reject and arraign it as undignified. Beginning then with that nativity you so strongly object to, orate, attack now, the nastinesses of genital elements in the womb, the filthy curdling of moisture and blood, and of the flesh to be for nine months nourished on that same mire. Draw a picture of the womb getting daily more unmanageable, heavy, self-concerned, safe not even in sleep, uncertain in the whims of dislikes and appetites. Next go all out against the modesty of the travailing woman, a modesty which at least because of danger ought to be respected and because of its nature is sacred. You shudder, of course, at the child passed out along with his afterbirth, and of course bedaubed with it. You think it shameful that he is straightened out with bandages, that he is licked into shape with applications of oil, that he is beguiled by coddling. This natural object of reverence you, Marcion, bespittle: yet how were you born? You hate man during his birth: how can you love any man? Yourself at least you evidently did

[1] Cf. John 1. 32–34.   [2] Cf. Luke 3. 22.

quomodo diligis aliquem? te quidem plane non amasti cum ab ecclesia et fide Christi recessisti. sed videris si tibi displices aut si aliter es natus: certe Christus dilexit hominem illum in immunditiis in utero coagulatum, illum per pudenda prolatum, illum per ludibria nutritum. propter eum descendit, propter eum praedicavit, propter eum omni se humilitate deiecit usque ad mortem, et mortem crucis. amavit utique quem magno redemit. si Christus creatoris est, suum merito amavit: si ab alio deo est, magis adamavit, quando alienum redemit. amavit ergo cum homine etiam nativitatem, etiam carnem eius: nihil amari potest sine eo per quod est id quod est. aut aufer nativitatem et exhibe hominem, adime carnem et praesta quem deus redemit. si haec sunt homo quem deus redemit, tu haec erubescenda illi facis qui redimit, et indigna, quae nisi dilexisset non redemisset? nativitatem reformat a morte regeneratione caelesti, carnem ab omni vexatione restituit: leprosam emaculat, caecam reluminat, paralyticam redintegrat, demoniacam expiat, mortuam resuscitat: et nasci in illam erubescit? si revera de lupa aut sue aut vacca prodire voluisset, et ferae aut pecoris corpore indutus regnum caelorum praedicaret, tua opinor illi censura praescriberet turpe hoc deo et indignum hoc dei filio, et stultum propterea qui ita credat. sit plane stultum: de nostro sensu iudicemus deum. sed circumspice, Marcion, si tamen non delesti: Stulta mundi elegit deus, ut confundat sapientia. quaenam haec stulta sunt? conversio hominum ad culturam veri dei, reiectio erroris, disciplina iustitiae pudicitiae

---

21 creatoris *A* creator eius *T* (*sec. man.*) *XB*.
22 adamavit *XB* amavit *AT*.
25 adime *TXB* aut adhibe *A*   *post* redemit *periodum faciebam*.
26 qui redemit *scribebam* (*ita T. sec. man.*) quem *F* quae *ceteri*.
29 reluminat *AT* perluminat *XB*.
30 nasci in illam erubescit *TXB Kroy.* nos illam erubescemus *A Oeh*.
34 sit *TXB* si *A*   de nostro *A* si de nostro *ceteri*.
37 sapientia *A* sapientiā *T* sapientes *XB*.
38 culturam *AT* cultum *XB*.

not love when you withdrew from the Church and the faith of Christ. But it is your own concern if you are an object of displeasure to yourself, or if you were born some other way. Christ, there is no doubt of it, did care for the sort of man who was curdled in uncleannesses in the womb, who was brought forth through organs immodest, who took nourishment through organs of ridicule. For his sake he came down, for his sake he preached the gospel, for his sake he cast himself down in all humility even unto death, yea, the death of the cross.[1] Evidently he loved him: for he redeemed him at a great price.[2] If Christ belongs to the Creator, with good reason he loved his own: if he is from another god his love was even greater, in that he loved one who was not his own. In any case, along with man he loved also his nativity, and his flesh besides: nothing can be loved apart from that by which it is what it is. Else you must remove nativity and show me man, you must take away flesh and present to me him whom God has redeemed. If these are the constituents of man whom God has redeemed, who are you to make them a cause of shame to him who redeemed them, or to make them beneath his dignity, when he would not have redeemed them unless he had loved them? Nativity he reshapes from death by a heavenly regeneration, flesh he restores from every distress: leprous he cleanses it, blind he restores its sight, palsied he makes it whole again, devil-possessed he atones for it, dead he brings it again to life: is he ashamed to be born into it? If indeed it had been his will to come forth of a she-wolf or a sow or a cow, and, clothed with the body of a wild or a domestic animal, he were to preach the kingdom of heaven, your censorship I suppose would make for him a ruling that this is a disgrace to God, that this is beneath the dignity of the Son of God, and consequently that any man is a fool who so believes. A fool, yes certainly: let us judge God in accordance with our own sentiments. But look about you, Marcion, if indeed you have not deleted the passage: *God hath chosen the foolish things of the world, that he may put to shame the things that are wise.*[3] What are these foolish things? The conversion of men to the worship of the true God, the rejection of error,

[1] Cf. Phil. 2. 8.   [2] Cf. 1 Cor. 6. 20.   [3] 1 Cor. 1. 27.

misericordiae patientiae, innocentiae omnis? haec quidem stulta
non sunt. quaere ergo de quibus dixerit: et si te praesumpseris
invenisse, num erit tam stultum quam credere in deum natum, et
quidem ex virgine, et quidem carneum, qui per illas naturae
contumelias volutatus sit? dicat haec aliquis stulta non esse, et alia
sint quae deus in aemulationem elegerit sapientiae saecularis: et
tamen apud illam facilius creditur Iuppiter taurus factus aut
cycnus, quam vere homo Christus penes Marcionem.

5 Sunt plane et alia tam stulta, quae pertinent ad contumelias et
passiones dei: aut prudentiam dicant deum crucifixum. aufer hoc
quoque, Marcion, immo hoc potius. quid enim indignius deo,
quid magis erubescendum, nasci an mori, carnem gestare an
crucem, circumcidi an suffigi, educari an sepeliri, in praesepe
deponi an in monimento recondi? sapientior eris si nec ista
credideris. sed non eris sapiens nisi stultus in saeculo fueris, dei
stulta credendo. an ideo passiones a Christo non rescidisti quia ut
phantasma vacabat a sensu earum? diximus retro aeque illum et
nativitatis et infantiae imaginariae vacua ludibria subire potuisse.
sed iam hic responde, interfector veritatis: nonne vere crucifixus
est deus? nonne vere mortuus est ut vere crucifixus? nonne vere
resuscitatus ut vere scilicet mortuus? falso statuit inter nos scire
Paulus tantum Iesum crucifixum, falso sepultum ingessit, falso
resuscitatum inculcavit? falsa est igitur et fides nostra, et phantasma erit totum quod speramus a Christo, scelestissime hominum,
qui interemptores excusas dei: nihil enim ab eis passus est Christus,

39 omnis. haec *A* omnia haec *TXB*.   40 te *om. A*.
41 num *TB*$^{mg.}$ non *AXB*.
5: 6 monimento *A* monumentum *ceteri*.
   7 in saeculo *AT* saeculo *XB*.
   9 a sensu *ATB*$^{mg.}$ ad sensum *XB* (*manifesto errore*).
  11 hic *TXB* hinc *A*.
  12 deus *AXB* dñs *T*.
  13 suscitatus *AT et hic et infra*   se statuit *A*.
  14 Iesum *A om. ceteri* Christum *potius expectasses*.
  15 inculcavit? *interrogandi signum ponebam*.
  17 dei *AXB* domini *T*.

instruction in righteousness, in chastity, in mercy, in patience, and in all manner of innocency? No, these are not foolish things. Inquire then to what things he did refer: and if you presume you have discovered them, can any of them be so foolish as belief in God who was born, born moreover of a virgin, born with a body of flesh, God who has wallowed through those reproaches of nature? Let someone say these are not foolish things: suppose it to be other things which God has chosen for opposition to the wisdom of the world—and yet, the professors of this world's wisdom find it easier to believe that Jupiter became a bull or a swan than Marcion finds it to believe that Christ veritably became man.

5 There are, I submit, other things too that are foolish enough, those concerned with the reproaches and sufferings of God. If not, let them call it prudence that God was crucified. Excise this also, Marcion—or rather, this for preference. For which is more beneath God's dignity, more a matter of shame, to be born or to die, to carry about a body or a cross, to be circumcised or to be crucified, to be fed at the breast or to be buried, to be laid in a manger or to be entombed in a sepulchre? You will be the wiser if you refuse to believe these either. Yet wise you cannot be, except by becoming a fool in the world through believing the foolish things of God. Or was your reason for not tearing out of your scriptures the sufferings of Christ that as a phantasm he was free from the perception of them? I have already suggested that he could equally well have undergone the unsubstantial ridicule of an imaginary nativity and infancy. But your answer is now required, murderer of the truth: was not God truly crucified? did he not, as truly crucified, truly die? was he not truly raised again, seeing of course he truly died? Was it by fraud that Paul determined to know nothing among us save Jesus crucified,[1] was it by fraud that he represented him as buried,[2] by fraud that he insisted that he was raised up again?[3] Fraudulent in that case is also our faith, and the whole of what we hope for from Christ will be a phantasm, you utter scoundrel, who pronounce innocent the assassins of God. For of them Christ suffered nothing, if he in

[1] Cf. 1 Cor. 2. 2.   [2] Cf. 1 Cor. 15. 4.   [3] Cf. 1 Cor. 15. 17–19.

si nihil vere est passus. parce unicae spei totius orbis: quid destruis necessarium dedecus fidei? quodcunque deo indignum est mihi
20 expedit: salvus sum si non confundar de domino meo: Qui me, inquit, confusus fuerit, confundar et ego eius. alias non invenio materias confusionis quae me per contemptum ruboris probent bene impudentem et feliciter stultum. crucifixus est dei filius: non pudet, quia pudendum est. et mortuus est dei filius: prorsus
25 credibile est, quia ineptum est. et sepultus resurrexit: certum est, quia impossibile. sed haec quomodo vera in illo erunt si ipse non fuit verus, si non vere habuit in se quod figeretur quod moreretur quod sepeliretur et resuscitaretur, carnem scilicet hanc sanguine suffusam ossibus substructam nervis intextam venis implexam,
30 quae nasci et mori novit, humanam sine dubio ut natam de homine? ideoque mortalis haec erit in Christo quia Christus homo et filius hominis. aut cur homo Christus et hominis filius si nihil hominis et nihil ex homine, nisi si aut aliud est homo quam caro, aut aliunde caro hominis quam ex homine, aut aliud est Maria
35 quam homo, aut homo deus Marcionis? aliter non diceretur homo Christus sine carne, nec hominis filius sine aliquo parente homine, sicut nec deus sine spiritu dei nec dei filius sine deo patre. ita utriusque substantiae census hominem et deum exhibuit, hinc natum inde non natum, hinc carneum inde spiritalem, hinc in-
40 firmum inde praefortem, hinc morientem inde viventem. quae proprietas conditionum, divinae et humanae, aequa utique naturae cuiusque veritate dispuncta est, eadem fide et spiritus et carnis:

18 quid *AT* qui *XB*.
20 me *libri* mei *Rig*.
23 crucifixus *ATB*$^{mg.}$ natus *XB* (*manifesto errore*).
24 prorsus *om. AT*.
30 humanam...natam *XB* humana...nata *AT*, *ut periodo post* implexam *facta ita quae sequuntur rescribas* quae nasci et mori novit, humana sine dubio ut nata de homine ideoque mortalis, haec erit in Christo etc.
31 quia Christus *TB om. ceteri*.
35 aliter *AT* haud aliter *B* aut aliter *X*   dicetur *T*.
42 cuiusque *om. X*.

reality suffered nothing. Spare the one and only hope of the whole world: why tear down the indispensable dishonour of the faith? Whatever is beneath God's dignity is for my advantage. I am saved if I am not ashamed of my Lord. *Whosoever is ashamed of me*, he says, *of him will I also be ashamed.*[1] I find no other grounds for shame, such as may prove that in contempt of dishonour I am nobly shameless and advantageously a fool. The Son of God was crucified: I am not ashamed—because it is shameful. The Son of God died: it is immediately credible—because it is silly. He was buried, and rose again: it is certain—because it is impossible. But how can these acts be true in him, if he himself was not true, if he had not truly in himself that which could be crucified, which could die, which could be buried and raised up again—this flesh, in fact, suffused with blood, scaffolded of bones, threaded through with sinews, intertwined with veins, competent to be born and to die, human unquestionably, as born of a human mother? And in Christ this flesh will be mortal precisely because Christ is man, and Son of Man. Else why is Christ called Man, and Son of Man, if he has nothing that is man's, and nothing derived from man?—unless perchance either man is something other than flesh, or man's flesh is derived from somewhere else than from man, or Mary is something other than human, or Marcion's god is a man. Unless one of these suppositions were true, Christ could not be described in the Scripture as man except with reference to his flesh, nor as Son of Man except with reference to some human parent: as neither could he be described as God without the Spirit of God, nor as the Son of God without God for his Father. Thus the official record of both substances represents him as both man and God: on the one hand born, on the other not born: on the one hand fleshly, on the other spiritual: on the one hand weak, on the other exceeding strong: on the one hand dying, on the other living. That these two sets of attributes, the divine and the human, are each kept distinct from the other, is of course accounted for by the equal verity of each nature, both flesh and spirit being in full degree what they claim to be: the powers of the Spirit of God proved him God, the sufferings

[1] Matt. 10. 33; Mark 8. 38; Luke 9. 26.

virtutes spiritus dei deum, passiones carnem hominis probaverunt.
si virtutes non sine spiritu, perinde et passiones non sine carne: si
caro cum passionibus ficta, et spiritus ergo cum virtutibus falsus.
quid dimidias mendacio Christum? totus veritas fuit. maluit,
credo, nasci quam ex aliqua parte mentiri, et quidem in semetipsum, ut carnem gestaret sine ossibus duram, sine musculis
solidam, sine sanguine cruentam, sine tunica vestitam, sine fame
esurientem, sine dentibus edentem, sine lingua loquentem, ut
phantasma auribus fuerit sermo eius per imaginem vocis. fuit
itaque phantasma etiam post resurrectionem cum manus et pedes
suos discipulis inspiciendos offert, Aspicite, dicens, quod ego sum,
quia spiritus ossa non habet sicut me habentem videtis—sine dubio
manus et pedes et ossa quae spiritus non habet, sed caro. quomodo
hanc vocem interpretaris, Marcion, qui a deo optimo et simplici et
bono tantum infers Iesum? ecce fallit et decipit et circumvenit
omnium oculos, omnium sensus, omnium accessus et contactus.
ergo iam Christum non de caelo deferre debueras sed de aliquo
circulatorio coetu, nec deum praeter hominem sed magum
hominem, nec salutis pontificem sed spectaculi artificem, nec
mortuorum resuscitatorem sed vivorum avocatorem: nisi quod et
si magus fuit, natus est.

6 Sed quidam iam discentes Pontici illius, supra magistrum
sapere compulsi, concedunt Christo carnis veritatem, sine prae-
iudicio tamen renuendae nativitatis: 'Habuerit, inquiunt, carnem,
dum omnino non natam.' pervenimus igitur de calcaria quod dici
solet in carbonariam, a Marcione ad Apellen, qui posteaquam a
disciplina Marcionis in mulierem carne lapsus et dehinc in virginem
Philumenen spiritu eversus est, solidum Christi corpus sed sine
nativitate suscepit ab ea praedicare. et angelo quidem illi Philumenes eadem voce apostolus respondebit qua ipsum illum iam

    43 spiritus dei deum *A* spiritum dei *TXB* (*forsan recte*).
    47 credo *scribebam* crede *AMPNRB* credi *F* credi et *TB^{mg}*.
    57 Iesum *om. TB^{mg}*.
    6: 1 quidam iam *T* quid iam *AXB* quidam *Urs*.

proved there was the flesh of man. If the powers postulate the Spirit, no less do the sufferings postulate the flesh. If the flesh along with the sufferings was fictitious, it follows that the Spirit also along with the powers was a fraud. Why make out that Christ was half a lie? He was wholly the truth. He thought it better, I am sure, to be born than to be partially a liar, a liar too against himself, by wearing flesh without bones yet hard, without muscles yet firm, without blood yet gory, without a cloak yet clothed, flesh that hungered without appetite, ate without teeth, and spoke without a tongue, so that his discourse should be a phantasm conveyed to the ears by the ghost of a voice. In such a case he was a phantasm even after the resurrection when he offered his hands and feet for his disciples to examine, saying, *Behold that I am I, because a spirit hath not bones as ye see me having*[1]— undoubtedly meaning hands and feet and bones which a spirit has not but flesh has. How do you interpret this saying, Marcion, when you deduce Jesus from a god who is supremely good and candid and free from all evil? See how he beguiles and deceives and circumvents the eyes of all, their perceptions, their approaches, their contacts. In that case you ought not to have brought Christ down from heaven, but from some band of strolling mountebanks, not as God without manhood but as a man and a magician, not as the high priest of salvation[2] but as the producer of a pantomime, not as the raiser of the dead but as a seducer of the living: except that even if he was a magician he was born.

6 Next we come to certain disciples of this man of Pontus, who, driven to be wise above their master, allow Christ veritable flesh, yet without prejudice to the denial of his nativity. 'We will admit,' they say, 'that he had flesh, provided it was in no sense born.' So we come, as the proverb has it, from the limekiln to the charcoal-furnace, from Marcion to Apelles. This person, after suffering a carnal fall from the school of Marcion in respect of a woman, and thereafter a spiritual overthrow in respect of the virgin Philumena, adopted from her the preaching of a three-dimensional body of Christ, yet without a nativity. Now the apostle will answer that angel of Philumena's in the same terms in

---
[1] Luke 24. 39.   [2] Cf. Heb. 9. 11.

tunc praecinebat dicens, Etiamsi angelus de caelis aliter evangelizaverit vobis quam nos evangelizavimus, anathema sit: his vero quae insuper argumentantur, nos resistemus. confitentur vere corpus habuisse Christum. unde materia si non ex ea qualitate in qua videbatur? unde corpus si non caro corpus? unde caro si non nata? quia nasci haberet, ea futura quae nascitur. De sideribus, inquiunt, et de substantiis superioris mundi mutuatus est carnem: et utique proponunt non esse mirandum corpus sine nativitate, cum et apud nos angelis licuerit nulla uteri opera in carne processisse. agnoscimus quidem ita relatum: sed tamen quale est ut alterius regulae fides ab ea fide quam impugnat instrumentum argumentationibus suis mutuetur? quid illi cum Moyse qui deum Moysi reicit? si alius deus est, aliter sint res eius. sed utantur haeretici omnes scripturis eius cuius utuntur etiam mundo—erit illis hoc quoque in testimonium iudicii quod de exemplis ipsius blasphemias suas instruunt—facile est veritati etiam nihil tale adversus eos praescribenti obtinere. igitur qui carnem Christi ad exemplum proponunt angelorum, non natam dicentes licet carnem, comparent velim et causas tam Christi quam et angelorum ob quas in carne processerint. nullus unquam angelus ideo descendit ut crucifigeretur, ut mortem experiretur, ut a morte suscitaretur. si nunquam eiusmodi fuit causa angelorum corporandorum, habes causam cur non nascendo acceperint carnem: non venerant mori, ideo nec nasci. at vero Christus mori missus nasci quoque necessario habuit ut mori posset. non enim mori

31 fuit *om. T.*

which, so long ago, he prophesied of the heretic himself, saying, *Even if an angel from heaven preach the gospel to you otherwise than we have preached it, let him be anathema:*[1] these further arguings of theirs, however, it shall be ours to resist. They admit that Christ truly had a body. From whence was its constituent matter, if not from matter of that quality in which it was present to sight? From whence the body, if the body was not flesh? From whence flesh, if the flesh was not born? For it had to be born if it was to be such flesh as is born. 'From the stars,' they say, 'and from the substances of the superior world, he took flesh on loan.' And they actually suggest that a body without a nativity is not to be wondered at, seeing that we too admit that angels were permitted, without any functioning of a womb, to appear on the scene in flesh.[2] Now we agree that that is what the scripture reports. Yet what sort of procedure is this, that a faith of a different rule should borrow documentary evidence for its arguings from the faith it is attacking? What has Apelles to do with Moses, when he repudiates the God of Moses? If the god is a different one, all that belongs to him must be differently dealt with. But even supposing we allow all the heretics to make use of the scriptures of that God whose world they also use—and this too will be for them a testimony of judgement, that they find support for their blasphemies from precedents he has provided—it is easy for the truth to win its case, even without raising this kind of objection to their use of the evidence. Therefore I would that these who claim that the flesh of Christ followed the precedent of the angels, alleging that though flesh it was not born, would compare also the reasons, Christ's no less than the angels', for which they made their appearance in flesh. No angel ever came down with the intention of being crucified, of obtaining experience of death, of being raised again from death. If there never was this kind of reason for angels becoming embodied, you have the very reason why they took to them flesh without being born. They had not come to die, and consequently had no need to be born. Christ, on the other hand, being sent to die, had of necessity also to be born, so that he might die. For customarily nothing dies except

[1] Gal. 1. 8.   [2] Cf. Gen. 19. 1.

solet nisi quod nascitur: mutuum debitum est nativitati cum mortalitate: forma moriendi causa nascendi est. si propter id quod moritur mortuus est Christus, id autem moritur quod et nascitur, consequens erat, immo praecedens, ut aeque nasceretur propter id quod nascitur, quia propter id ipsum mori habebat quod quia nascitur moritur: non competebat non nasci pro quo mori competebat. atquin tunc quoque inter angelos illos ipse dominus apparuit Abrahae sine nativitate, cum carne scilicet, pro eadem causae diversitate: sed vos hoc non recipitis, non eum Christum recipientes qui iam tunc et adloqui et liberare et iudicare humanum genus ediscebat in carnis habitu, non natae adhuc quia nondum moriturae nisi prius et nativitas eius et mortalitas annuntiarentur. igitur probent angelos illos carnem de sideribus concepisse: si non probant, quia nec scriptum est, nec Christi caro inde erit, cui angelorum accommodant exemplum. constat angelos carnem non propriam gestasse utpote natura substantiae spiritalis—etsi corporis alicuius, sui tamen generis—in carnem autem humanam transfigurabiles ad tempus videri et congredi cum hominibus posse. igitur cum relatum non sit unde sumpserint carnem, relinquitur intellectui nostro non dubitare hoc esse proprium angelicae potestatis, ex nulla materia corpus sibi sumere. Quanto magis, inquis, ex aliqua. certum est: sed nihil de hoc constat, quia scriptura non exhibet. ceterum qui valent facere semetipsos quod natura non sunt, cur non valeant ex nulla substantia facere? si fiunt quod non sunt, cur non ex eo fiant quod non est? quod autem non est, cum fit, ex nihilo est. propterea nec requiritur nec ostenditur

39 quia nascitur *AT* quia id quod nascitur *XB*.
40 pro quo *AXB* propter quod *T*.
47 carnem de sideribus concepisse *A Rig. Oeh.* de sideribus accepisse substantiam carnis *TXB Kroy*.
50 gestasse *TXB edd.* portasse *A*.
52–53 transfigurabiles ad tempus videri...posse *A Oeh.* transfigurabilis ad tempus ut videri...possent *TF Kroy*. transfigurabiles ad tempus ut videri...possent *MPNRB*.

what is born. Nativity and mortality have a debt they owe each to the other. The project of dying is the reason for being born. If Christ died on behalf of that which does die, and if that does die which also is born, it followed—or rather, it preceded—that he no less must be born on behalf of that which is born, since he had to die on behalf of that which, because it is born, does die: it was not competent for him not to be born on behalf of that for which it was competent for him to die. Moreover, on the occasion in question, the Lord himself was one of those angels who appeared to Abraham:[1] he appeared without nativity, but certainly with flesh, for the same difference of purpose—though you do not accept this, since you do not accept that Christ who as early as this was habituating himself both to address and to liberate and to judge the human race,[2] in the guise of flesh not as yet born because not yet to die, except first there should be an annunciation both of his nativity and of his mortality. Let them then show proof that those angels received the substance of their flesh from the stars. As they do not prove it—because neither is it written— neither will the stars be the origin of Christ's flesh, to which they apply the precedent of the angels. It is agreed between us that the angels wore flesh not their own, seeing they are by nature of spiritual substance—though they have a body, albeit of its own kind—but yet are transfigurable into human flesh, and can on occasion come into sight and into contact with men. Since then it is not reported from what source they took their flesh, it is left for our understanding not to doubt that it is a property of angelic power to take to itself a body from a source not material. 'How much more,' you say, 'from a source which is material.' Certainly. But on this there is no agreement, because the Scripture offers no evidence. Yet why should those who have the power to make themselves into that which by nature they are not, not have the power to make themselves so out of that which is no substance? If they are made into something they are not, why should they not be made into it out of that which is not? But when that which is not comes into existence, it exists out of nothing. For this reason one does not ask, and we are not told,

[1] Cf. Gen. 18. 1.   [2] Cf. Gen. 18. 5 etc.; 19. 16; 18. 20; 19. 24.

quid postea factum sit corporibus illorum: quod de nihilo fuit, nihil factum est. possunt nihil ipsum convertere in carnem qui semetipsos potuerunt convertere in carnem: plus est naturam demutare quam facere materiam. sed et si de materia necesse fuit
65 angelos sumpsisse carnem, credibilius utique est de terrena materia quam de ullo genere caelestium substantiarum, cum adeo terrenae qualitatis extiterit ut terrenis pabulis pasta sit. fuerit: sit nunc quoque siderea eodem modo terrenis pabulis pasta quando terrena non esset, quo terrena caelestibus pasta est quando caelestis non
70 esset—legimus enim manna esui populo fuisse: Panem, inquit, angelorum edit homo—non tamen infringitur semel separata condicio dominicae carnis ex causa alterius dispositionis. homo vere futurus usque ad mortem, eam carnem oportebat indueret cuius et mors: eam porro carnem cuius est mors nativitas ante-
75 cedit.

7 Sed quotiens de nativitate contenditur omnes qui respuunt eam ut praeiudicantem de carnis in Christo veritate ipsum dominum volunt negare esse ⟨se⟩ natum quia dixerit, Quae mihi mater et qui mihi fratres? audiat igitur et Apelles quid iam
5 responsum sit a nobis Marcioni eo libello quo ad evangelium ipsius provocavimus, considerandam scilicet materiam pronuntiationis istius. primo quidem nunquam quisquam adnuntiasset illi matrem et fratres eius foris stantes qui non certus esset et habere illum matrem et fratres et ipsos esse quos tunc nuntiabat,
10 vel retro cognitos vel tunc ibidem compertos: licet propterea abstulerint haereses ista de evangelio quod et creditum patrem eius Ioseph fabrum et matrem Mariam et fratres et sorores eius optime notos sibi esse dicebant qui mirabantur doctrinam eius. 'Sed

67 fuerit *om. X.*
71 semel *om. T.*
72 condicio *A* conditio *ceteri (forsan recte).*
74 et *AT Kroy.* est *ceteri.*   est *TXB* et *A Kroy.*
7: 3 dominum *AT* deum *X (vulgo).*   negare esse se *scribebam* negasse* *A* negare *T* negare esse *XB vulgo.*
8 stantes *A* stare *TXB.*

what afterwards became of their bodies. That which was from nothing became nothing. Being able to change themselves into flesh, they are able to change nothingness itself into flesh. It is a bigger thing to change one's nature than to make matter. But even supposing it was necessary for the angels to have taken flesh from matter it is certainly easier to believe that they took it from terrestrial matter than from any species of celestial substances, since it was to such an extent of terrestrial quality that it fed on terrestrial food. And further, suppose now we grant that sidereal flesh, while not terrestrial, may have fed on terrestrial food in the same manner as terrestrial flesh, while not celestial, fed on celestial food—for we read that manna was meat for the people, and it says, *Man did eat angels' food*[1]—yet the attributes of the Lord's flesh, once they are set in a class by themselves, are not affected by a reason which belongs to a different dispensation. As he was to be truly man even unto death, he was under necessity of clothing himself with that flesh to which death belongs: and that flesh to which death belongs has nativity for its antecedent.

7 But as often as there is discussion of the nativity, all those who reject it as prejudging the issue concerning the verity of the flesh in Christ, claim that the Lord himself denies having been born, on the ground that he asked, *Who is my mother and who are my brethren?*[2] So let Apelles too hear what answer I have already given to Marcion in that work in which I have made appeal to the Gospel which he accepts, namely that the background of that remark must be taken into consideration. Well then, in the first place no one would ever have reported to him that his mother and his brethren were standing without unless he were sure that he had a mother and brethren and that it was they whose presence he was then announcing, having either previously known them, or at least then and there made their acquaintance. This I say, in spite of the fact that the heresies have deliberately removed from the Gospel the statements that those who marvelled at his doctrine said that both Joseph the carpenter, his reputed father, and Mary his mother, and his brothers and sisters, were very well known to

[1] Ps. 78. 25.
[2] Matt. 12. 48; cf. Mark 3. 33; Luke 8. 20, 21.

temptandi gratia nuntiaverant ei matrem et fratres quos non habebat.' hoc quidem scriptura non dicit, alias non tacens cum quid temptationis gratia factum est erga eum: Ecce, inquit, surrexit legis doctor temptans eum: et alibi, Et accesserunt ad eum pharisaei temptantes eum: quod nemo prohibebat hic quoque significari temptandi gratia factum. non recipio quod extra scripturam de tuo infers. dehinc materia temptationis debet subesse. quid temptandum putaverint in illo? 'Utique natusne esset annon: si enim hoc negavit responsio eius, hoc captavit nuntiatio temptatoris.' sed nulla temptatio tendens ad agnitionem eius de quo dubitando temptat ita subito procedit ut non ante praecedat quaestio quae dubitationem inferens cogat temptationem. porro si nusquam de nativitate Christi volutatum est, quid tu argumentaris voluisse illos per temptationem sciscitari quod nunquam produxerunt in quaestionem? eo adicimus, etiam si temptandus esset de nativitate, non utique hoc modo temptaretur, earum personarum adnuntiatione quae poterant etiam nato Christo non fuisse. omnes nascimur, et tamen non omnes aut fratres habemus aut matrem: adhuc potest ⟨quis⟩ et patrem magis habere quam matrem et avunculos magis quam fratres. adeo non competit temptatio nativitatis, quam licebat et sine matris et sine fratrum nominatione constare. facilius plane est ut certi illum et matrem et fratres habere divinitatem potius temptaverint eius quam nativitatem, an intus agens sciret quid foris esset mendacio petitus praesentiae adnuntiatae eorum qui in praesentia non erant. nisi

16 erga *AT* circa *X*.
21 putaverint *A Oeh.* putaverunt *TXB Kroy.*   utique etc. *interlocutori assignabam.*
32 quis *om. libri.*
38 adnuntiatae *AT om. XB.*

them.¹ 'But,' they say, 'it was for the sake of tempting him that they announced to him the mother and the brethren whom actually he had not.' Now the Scripture does not say this, though elsewhere it is not silent when any action respecting him was taken with a view to temptation. *Behold*, it says, *there stood up a doctor of the law, tempting him*:² and in another place, *And there came to him the Pharisees, tempting him*.³ And there was no reason why it should not have been indicated here that this was done to tempt him. I refuse to accept an inference of your own, which is not in Scripture. Secondly, there has to be some ground beneath the temptation. What was it they could think worth tempting in him? 'Whether, of course, he had been born or not: for as his answer constituted a denial of this, this was what the tempter's announcement angled for.' But no temptation, which has in view the ascertainment of that in doubt of which it makes the temptation, proceeds with such abruptness as to dispense with a precedent question which by suggesting doubt may give point to the temptation. Consequently, as there had nowhere been any canvassing of Christ's nativity, how can you argue that these people wished by means of a temptation to elicit something they had never brought into question? To this we add that, even if there had been a case for tempting him in respect of his nativity, the temptation would certainly not have proceeded on the lines of an announcement of the arrival of persons whose present existence was no necessary consequence of Christ's having been born. All of us are born, yet not all of us have either brothers or a mother: one is more likely at any point to have a father than a mother, and maternal uncles than brothers. Thus there is here no room for a temptation respecting his nativity, for this could quite well be a fact apart from any mention either of mother or of brethren. It is in fact easier to suppose that, being assured that he had both a mother and brethren, they were making trial of his divinity rather than of his nativity, by attempting to discover whether while busy indoors he knew what there was out of doors, when assailed with a lying report of the presence of people

---

¹ Cf. Luke 3. 23; Mark 6. 2–4; Matt. 13. 55, 56.
² Luke 10. 25. ³ Matt. 19. 3.

quod et sic vacuisset temptationis ingenium: poterat enim
evenire ut quos illi nuntiabant foris stare, ille eos sciret absentes
esse vel valetudinis vel negotii vel peregrinationis nota *ei* iam
necessitate. nemo temptat eo modo quo sciat posse se ruborem
temptationis referre. nulla igitur materia temptationis com-
petente liberatur simplicitas nuntiatoris, quod vere mater et
fratres eius supervenissent. sed quae ratio responsi matrem et
fratres ad praesens negantis discat etiam Apelles. fratres domini
non crediderant in illum, sicut et in evangelio ante Marcionem
edito continetur: mater aeque non demonstratur adhaesisse illi,
cum Martha et Mariae aliae in commercio eius frequententur.
hoc denique in loco apparet incredulitas eorum: cum Iesus doceret
viam vitae, cum dei regnum praedicaret, cum languoribus et
vitiis medendis operaretur, extraneis defixis in illum tam proximi
aberant: denique superveniunt et foris subsistunt nec introeunt,
non computantes scilicet quid intus ageretur, nec sustinent saltem,
quasi necessarius aliquid afferrent eo quod ille cum maxime age-
bat, sed amplius interpellant et a tanto opere revocatum volunt.
oro te Apelle, vel tu Marcion, si forte tabula ludens vel de histrio-
nibus aut aurigis contendens tali nuntio avocareris nonne dixisses,
Quae mihi mater aut qui fratres? deum praedicans et probans
Christus, legem et prophetas adimplens, tanti retro aevi caliginem
dispergens, indigne usus est hoc dicto ad percutiendam increduli-
tatem foris stantium vel ad excutiendam importunitatem ab opere

40 stare *XB vulgo om. A* esse *T*.
41 nota ei iam *Kroy.* notae iam *AT* nota *XB*.
44 nuntiatoris *TXB* enuntiationis *A Kroy.* nuntiationis *Rig. Oeh.*
49 Martha et Mariae aliae *scribebam* martha et maria aliae quae *T* (que *Kroy.*) marte et marie alie *A* marthae et mariae aliae *XB vulgo.*
56 revocatum *XB* vocatum *A* avocatum *T Kroy.*
59 qui *AXB* qui mihi *T*.

who actually were not there. And yet, even in this case the device behind the temptation would have failed of its purpose: for it could have been the case that those whom they reported standing without were known by him to be absent, through the claims of illness or of business or of a long journey, which he was already aware of. No one frames a temptation in terms through which he knows that the embarrassment of the temptation may recoil upon himself. As therefore there existed no pertinent ground of temptation, it remains for us to admit the candour of the messenger and to acknowledge that his mother and his brethren really had come for him. But let Apelles, as well as Marcion, hear from me what was the reason behind the reply which for the moment denied mother and brethren. Our Lord's brethren did not believe in him:[1] this also is included in the Gospel as it was published before Marcion's day. His mother likewise is not shown to have adhered to him, though Martha and other Marys are often mentioned as being in his company.[2] At this juncture their unbelief at last comes into the open. When Jesus was teaching the way of life, when he was preaching the Kingdom of God, when he was occupied in healing infirmities and sicknesses, though strangers were intent upon him these near relations were absent. At length they come for him, they stand without and will not enter, evidently not valuing what was being done inside. They do not so much as even wait, but, as though bringing more important business than what he was then engaged upon, they go so far as to interrupt, and wish him to be called away from so great a work. I put it to you, Apelles, or you if you like, Marcion, if perchance when playing dice or laying bets on actors or jockeys you were called away by such a message, would you not ask, 'Who is my mother, and who are my brethren?'? When Christ was preaching God and giving proof of him, was fulfilling the Law and the Prophets, and was dispelling the darkness of long ages past, was it without justification that he used this expression to castigate the unbelief of those who stood without, or at least to expose their unseasonableness in calling him back from his work?

[1] Cf. John 7. 5.
[2] Luke 10. 38–41; John 11. 5, 19 sqq., 24, 39; Matt. 27. 56; Mark 16. 1.

revocantium? ceterum ad negandam nativitatem alius fuisset ei locus et tempus et ordo sermonis, non eius qui possit pronuntiari etiam ab eo cui et mater esset et fratres: cum indignatio parentes negat, non negat sed obiurgat. denique potiores fecit alios, et meritum praelationis ostendens, audientiam scilicet verbi, demonstrat qua condicione negaverit matrem et fratres: qua enim alios sibi adoptavit qui ei adhaerebant, ea abnegavit illos qui ab eo absistebant. solet etiam adimplere Christus quod alios docet. quale ergo erat si docens non tanti facere matrem aut patrem aut fratres quanti dei verbum ipse dei verbum adnuntiata matre et fraternitate desereret? negavit itaque parentes quomodo docuit negandos, pro dei opere. sed et alias figura est synagogae in matre abiuncta, et Iudaeorum in fratribus incredulis. foris erat in illis Israel: discipuli autem novi, intus audientes et credentes, cohaerentes Christo ecclesiam deliniabant, quam potiorem matrem et digniorem fraternitatem recusato carnali genere nuncupavit. eodem sensu denique et illi exclamationi respondit, non matris uterum et ubera negans sed feliciores designans qui verbum dei audiunt.

8 Solis istis capitulis quibus maxime instructi sibi videntur Marcion et Apelles secundum veritatem integri et incorrupti evangelii interpretatis, satis esse debuerat ad probationem carnis humanae in Christo per defensionem nativitatis. sed quoniam et isti Apelleiaci carnis ignominiam praetendunt maxime, quam volunt ab igneo illo praeside mali sollicitatis animabus adstructam et idcirco indignam Christo et idcirco de sideribus illi substantiam

---

63 alius *ATMPN* alius necessarius *FRB*.
64 possit *TXB* posset *A Oeh. Kroy*.
65 indignatio *AN Oeh. Kroy*. indignatione *T alii alia*.
66 fecit sibi alios *T Kroy*.
79 *quaero an scribendum* illi mulieris cuiusdam exclamationi.
8: 6 animabus *AXB* animalibus *TB^{mg}*.   abstructam *TMPNF*.

For repudiating nativity, on the other hand, he could have chosen the place and time and occasion of a different discourse, not such as could be uttered by one who had both a mother and brethren. When indignation denies kindred, this is not a denial but a reproof. Besides, he gave others prior place, and when he reveals what has caused these to deserve preference, namely the hearing of the word, he makes it clear on what terms he has denied having a mother and brethren: for on the terms on which he adopted to himself those others who clave to him, on these he repudiated those who stood apart from him. It is Christ's custom himself to put into practice the teaching he gives to others. Then how could it be possible for him, when teaching men not to value mother or father or brethren so highly as the word of God, himself to desert the word of God when his mother and brethren were reported waiting? So then, he denied his kinsfolk for the reason for which he taught they ought to be denied, for God's work's sake. And further: in another sense there is in his mother's estrangement a figure of the Synagogue, and in his brethren's unbelief a figure of the Jews. Outside, in them, was Israel: whereas the new disciples, hearing and believing, and being inside, by cleaving to Christ depicted the Church which, repudiating carnal kinship, he designated a preferable mother and a worthier family of brothers. To conclude, it was in this same sense that he answered also that other exclamation[1]—not as denying his mother's womb and breasts, but as indicating that those are more blessed who hear the word of God.

8   We have expounded, in terms of the truth of the Gospel as it was until Marcion and Apelles mutilated and corrupted it, those passages which these regard as their most effective armoury: and this by itself ought to have been enough to establish the fact of Christ's nativity, and thereby to prove his possession of human flesh. But inasmuch as these Apelleasts make a special point of sheltering behind the dishonour of the flesh, alleging that it was constructed for seduced souls by that fiery prince of evil and therefore is unworthy of Christ, and therefore he must needs have got him a substance from the stars, I have the task of

---

[1] Cf. Luke 11. 27, 28.

competisse, debeo eos de sua paratura repercutere. angelum
quendam inclitum nominant qui mundum hunc instituerit et
instituto eo paenitentiam admiserit. et hoc suo loco tractavimus—
nam est nobis et ad illos libellus—an qui spiritum et voluntatem et
virtutem Christi habuerit ad ea opera dignum aliquid paenitentia
fecerit. eum angelum etiam de figura erraticae ovis interpre-
tantur. teste igitur paenitentia institutoris sui peccatum erit
mundus, siquidem omnis paenitentia confessio est delicti quia
locum non habet nisi in delicto. si mundus delictum est, qua
corpus et membra delictum erit perinde et caelum et caelestia cum
caelo: si caelestia, et quicquid inde conceptum prolatumque est.
mala arbor malos fructus edat necesse est. caro igitur Christi de
caelestibus structa de peccati constat elementis, peccatrix de
peccatorio censu, et pars iam erit eius substantiae, id est nostrae,
quam ut peccatricem Christo dedignantur inducere. ita si nihil de
ignominia interest, aut aliquam purioris notae materiam excogi-
tent Christo quibus displicet nostra, aut eam agnoscant qua etiam
caelestis melior esse non potuit. legimus plane, Primus homo de
terrae limo, secundus homo de caelo: non tamen ad materiae
differentiam spectat, sed tantum terrenae retro substantiae carnis
primi hominis, id est Adae, caelestem de spiritu substantiam
opponit secundi hominis, id est Christi. et adeo ad spiritum, non
ad carnem, caelestem hominem refert, ut quos ei comparat constet
in hac carne terrena caelestes fieri, spiritu scilicet: quodsi secundum
carnem quoque caelestis Christus, non compararentur illi non
secundum carnem caelestes. si ergo qui fiunt caelestes, qualis et
Christus, terrenam carnis substantiam gestant, hinc quoque con-

13-14 eum...interpretantur *A Kroy.* cum...interpretentur *TXB vulgo.*
14 peccatum *AT* delictum *XB.*
17-18 cum caelo: si caelestia, *om. A Oeh.*
19 et mala *A Oeh.*
20 constat *A Oeh. Kroy.* consistit *TXB.*
22 Christo dedignantur inducere *AT* Christus dedignatur induere *XB.*
23 aliquam *AT* aliam *XB.*
24 eam *TXB* eandem *A Rig. Oeh.*
33 et *AT Oeh. Kroy.* est *XB.*

beating them back with the aid of their own ordnance. They tell us the name of a certain mighty angel, and allege that he founded this world, and did penance for founding it. This also I have discussed in its proper place—for I have also a book addressed to them—asking whether one who, according to them, had the spirit and will and power of Christ with a view to those works did anything worthy of penance. This angel they go so far as to interpret by the figure of the Lost Sheep. So, on the evidence of the penance of its founder, the world must be a mistake, since all penance is a confession of sin, seeing it has no place except in case of sin. If the world is a sin, then on the analogy of body and members the sky, and along with the sky the things in it, must equally be a sin, and, if the things in the sky, so also whatever has been conceived and brought forth from them. An evil tree cannot but bring forth evil fruits.[1] In that case the flesh of Christ, being composed of things from the sky, consists of elements of sin, and is sinful by reason of its sinful origin, and will from its very nature be part of that substance, our substance, with which, as being sinful, they think shame to besmirch Christ. As then there is no difference in respect of the dishonour involved, either let them, since they are displeased with ours, think out for Christ a material of purer brand, or else let them acknowledge this, than which even that from the sky cannot be better. I am aware that it is written, *The first man is from the mud of the earth, the second man is from heaven:*[2] but this has not in view a difference of material, but is merely opposing to the previous earthy substance of the flesh of the first man, which is Adam, the celestial spiritual substance of the second Man, which is Christ. And so closely does he relate the celestial Man to spirit and not to flesh, that beyond question those whom he brings into parity with him are in this earthly flesh being made celestial, by spirit of course: whereas if Christ were celestial according to the flesh as well, those not celestial according to the flesh could not be brought into parity with him. If therefore those who are being made celestial, as Christ is already celestial, wear an earthly substance of flesh, this provides a further

---

[1] Cf. Matt. 7. 17; 12. 33; Luke 6. 43.
[2] 1 Cor. 15. 47.

firmatur ipsum etiam Christum in carne terrena fuisse caelestem sicut ii sunt qui ei adaequantur.

9 Praetendimus adhuc nihil quod ex alio acceptum sit, ut aliud sit quam id de quo sit acceptum, ita aliud esse ut non suggerat unde sit acceptum. omnis materia sine testimonio originis suae non est, etsi demutetur in novam proprietatem. ipsum certe corpus hoc nostrum, quod de limo figulatum etiam ad fabulas nationum veritas transmisit, utrumque originis elementum confitetur, carne terram, sanguine aquam. nam licet alia sit species qualitatis, hoc est quod ex alio aliud fit. ceterum quid est sanguis quam rubens humor, quid caro quam terra conversa in figuras suas? considera singulas qualitates, musculos ut glebas, ossa ut saxa, etiam circum papillas calculos quosdam: aspice nervorum tenaces conexus ut traduces radicum et venarum ramosos discursus ut ambages rivorum et lanugines ut muscos et comam ut caespitem et ipsos medullarum in abdito thesauros ut metalla carnis. haec omnia terrenae originis signa et in Christo fuerunt, et haec sunt quae illum dei filium celaverunt, non alias tantummodo hominem existimatum quam humana extantem substantia corporis. aut edite aliquid in illo caeleste de Septentrionibus et Virgiliis et Suculis emendicatum: nam quae enumeravimus adeo terrenae testimonia carnis sunt ut et nostrae. sed nihil novum nihilque peregrinum deprehendo. denique verbis et factis tantum, doctrina et virtute sola, Christum hominem obstupescebant: notaretur autem etiam carnis in illo novitas miraculo habita. sed carnis terrenae non mira condicio ipsa erat quae cetera eius miranda faciebat cum dicerent, Unde huic doctrina et signa ista? etiam despicientium formam eius haec erat vox: adeo nec

36 ii *om. TXB* (*forsan recte*).

9: 6 utrumque originis elementum *TXB Kroy.* utriusque originem elementi *A Oeh.*

7 species *A Oeh.* facies *TXB* (*quod forsan scribendum*).

9 conversa *om. A Oeh.*

9–10 figuras suas *TXB Rig. Kroy.* figura sua *A Oeh.*

15–16 et haec *F Kroy.* et *A Oeh.* haec *MPNRB deficit T. tota omissa incisione.*

17 humana extantem *scribebam* ex humana tantum *T Kroy.* extantem humana *A Oeh.* ex humana *XB.*

21 et factis tantum *AT Oeh. Kroy.* tantummodo et factis *XB.*

proof of our case that Christ himself also was celestial, yet in earthly flesh, as are those who are classed with him.

9 My next contention is that nothing that is derived from something else, though it be other than that from which it is derived, is to such an extent other as not to suggest that from which it is derived. No material loses all evidence of its origin, though it be changed into a new identity. Certainly this body of ours, the fact of whose formation from clay the truth has passed on even to the mythologies of the Gentiles, confesses both elements of its origin, earth by its flesh, water by its blood. For though its quality manifests itself under another aspect, this is because it comes into existence as one thing derived from another. Yet what is blood but reddened water, and what is flesh but earth transformed into shapes still its own? Consider its attributes one by one, the muscles as turf, the bones as rocks, even a sort of pebbles round the nipples. Look upon the clinging bands of the sinews as the fibres of roots, the branching meanderings of the veins as the twistings of rivers, the down as moss, the hair as grass, even the very treasures of the marrow in its secret place as the goldmines of the flesh. All these tokens of a terrestrial origin were also in Christ, and these it is which hid the fact that he was the Son of God, since for no other reason was he supposed to be merely man than because he consisted of a human bodily substance. If not, point to something in him that was celestial, begged and borrowed from the Great Bear or the Pleiades or the Hyades: for the things I have enumerated are no less evidences that his flesh was terrestrial than that it was ours. I find no trace of anything novel or anything outlandish. In fact it was only for his words and works, solely for his doctrine and power, that they were astonished at Christ as man: whereas a new kind of flesh in him would even have been remarked upon and taken for a marvel. But it was precisely the non-marvellous character of his terrestrial flesh which made the rest of his activities things to marvel at, when they asked, *Whence hath this man this doctrine and these signs?*[1] These were the words of men who even despised his outward appearance, so far was his body from being of human comeliness,

[1] Matt. 13. 54.

humanae honestatis corpus fuit, nedum caelestis claritatis.
tacentibus apud vos quoque prophetis de ignobili aspectu eius,
ipsae passiones ipsaeque contumeliae loquuntur: passiones quidem
humanam carnem, contumeliae vero inhonestam probaverunt.
an ausus esset aliqui ungue summo perstringere corpus novum,
sputaminibus contaminare faciem nisi merentem? quid dicis
caelestem carnem quam unde caelestem intellegas non habes, quid
terrenam negas quam unde terrenam agnoscas habes? esurit sub
diabolo, sitit sub Samaritide, lacrimatur super Lazarum, trepidat ad
mortem—Caro enim inquit infirma—sanguinem fundit postremo:
haec sunt opinor signa caelestia. sed quomodo, inquam, contemni et pati posset sicut et dixit, si quid in illa carne de caelesti
generositate radiasset? ex hoc ergo convincimus nihil in illa de
caelis fuisse, propterea ut contemni et pati posset.

10 Convertor ad alios aeque sibi prudentes qui carnem Christi
animalem adfirmant, quod anima caro sit facta: ergo et caro
anima, et sicut caro animalis ita et anima carnalis. et hic itaque
causas requiro. si ut animam salvam faceret in semetipso suscepit
animam Christus, quia salva non esset nisi per ipsum dum in ipso,
non video cur eam carnem fecerit animalem induendo carnem,
quasi aliter animam salvam facere non posset nisi carnem factam.
cum enim nostras animas non tantum non carneas sed etiam a
carne disiunctas salvas praestet, quanto magis illam quam ipse

28 vos *vulgo* nos *FB Oeh. perperam.*
30 probaverunt *om. AT.*
34-5 esurit...sitit *T*: esuriit...sitiit *ceteri*   lacrimatur *XB* lacrimat* *T*: lacrimatus est *A*.
37 inquam *XB vulgo* inquitis *A Kroy. (manifesto errore)* inquit is *TB^{mg}*.
38 dixit *AT Kroy.* dixi *XB vulgo*   ex illa carne *T*.

not to speak of celestial glory.¹ Also, though among you the prophets are silent regarding his ignoble presence, the very sufferings, the very revilings tell the tale: the sufferings proved his flesh human, the revilings proved it uncomely. Would any one have dared even to scratch a novel kind of body with the end of his finger-nail, or to defile his face with spittings unless it seemed to deserve it?² Why do you allege that that flesh is celestial which you have no data for thinking celestial, why deny that that is terrestrial which you have data for recognizing as terrestrial? It hungers when with the devil,³ is athirst with the Samaritan woman,⁴ weeps over Lazarus,⁵ trembles at the prospect of death— *The flesh*, he says, *is weak*⁶—and at last sheds its blood. You take these, I suppose, for celestial signs. But, say I, how could he, as he said would happen, be despised and suffer,⁷ if in that flesh there had shone any radiance from his celestial nobility? By this means, then, we prove our case that in that flesh there was nothing brought down from the skies, and that that was so for the express purpose that it should be capable of being despised and of suffering.

10 I turn to others, equally wise in their own eyes, who insist that Christ's flesh was composed of soul, in that soul was made into flesh.⁸ In that case his soul was flesh, and as his flesh was composed of soul, so also his soul was turned into flesh. Here, as before, I ask for reasons. If it was for the salvation of soul in himself that Christ assumed soul—because it could not have been saved except through him, by being in him—I do not see why he made it into flesh by clothing himself with flesh composed of soul, as though he were unable to save soul except it were turned into flesh. For seeing that he affords salvation to our souls when they are not only not fleshly but are even disjoined from the flesh,

---

¹ Cf. Isa. 53. 2. ² Cf. Matt. 27. 30; Mark 15. 19; Luke 22. 64.
³ Cf. Matt. 4. 2–4. ⁴ Cf. John 4. 7.
⁵ Cf. John 11. 35. ⁶ Matt. 26. 41; Mark 14. 38.
⁷ Cf. Matt. 16. 21; Mark 8. 31; Luke 9. 22.
⁸ Throughout this chapter 'composed of soul' stands for *animalis*, 'turned into flesh' for *carnalis*, 'fleshly' for *carneus*. *Carneus* seems to differ from *carnalis* as referring to form rather than matter.

10 suscepit etiam non carneam redigere potuit in salutem. item cum praesumant non carnis sed animae nostrae solius liberandae causa processisse Christum, primo quam absurdum est ut animam solam liberaturus id genus corporis eam fecerit quod non erat liberaturus. deinde si animas nostras per illam quam gestavit liberare sus-
15 ceperat, illam quoque quam gestavit nostram gestasse debuerat, id est nostrae formae, cuiuscunque formae est in occulto anima nostra, non tamen carneae. ceterum non nostram animam liberavit si carneam habuit: nostra enim carnea non est. porro si non nostram liberavit quia carneam liberavit, nihil ad nos, quia
20 non nostram liberavit. sed nec liberanda erat quae non erat nostra, ut scilicet carnea: non enim periclitabatur si non erat nostra, id est non carnea. sed liberatam constat illam. ergo non fuit carnea, et fuit nostra, si ea fuit quae liberaretur, quoniam periclitabatur. iam ergo si anima non fuit carnalis in Christo, nec
25 caro potest animalis fuisse.

11 Sed aliam argumentationem eorum convenimus, exigentes cur animalem carnem subeundo Christus animam carnalem videatur habuisse. 'Deus enim inquiunt gestivit animam visibilem hominibus exhibere faciendo eam corpus quae retro invisibilis
5 extiterit, natura nihil sed nec semetipsam videns prae impedimento carnis huius, ut etiam disceptaretur nata sit anima an non, mortalis an non: itaque animam corpus effectam in Christo ut eam nascentem et morientem et, quod sit amplius, resurgentem videremus.' et hoc autem quale erit, ut per carnem demonstraretur
10 anima sibi aut nobis, quae per carnem non poterat agnosci, ut sic ostenderetur dum id fit cui latebat, id est caro? tenebras videlicet

10: 11 *post* animae nostrae *deficit A.*
  15 illa quoque...nostra quaeque *T Kroy.*
  19–20 quia non nostram *TB* quia carnea non est quia non nostram *X.*
  23 et *X vulgo* sed *T Kroy.*
11: 5 sed *T Kroy. om. ceteri.*
  7 mortalis an non *TB om. ceteri.*
  9 erit *libri* erat *Urs. Rig. Oeh. qui et infra* posset *pro* possit *rescribunt.*

how much more was he able to bring to salvation that soul which he himself assumed, even without its being fleshly. Also, seeing that they premise that Christ came forth for the purpose of delivering not our flesh but our soul alone, in the first place how absurd it is that when intending to deliver soul alone, he should have made it into that sort of body which he was not going to deliver. And again, if the task he took upon him was to deliver our souls by the agency of that soul with which he clothed himself, that too with which he clothed himself must have been ours when he clothed himself with it, that is, of our fashion—of whatever fashion our soul in secret is, at any rate not a fleshly fashion. But if the soul he had was fleshly, it was not our soul that he delivered: for ours is not fleshly. So then, if it was not ours that he delivered, it being a fleshly one that he delivered, it is no concern of ours, because it was not ours that he delivered. In fact it did not even need to be delivered, seeing it was not ours, being fleshly: for it was not in peril if it was not ours, that is, was not non-fleshly. But it is agreed that it was delivered. Consequently it was not fleshly, and it was ours, seeing it was such as to need deliverance, because it was ours that was in peril. So then if in Christ soul was not turned into flesh, neither can his flesh have been composed of soul.

11 But we are faced with a further argument of theirs when we demand why it should be supposed that Christ, by taking upon him flesh made out of soul, was in possession of a soul turned into flesh. 'It was,' they say, 'because God was anxious to display soul visibly to men by making it into body: for it had previously been invisible, by nature seeing nothing, not even itself, by reason of the impediment of this flesh, with the result that it was even argued whether soul was born or not, was mortal or not: and so in Christ soul was made into body with a view to our seeing it both being born, and dying, and, what is more, rising again.' But it would be a very strange thing if by means of flesh either itself or we should obtain proof of that soul whose existence the flesh precluded from recognition, and if soul should be brought into view only by becoming that to which it was invisible, namely flesh. In that case it has had darkness conferred upon it so that it

accepit ut lucere possit. denique ad hoc prius retractemus an isto modo ostendenda fuerit anima, dehinc an in totum invisibilem eam retro allegent, utrum quasi incorporalem an etiam habentem aliquod genus corporis proprii. et tamen cum invisibilem dicant corporalem constituunt, habentem quod invisibile sit: nihil enim habens invisibile quomodo potest invisibilis dici? sed nec esse quidem potest, nihil habens per quod sit: cum autem sit, habeat necesse est aliquid per quod est. si habet aliquid per quod est, hoc erit corpus eius. omne quod est corpus est sui generis: nihil est incorporale nisi quod non est. habente igitur anima invisibile corpus, qui visibilem eam facere susceperat utique dignius id eius visibile fecisset quod invisibile habebatur, quia nec hic mendacium aut infirmitas deo competit, mendacium si aliud animam quam quod erat demonstravit, infirmitas si id quod erat demonstrare non valuit. nemo ostendere volens hominem cassidem aut personam ei inducit: hoc autem factum est animae si in carne conversa alienam induit superficiem. sed et si incorporalis anima deputetur, ut aliqua vi rationis occulta sit quidem anima, corpus tamen non sit quicquid est anima, proinde et impossibile deo non erat, et proposito eius congruentius competebat, nova aliqua corporis specie eam demonstrare quam ista communi omnium, alterius iam notitiae, ne sine causa visibilem ex invisibili facere gestisset animam, istis scilicet quaestionibus opportunam per carnis in illam humanae defensionem. 'Sed non poterat Christus inter homines nisi homo videri.' redde igitur Christo fidem suam, ut qui homo voluit incedere animam quoque humanae condicionis ostenderit, non faciens eam carneam sed induens eam carne.

12 Ostensa sit nunc anima per carnem, si constiterit illam ostendendam quoquo modo fuisse, id est incognitam sibi et nobis:

12 ad hoc *vulgo* adhuc *TB*^{*mg*}· *Kroy*. prius *TMPRB* potius *N om. F* pressius *Kroy*.
18 nihil *TMFR*^{*mg*}· nisi *PNRB vulgo*.
27 carnem *Kroy*.
30 et *T Kroy. om. ceteri*.
34 istis *libri* iustis *Kroy* (*forsan recte*).
35–6 in illam *om. X*   sed non poterat etc. *interlocutori assignabam*.

may be able to shine. So then in this connexion let us first discuss whether there was any need for soul to be brought into view in such a manner: and next, when they allege that it was formerly totally invisible, whether they mean it was incorporeal, or even that it possessed some sort of body of its own. Yet even when they affirm that it was invisible, they define it as corporeal, as possessing that which is invisible: for if it possesses nothing invisible how can it be described as invisible? Indeed it cannot even exist if it possesses nothing by which to exist. But since it does exist it must of necessity possess something by which it exists. If it does possess something by which it exists, this must be its body. Everything that exists is body of some kind or another. Nothing is incorporeal except what does not exist. Seeing then that soul possesses an invisible body, he who took upon himself to make it visible might with much more dignity have made visible that of it which it already possessed, though invisible: because in this matter also neither falsehood nor infirmity should attach to God—falsehood if he had displayed soul as other than what it was, infirmity if he had not power to display it as what it was. No one, with the intention of bringing a man into view, pulls a helmet or a mask over his face. Yet this was done to soul if by being changed into flesh it put on a top layer which was not its own. Moreover, even if soul be reckoned incorporeal, so that by some occult violation of reason soul exists while whatever it is that soul is is not body, it was not on that account impossible for God—and it did more appropriately befit his purpose—to display it in some new aspect of body, not in this which is common to all and is already of a different significance: otherwise his anxiety to make soul visible instead of invisible would have failed of its purpose, and an action for trespass would have lain against soul at the instance of human flesh. 'But it was impossible for Christ to be seen among men except as man.' Then give back to Christ his trustworthiness, and it will follow that he whose will it was to walk as man also made soul perceptible under human conditions, not making it fleshly, but clothing it with flesh.

12 We might at this juncture be prepared to admit that soul was made visible by means of flesh, if it were sufficiently proved that

quanquam in hoc vana distinctio est, quasi nos seorsum ab anima simus, cum totum quod sumus anima sit. denique sine anima nihil sumus, ne hominis quidem sed cadaveris nomen. si ergo ignoramus animam, ipsa se ignorat. ita superest hoc solummodo inspicere, an se anima sic ignorarit ut nota quoquo modo fieret. opinor sensualis est animae natura: adeo nihil animale sine sensu, nihil sensuale sine anima, et ut impressius dixerim animae anima sensus est. igitur cum omnibus anima sentire praestet et ipsa sentiat omnium etiam sensus, nedum qualitates, cui verisimile est ut ipsa sensum sui ab initio sortita non sit? unde illi scire quod interdum sibi sit necessarium ex naturalium necessitate, si non scit suam qualitatem, cui quid necessarium est? hoc quidem in omni anima recognoscere est, notitiam sui dico, sine qua notitia sui nulla anima se ministrare potuisset. puto autem magis hominem, animal solum rationale, compotem et animam esse sortitum quae illum faciat animal rationale, ipsa in primis rationalis. porro quomodo rationalis quae efficit hominem rationale animal, si ipsa rationem suam nescit ignorans semetipsam? sed adeo non ignorat, ut auctorem et arbitrum et statum suum norit. nihil adhuc de deo discens deum nominat: nihil adhuc de iudicio eius admittens deo commendare se dicit: nihil magis audiens quam spem nullam esse post mortem et bene et male defuncto cuique imprecatur. plenius haec prosequitur libellus quem scripsimus DE TESTIMONIO ANIMAE. alioquin si anima semetipsam ignorans erat ab initio, nihil a Christo cognovisse debuerat nisi qualis esset. nunc autem non effigiem suam didicit a Christo sed salutem.

12: 7 sic *Kroy*. hic *TB* om. *X*.
    12 quod *PRB vulgo* quid *TMNF Kroy*.
    15–16 notitia sui...se *XB* sibi...a se *T Kroy*.
    17 compotem *TB Kroy*. computes *X* competere *Oeh. suo marte*.
    18–19 porro quomodo rationalis *om. X (manifesto errore)*.

it needed in some way or other to be made visible—that is, that it was till then unknown either to itself or to us: although in this context the distinction is idle, as though we were here and soul there, the truth being that the whole of what we are is soul. In fact, without soul we are nothing, a mere name, not even of a man, but of a corpse. If, therefore, we are ignorant of soul, it is soul that is ignorant of itself. So it remains only to examine this question, whether soul was in such sense ignorant of itself as to need by all possible means to be made known. The nature of soul, I imagine, is perceptive. Certainly nothing that has a soul is without perception, and nothing is perceptive apart from soul: and, to speak more precisely, perception is the soul of the soul. Therefore, since soul enables all to be perceptive, and is itself perceptive even of the perceptions of all, not to speak of their attributes, can anyone think it likely that it has not from the beginning been endowed with perception of itself? Whence its faculty of knowing that which from time to time is necessary to it from the necessity imposed by its natural characteristics, if it knows not its own attributes and what is necessary to each? This indeed one can observe in every soul, knowledge of itself: for without this knowledge of itself no soul would have been able to cause itself to function. But even more I think that man, the only rational animal, is endowed also with a soul competent to make him a rational animal, being itself in first instance rational. Yet how is it rational, this which makes man a rational animal, if while ignorant of itself it knows not its own reason? So far however is it from being ignorant of itself, that it knows its Author, and its Judge, and its own estate. While as yet it learns nothing of God, it mentions God's name: while as yet it makes no acknowledgement of his judgement, it professes to commend its cause to God: while it hears at every turn that there is no hope after death, it utters either a blessing or a curse upon this dead man or that. This theme is more fully pursued in the book I have written ON THE TESTIMONY OF THE SOUL. Another point: if soul had been ignorant of itself from the beginning, there is nothing it had more need to obtain knowledge of from Christ than its own qualities. In fact, however, what it has learned from Christ, is not what it

propterea filius dei descendit et animam subiit, non ut ipsa se
30 anima cognosceret in Christo sed Christum in semetipsa: non
enim se ignorando de salute periclitabatur sed dei verbum. *Vita
inquit manifestata est,* non anima: et *Veni inquit animam salvam
facere,* non dixit ostendere. ignorabamus nimirum animam, licet
invisibilem, nasci et mori, nisi corporaliter exhiberetur. ignora-
35 vimus plane resurrecturam cum carne. hoc erit quod Christus
manifestavit: sed et hoc non aliter in se quam in Lazaro aliquo,
cuius caro non erat animalis, ita nec anima carnalis. quid ergo
amplius innotuit nobis de animae ignoratae retro dispositione?
quid invisibile eius fuit quod visibilitatem per carnem desideraret?

13 'Caro facta est anima ut anima ostenderetur.' numquid ergo
et caro anima facta est ut caro manifestaretur? si caro anima est,
iam non anima est sed caro: si anima caro est, iam non caro est sed
anima. ubi ergo caro, et ubi anima, si alterutro alterutrum facta
5 sunt, immo si neutrum sunt dum alterutro alterutrum fiunt? certe
perversissimum ut carnem nominantes animam intellegamus et
animam significantes carnem interpretemur. omnia periclita-
buntur aliter accipi quam sunt, et amittere quod sunt dum aliter
accipiuntur, si aliter quam sunt cognominantur. fides nominum
10 salus est proprietatum. etiam cum demutantur qualitates accipiunt
vocabulorum possessiones. verbi gratia, argilla excocta testae
vocabulum suscipit, nec communicat cum vocabulo pristini
generis quia nec cum ipso genere. proinde et anima Christi caro
facta non potest non id esse quod facta est et id non esse quod
15 fuerat, aliud scilicet facta. et quoniam proximum adhibuimus

  31 periclitabatur *T Kroy.* periclitatur *X vulgo.*
  34 nasci et mori nisi corporaliter *X vulgo* nasci et non mori incorporaliter
  ut nobis nascens et moriens corporaliter *TB^{mg}·, quos paene sequitur Kroy.*
  37 cuius *XB* cuiusque *T* (*male intellecto scriptoris sensu*).
  13: 1 ante caro *lacunam signavit Kroy., sed haud opus erat.*
   2–4 si caro etc. *XB* si caro est anima iam non est caro sed anima, si anima
   caro est iam non anima est sed caro *T Kroy. ambiguitates a scriptore
   relictas resolvere conatus esse videtur librarius quispiam.*
   4 ubi anima *T add.* est *XB vulgo*   si alterutro *T om. XB vulgo.*
   5 alterutro alterutrum *T* alterutrum alterum *XB vulgo*   post fiunt
   quaerendi signum posuit Kroy.
   15 fuerat *T* fuerit *XB vulgo.*

looks like but how it is saved. For this cause did the Son of God come down and submit to having a soul, that soul might obtain knowledge, not of itself in Christ but of Christ in itself. For it was through ignorance, not of itself but of the Word of God, that it was in peril of its salvation. *The life*, it says, not 'the soul', *was made manifest*:[1] and *I came*, he says, *to save the soul*;[2] he did not say 'to make it visible'. We were ignorant, were we, that the soul, though invisible, is born and dies, and should have continued so unless it were displayed in the form of a body? We were ignorant, surely, that it will rise again, and the flesh along with it. This it must be that Christ made manifest: yet even this not otherwise in himself than in such a one as Lazarus, whose flesh was not composed of soul, any more than his soul was turned into flesh. What further information did we then acquire of the state of the soul hitherto unknown? What invisible attribute had it that stood in need of visibility by means of flesh?

13 'Soul was made into flesh so that soul might be made visible.' Then was flesh also made into soul, so that flesh might be made manifest? If soul is flesh, it is no longer soul, but flesh: if flesh is soul, it is no longer flesh, but soul. Where then is the flesh, and where is the soul, if both have been made out of each other—nay more, if they are neither, in that each is made into the other? Evidently it is most perverse that while using the word 'flesh' we should understand 'soul', and while talking of soul should interpret it as flesh. All things will be in danger of being taken for other than they are, losing their own identity by being taken for that other, if they are termed otherwise than they are. Fidelity of terms is the safeguard of things being what they are. Even when qualities are changed, things receive new endowments of names. For example, baked clay takes up the name of crockery, and has no joint interest in the name belonging to its original species, seeing it has none in the species itself. Consequently also the soul of Christ, if made into flesh, cannot but be that which it has been made into, and have ceased to be that which it was, now that it has been made into something else. And since I have adduced a closely related illustration, I shall make fuller use of it. For

[1] I John 1. 2.   [2] Luke 9. 56.

exemplum plenius eo utemur. certe enim testa ex argilla unum est corpus, unumque vocabulum unius scilicet corporis: nec potest testa dici et argilla, quia quod fuit non est, quod autem non est et ⟨nomen⟩ non adhaeret. ergo et anima caro facta uniformis soli-
20 ditas et singularitas tota est, et indiscreta substantia. in Christo vero invenimus animam et carnem simplicibus et nudis vocabulis editas, id est animam animam et carnem carnem, nusquam animam-carnem aut carnem-animam, quando ita nominari debuissent si ita fuissent, sed etiam sibi quamque substantiam
25 divise pronuntiatas ab ipso, utique pro duarum qualitatum distinctione, seorsum animam et seorsum carnem. quid? Anxia est, inquit, anima mea usque ad mortem: et, Panis quem ego dedero pro salute mundi caro mea est. porro si anima caro fuisset, unum esset in Christo carnea anima aut caro animalis: at cum dividit
30 species, carnem et animam, duo ostendit. si duo, iam non unum: si non unum, iam nec anima carnalis nec caro animalis: unum enim est anima-caro aut caro-anima. nisi si et seorsum aliam gestabat animam praeter eam quae caro erat, et aliam circumferebat carnem praeter illam quae anima erat. quodsi una caro et
35 una anima, illa tristis usque ad mortem et illa panis pro mundi salute, salvus est numerus duarum substantiarum in suo genere distantium, excludens carneae animae unicam speciem.

14 'Sed et angelum,' aiunt, 'gestavit Christus.' qua ratione? 'Qua et hominem.' eadem ergo est et causa. ut hominem gestaret Christus salus hominis fuit causa, scilicet ad restituendum quod perierat. homo perierat, hominem restitui opor-
5 tuerat. ut angelum gestaret Christus nihil tale de causa est. nam etsi angelis perditio reputatur in ignem praeparatum diabolo et angelis eius, nunquam tamen illis restitutio repromissa est: nullum

18–19 quod autem non est et non adhaeret *TB*   *om. X* nomen *inserendum putabam.*
26 quid? *ita pungebam.*
32 nisi si *T om.* si *XB vulgo.*
14: 2 est *XB* sit *T.*

certainly crockery made out of clay is one body, and there is one term for it, as being one body: crockery cannot also be called clay, because what it was it is not, and of that which it is not the name also ceases to be applicable. So also, soul made into flesh is wholly a uniform solidity and singularity, a substance undifferentiated. But in Christ we observe soul and flesh set forth in plain and undisguised terms, that is, soul as soul, and flesh as flesh, never soul-flesh or flesh-soul—though they would have needed to be so described, if such they had been—and even each substance for itself separately named by him, strictly in accordance with the distinction between their two sets of attributes, soul on the one hand, flesh on the other. For example: *My soul*, he says, *is troubled even unto death*:[1] and, *The bread which I shall give for the salvation of the world is my flesh*.[2] But if his flesh had been soul, there would in Christ be one thing, fleshly soul or else flesh composed of soul: but now that he distinguishes their aspects, flesh and soul, he shows them to be two things. If two, of course not one: if not one, evidently the soul is not turned into flesh, nor the flesh composed of soul—for 'one thing' amounts to 'soul-flesh' or 'flesh-soul'—unless perchance he was also carrying about another soul apart by itself, in addition to the one which was flesh, and was carrying round another flesh in addition to the one which was soul. But if there is one flesh and one soul, the latter sorrowful even unto death and the former bread for the salvation of the world, there is conserved the duality of two substances each distinct in its own species, a duality which precludes the singular aspect of a fleshly soul.

14 'But,' say they, 'Christ was also clothed upon with an angel.' By what method? 'The same by which he might have been clothed with man.' Then the reason for it also is the same. For Christ to be clothed with manhood, man's salvation was the reason, the restitution of that which had perished. Man had perished: it was man that must be restored. For Christ to be clothed with an angel there was nothing of this sort by way of reason. For even though perdition is reckoned to angels—*into the fire prepared for the devil and his angels*[3]—yet never to them has

[1] Matt. 26. 38; Mark 14. 34.   [2] John 6. 51.   [3] Matt. 25. 41.

mandatum de salute angelorum suscepit Christus a patre. quod
pater neque repromisit neque mandavit, Christus administrare
non potuit. cui igitur rei angelum quoque gestavit nisi ut satel-
litem forte cum quo salutem hominis operaretur? idoneus enim
non erat dei filius qui solus hominem liberaret, a solo et singulari
serpente deiectum? ergo iam non unus deus nec unus salutificator,
sed duo salutis artifices, et utique alter altero indigens. an vero ut
per angelum liberaret hominem? cur ergo ipse descendit, ad id
quod per angelum erat expediturus? si per angelum, quid et ipse?
si per se, quid et angelus? dictus est quidem magni consilii
angelus, id est nuntius, officii non naturae vocabulo: magnum
enim cogitatum patris, super hominis scilicet restitutionem,
adnuntiaturus saeculo erat. non ideo tamen sic angelus intelle-
gendus ut aliqui Gabriel aut Michael. nam et filius a domino
vineae mittitur ad vinitores, sicut et famuli, de fructibus petitum:
sed non propterea unus ex famulis deputabitur filius quia famu-
lorum successit officio. facilius ergo dicam, si forte, ipsum filium
angelum (id est nuntium) patris, quam angelum in filio. sed cum
de [filio] ipso sit pronuntiatum, Minuisti eum modicum quid
citra angelos, quomodo videbitur angelum induisse, sic infra
angelos deminutus dum homo fit, qua caro et anima, et filius
hominis? qua autem spiritus dei et virtus altissimi non potest
infra angelos haberi, deus scilicet et dei filius. quanto ergo, dum
hominem gestat, minor angelis factus est, tanto non, dum angelum
gestat. poterit haec opinio Hebioni convenire qui nudum
hominem et tantum ex semine David, id est non et dei filium,

10 igitur *XB* ergo *T*.
11 forte *T Kroy*. fortem *XB vulgo*.
13 deus *XB* dominus *T*.
14 sed *T* si *XB*.
15 ipse *om. XB*.
17–18 magni consilii angelus *XB* angelus magni cogitatus *T*.
22 vinitores *T* cultores *XB quaero an legendum* viticultores.
26 filio *PR vulgo*.
27 angelum induisse *XB* angelus *T*.
29 qua *R³* quia *libri*.
32 poterit *XB* poterat *T*.

restitution been promised: no commandment concerning the salvation of angels has Christ received from the Father. That which the Father has neither promised nor commanded, Christ cannot have administered. To what purpose then was he also clothed with an angel, except perhaps as an attendant to help him in the accomplishment of man's salvation? Then was not the Son of God competent by himself to deliver man whom the serpent by himself and unattended had overthrown? In that case there is no longer one God, nor one Saviour, if there are two artificers of salvation, the one quite powerless without the other. Or perhaps it was that he might deliver man by the agency of the angel? Then why did he himself come down for a task which he was going to accomplish by the agency of the angel? If by the angel, why also himself? If by himself, why also the angel? Certainly he is described as *the angel of great counsel*,[1] 'angel' meaning 'messenger', by a term of office, not of nature: for he was to announce to the world the Father's great project, that concerned with the restitution of man. Yet he is not on that account to be understood as an angel, in the sense of a sort of Gabriel or Michael. For the son also is sent by the lord of the vineyard to the husbandmen, as the servants too had been, to fetch of the fruits of it: but the son must not be reckoned one of the servants just because he succeeded to the servants' task.[2] So I shall find it easier to say, if I have to, that the Son himself was the angel (that is, the messenger) of the Father, than that there was an angel in the Son. But seeing that the Son himself is the subject of the pronouncement, *Thou hast made him a little lower than the angels*,[3] how shall he be thought to have clothed himself with an angel when he is made lower than the angels by being made man (as being flesh and soul) and the Son of Man? For as the Spirit of God, and the Power of the Most High, he cannot be held to be lower than the angels, seeing he is God, and the Son of God. So then, even as he is made less than the angels while clothed with manhood, even so he is not less if clothed with an angel. This view of the matter could have suited Ebion, who determines that Jesus is a bare man, merely of the seed of David, and therefore not also the Son of God—though

[1] Isa. 9. 5 (LXX). [2] Cf. Matt. 21. 33 *seqq*. [3] Ps. 8. 5.

constituit Iesum—plane prophetis aliquo gloriosiorem—ut ita in
35 illo angelum fuisse dicatur quemadmodum in aliquo Zacharia:
nisi quod a Christo nunquam est dictum, Et ait mihi angelus qui
in me loquebatur. sed nec quotidianum illud omnium prophetarum, Haec dicit dominus: ipse enim erat dominus, coram et ex
sua auctoritate pronuntians, Ego autem dico vobis. quid ultra ad
40 haec? Esaiam exclamantem audi, Non angelus neque legatus sed
ipse dominus salvos eos fecit.

15 Licuit et Valentino ex privilegio haeretico carnem Christi
spiritalem comminisci. quidvis eam fingere potuit quisquis
humanam credere noluit, quando, quod ad omnes dictum sit, si
humana non fuit nec ex homine non video ex qua substantia ipse
5 Christus et hominem se et filium hominis pronuntiarit: Nunc
autem vultis occidere hominem veritatem ad vos locutum: et,
Dominus est sabbati filius hominis. de ipso enim Esaias, Homo in
plaga et sciens ferre imbecillitatem: et Hieremias, Et homo est et
quis cognovit illum? et Daniel, Et ecce super nubes tanquam
10 filius hominis: etiam Paulus apostolus, Mediator dei et hominum
homo Christus Iesus: item Petrus in actis apostolorum, Iesum
Nazarenum virum vobis a deo destinatum, utique hominem.
haec sola sufficere vice praescriptionis debuerunt ad testimonium
carnis humanae et ex homine sumptae et non spiritalis sicut nec
15 animalis nec sidereae nec imaginariae, si sine studio et artificio
contentionis haereses esse potuissent. nam, ut penes quendam ex
Valentini factiuncula legi, primo non putant terrenam et humanam
Christo substantiam informatam ne deterior angelis dominus

    35 dicatur *TB* edicat *X*.
    36 a Christo *TB* Christo *X*.
    40 Esaiam exclamantem audi *XB* Esaia exclamante *T*.
 15: 2 quidvis *XB* quidquidvis *T*.
    3 sit *T Urs. Kroy.* est *XB*.
    5 et hominem se *T* hominem *XB*.
    9 cognovit illum *MPNRB* cognoscet eum *TN*.   ecce *om. XB*.
    15 imaginariae *XB* putative imaginarie *T*.

clearly he speaks of himself in somewhat higher terms than the prophets use concerning themselves—so as to state that an angel was in him in the same way as in Zechariah, for example: though we object that the words, *And the angel that spake in me said unto me*,[1] were never used by Christ. Nor indeed was that habitual expression of all the prophets, *Thus saith the Lord*: for he was himself the Lord, declaring openly and on his own authority, *But I say unto you*.[2] What more do we need, when we hear Isaiah crying out, *Not an angel nor a delegate, but the Lord himself hath saved them*?[3]

15 Valentinus, by heretical privilege, allowed himself to invent a spiritual flesh of Christ. One who has refused to believe it human can fashion it into anything he likes, since (and let this remark be addressed to them all) if it was not human and not derived from man, I cannot see what substance Christ himself was referring to when he declared himself both man and the Son of Man: *Now therefore ye seek to kill a man who hath spoken to you the truth*,[4] and, *The Son of Man is lord of the sabbath*.[5] Moreover it is of him that Isaiah says, *A man under chastisement, and knowing how to bear weakness*:[6] and Jeremiah, *And he is a man, and who hath known him?*[7] and Daniel, *And behold, above the clouds as it were a son of man*:[8] also Paul the Apostle, *A mediator of God and men, the man Christ Jesus*:[9] again Peter in the Acts of the Apostles, *Jesus of Nazareth, a man appointed by God for you*[10]—where there is another word for 'man', but it still implies humanity. These texts by themselves ought to have been sufficient to non-suit them—as evidence of his flesh being human and derived from man, not composed of spirit, any more than it is composed of soul or of the stars, or is imaginary—if heresies had been able to rid themselves of special pleading and of the tricks of contentiousness. For, as I have read in the works of one of Valentinus' faction, in the first place they refuse to admit that terrestrial and human substance was brought into shape for Christ, lest the Lord should turn out

---

[1] Zech. 1. 14. [2] Matt. 5. 20 etc. [3] Isa. 63. 9 LXX.
[4] John 8. 40. [5] Matt. 12. 8. [6] Isa. 53. 3.
[7] Jer. 17. 9 LXX. [8] Dan. 7. 13. [9] 1 Tim. 2. 5.
[10] Acts 2. 22.

deprehendatur qui non terrenae carnis extiterunt, dehinc quod
20 oporteret similem nostrae carnem similiter nasci, non de spiritu
nec de deo, sed ex viri voluntate. 'Et cur, Non de corruptela sed
de incorruptela? et quare non, sicut et illa resurrexit et in caelo
resumpta est, ita et nostra par eius statim adsumitur? aut cur illa
par nostrae non aeque in terram dissoluta est?' talia et ethnici
25 volutabant: 'Ergo dei filius in tantum humilitatis exhaustus?' et,
'Si resurrexit in exemplum spei nostrae cur nihil tale de nobis
probatum est?' merito ethnici talia: sed merito et haeretici. numquid enim inter illos distat nisi quod ethnici non credendo credunt
at haeretici credendo non credunt? legunt denique, Minorasti
30 eum modico citra angelos, et negant inferiorem substantiam
Christi nec hominem se sed vermem pronuntiantis, qui nec formam habuit nec speciem, sed forma eius ignobilis, defecta citra
omnes homines, homo in plaga et sciens ferre imbecillitatem.
agnoscunt hominem deo mixtum, et negant hominem: mortuum
35 credunt, et quod est mortuum ex incorruptela natum esse contendunt, quasi corruptela aliud sit a morte. 'Sed et nostra caro
statim resurgere debebat.' exspecta: nondum inimicos suos
Christus oppressit, ut cum amicis de inimicis triumphet.

16 Insuper argumentandi libidine ex forma ingenii haeretici
locum sibi fecit Alexander ille quasi nos affirmemus idcirco
Christum terreni census induisse carnem ut evacuaret in semetipso
carnem peccati. quod etsi diceremus, quacunque ratione muni-
5 remus sententiam nostram, dum ne tanta amentia qua putavit
tanquam ipsam carnem Christi opinemur ut peccatricem evacua-

---

20 nostrae carnem *scribebam* nostri carnem *XB* nostrae carnis *T*.
25 exhaustus *XB* exhibitus est *T*.
30 modico *XB* modicum *T*.
32 defecta *TF Kroy*. despecta *MPNRB vulgo*.

to be of less worth than the angels, who do not consist of terrestrial flesh: and secondly, because flesh like ours would have needed to be born like us, not of the Spirit, nor of God, but of the will of a man. 'And what,' they ask, 'is the meaning of *Not of corruption but of incorruption*?[1] And why, even as that flesh rose again and was received up into heaven, is not ours, if it is like his, straightway taken up? Or else why was not his, if it is like ours, likewise dissolved into the earth?' These are the sort of questions the Gentiles also used to canvass: 'Was then the Son of God emptied out to such a degree of humility?' and, 'If he rose again for an example of our hope, why is there no evidence of anything of the kind happening to us?' You might expect such things of Gentiles: yes, you might expect them of heretics too. For is there any difference between them, except that Gentiles by not believing believe, while heretics by believing believe not? They find it written, *Thou hast made him a little less than the angels*,[2] yet they deny the inferior substance of Christ, though he declares himself not even a man but a worm,[3] though he had *no form nor comeliness*, but his aspect was ignoble, *worn out more than all men*, and he was *a man under chastisement, and knowing how to bear weakness*.[4] They acknowledge a man mingled with God, yet deny the manhood: they believe he died, yet that which died they claim was born of incorruption—as though corruption were anything else but death. 'But our flesh too ought to be immediately rising again.' Have patience. Christ has not yet put down all his enemies,[5] so as to triumph over his enemies, with his friends to share his victory.

16 Yet once more that Alexander person, through lust of arguing, has, according to the rules of heretical trickery, made himself noteworthy by his suggestion that we affirm that Christ's purpose in clothing himself with flesh of human origin was that in himself he might bring to nought the flesh of sin.[6] Now though we should say this we might by some reasoning or other defend our judgement, provided it was not with that great folly by which he supposes that our opinion is that the very flesh of

---

[1] 1 Pet. 1. 23.   [2] Ps. 8. 5.   [3] Cf. Ps. 22. 6.
[4] Isa. 53. 3.   [5] Cf. Ps. 8. 8; 1 Cor. 15. 27, 28.   [6] Cf. Rom. 6. 6.

tam in ipso, cum illam et ad dexteram patris in caelis praesidere meminerimus et venturam inde in suggestu paternae claritatis praedicemus. adeo, ut evacuatam non possumus dicere ⟨quae in
10 caelis est⟩, ita nec peccatricem in qua dolus non fuit. defendimus autem non carnem peccati evacuatam esse in Christo sed peccatum carnis, non materiam sed naturam, nec substantiam sed culpam, secundum apostoli auctoritatem dicentis, Evacuavit peccatum in carne. nam et alibi in similitudine inquit carnis peccati fuisse
15 Christum, non quod similitudinem carnis acceperit quasi imaginem corporis et non veritatem, sed similitudinem peccatricis carnis vult intellegi quod ipsa non peccatrix caro Christi eius fuit par cuius erat peccatum, genere non vitio Adae aequanda. hinc etiam confirmamus eam fuisse carnem in Christo cuius natura est
20 in homine peccatrix, et sic in illa peccatum evacuatum, dum in Christo sine peccato habetur quae in homine sine peccato non habebatur. at neque ad propositum Christi faceret evacuantis peccatum carnis non in ea carne evacuare illud in qua erat natura peccati, neque ad gloriam: quid enim magnum si in carne meliore
25 et alterius (id est non peccatricis) naturae naevum peccati peremit? 'Ergo, inquies, si nostram induit, peccatrix fuit caro Christi.' noli constringere explicabilem sensum: nostram enim induens suam fecit, suam faciens non peccatricem eam fecit. ceterum, quod ad omnes dictum sit qui ideo non putant carnem nostram in Christo
30 fuisse quia non fuit ex viri semine, recordentur Adam ipsum in hanc carnem non ex semine viri factum: sicut terra conversa est

16: 9 *post* praedicemus *gravius pungebam* (*ita Kroy.*).   quae in caelis est *addenda putabam*   *postea* peccatricem [quia] nec evacuatam *libri*.
   18 Adae aequanda *iamdudum scribebam*   adaequanda *T Kroy.* Adae, quando *XB vulgo.*
   20 dum *T* quod *XB.*
   21 habetur *TNF* habeatur *MP.*
   25 naevum peccati peremit *scribebam*   vim peccati peremit *T Kroy.* naevum peccati redemit *XB vulgo.*
   26 inquies *T* inquis *XB.*
   30 fuit *XB* fuerit *T.*

Christ, as being sinful, was brought to nought in him: for we remember that it sits on high in heaven at the right hand of the Father,[1] and we proclaim that it will come from thence in the eminence of the Father's glory:[2] and consequently, as we cannot say it has been brought to nought, when it is in heaven, so neither can we say it was sinful, when in it there was no guile.[3] Our contention, however, is not that the flesh of sin, but that the sin of the flesh, was brought to nought in Christ, not the material but its quality, not the substance but its guilt, according to the apostle's authority when he says, *He brought to nought sin in the flesh.*[4] For in another place also [5] he says that Christ was in the likeness of the flesh of sin: not that he took upon him the likeness of flesh, as it were a phantasm of a body and not its reality: but the apostle will have us understand by 'the likeness of sinful flesh' that the flesh of Christ, itself not sinful, was the like of that to which sin did belong, and is to be equated with Adam in species but not in defect. From this text we also prove that in Christ there was that flesh whose nature is in man sinful, and that it is by virtue of this that sin has been brought to nought, while in Christ that same flesh exists without sin which in man did not exist without sin. Moreover it would not suit Christ's purpose, when bringing to nought the sin of the flesh, not to bring it to nought in that flesh in which was the nature of sin: neither would it be to his glory. For what would it amount to if it was in a better kind of flesh, of a different (that is, a non-sinful) nature, that he destroyed the birthmark of sin?[6] 'In that case,' you will reply, 'if it was our flesh Christ clothed himself with, Christ's flesh was sinful.' Forbear to tie up tight a conception which admits of unravelling. By clothing himself with our flesh he made it his own, and by making it his own he made it non-sinful. Moreover—and let this be addressed to all those who suppose that because he was not of a man's seed, it was not our flesh that was in Christ—let them remember that Adam himself was made into this flesh, though not of a man's seed: as earth was changed into this flesh without a man's seed,

---

[1] Cf. Mark 16. 19.   [2] Cf. Matt. 16. 27; Mark 8. 38.
[3] Cf. 1 Pet. 2. 22.   [4] Rom. 8. 3.   [5] Ibid.
[6] Or, by another reading, 'overcame the power of sin'.

in hanc carnem sine viri semine, ita et dei verbum potuit sine coagulo in eiusdem carnis transire materiam.

17 Sed remisso Alexandro cum suis syllogismis quos in argumentationibus torquet, etiam cum psalmis Valentini quos magna impudentia quasi idonei alicuius auctoris interserit, ad unam iam lineam congressionem dirigamus an carnem Christus ex virgine acceperit, ut hoc praecipue modo humanam eam constet si ex humana matrice substantiam traxit: quanquam licuit iam et de nomine hominis et de statu qualitatis et de sensu tractationis et de exitu passionis humanam constitisse. ante omnia autem commendanda erit ratio quae praefuit ut dei filius de virgine nasceretur: nove nasci debebat novae nativitatis dedicator de qua signum daturus dominus ab Esaia praedicabatur. quod est istud signum? Ecce virgo concipiet in utero et pariet filium. concepit igitur virgo et peperit Emmanuelem, nobiscum deum. haec est nativitas nova, dum homo nascitur in deo, ex quo in homine deus natus est carne antiqui seminis suscepta sine semine antiquo, ut illam novo semine, id est spiritali, reformaret exclusis antiquitatis sordibus expiatam. sed tota novitas ista, sicut et in omnibus, de veteri figurata est, rationali per virginem dispositione homine domino nascente. virgo erat adhuc terra, nondum opere compressa, nondum sementi subacta: ex ea hominem factum accipimus a deo in animam vivam. igitur si primus Adam ita traditur, merito sequens vel novissimus Adam, ut apostolus dixit, proinde de terra (id est carne) nondum generationi resignata in spiritum vivificantem a deo est prolatus. et tamen ne mihi vacet incursus nominis Adae, unde Christus Adam ab apostolo dictus est si terreni non fuit census homo eius? sed et hic ratio defendit, quod

17: 5 hoc praecipue modo *XB* praecipue *T*.
   6 licuit *TX* liquuit *B*.
   11 est *om. T*.
   13 Emmanuel quod est nobiscum deus *T*.
   14 ex quo in homine *T Kroy.* in quo homine *XB*.
   16 spiritali *T* spiritaliter *XB*.
   19 *pro* opere *quaero an scribendum* vomere.

ON THE FLESH OF CHRIST 59

so also the Word of God was able, without coagulation, to pass into the material of that same flesh.

17 But, dismissing Alexander, along with those syllogisms of his which he tortures in his arguings, also along with those psalms of Valentinus which with supreme impudence he interpolates as though they were the work of some competent author, let us now concentrate our attack at one single point, whether it was from the Virgin that Christ took to himself flesh: for by this method, if by no other, it will be established that his flesh was human, if it derived its substance from a human womb: although it has already become clear that it was of human constitution, both from the appellation 'man' and from its natural characteristics, from the sense-perception of handling and from the issue of the passion. Yet before all else we shall need to adduce the reason which prescribed that the Son of God should be born of a virgin: which was, that he must needs be born in a new manner, as being the founder of that new birth concerning which it was proclaimed by Isaiah that the Lord would give a sign. What sign is that? *Behold, a virgin shall conceive in the womb and shall bear a son.*[1] And so a virgin did conceive, and bore Emmanuel, God with us. This is the new birth, that man is being born in God, since the day when God was born in man, taking to himself flesh of the ancient seed without the agency of the ancient seed, so that he might reshape it with new (that is, spiritual) seed when he had first by sacrifice expelled its ancient defilements. But that newness in its totality, as also in all its bearings, was prefigured of old, when by a reasonable ordinance by means of a virgin man was born to the Lord. The earth was still virgin, not yet deflowered by husbandry, not yet subdued to seedtime: of it we are told that man was made by God into a living soul. Therefore, seeing that of the first Adam it is so related, naturally the second or last Adam, as the apostle has called him, was likewise from earth (that is, flesh) not yet unsealed to generation brought forth by God to be a life-giving spirit. And yet—that I leave not otiose the introduction of the name of Adam—why was Christ called Adam by the apostle[2] if his manhood was not of terrestrial origin? Here also reason gives

[1] Isa. 7. 14. [2] Cf. 1 Cor. 15. 45.

deus imaginem et similitudinem suam a diabolo captam aemula operatione recuperavit. in virginem enim adhuc Evam irrepserat verbum aedificatorium mortis: in virginem aeque introducendum erat dei verbum exstructorium vitae, ut quod per eiusmodi sexum abierat in perditionem per eundem sexum redigeretur in salutem. crediderat Eva serpenti, credidit Maria Gabrieli: quod illa credendo deliquit haec credendo delevit. 'Sed Eva nihil tunc concepit in utero ex diaboli verbo.' immo concepit. nam exinde ut abiecta pareret et in doloribus pareret verbum diaboli semen illi fuit: enixa est denique diabolum fratricidam. contra Maria eum edidit qui carnalem fratrem Israel interemptorem suum salvum quandoque praestaret. in vulvam ergo deus verbum suum detulit bonum fratrem, ut memoriam mali fratris eraderet: inde prodeundum fuit Christo ad salutem hominis quo homo iam damnatus intraverat.

18 Nunc et simplicius respondeamus. non competebat ex semine humano dei filium nasci, ne si totus esset filius hominis non esset et dei filius nihilque haberet amplius Salomone et amplius Iona, ut de Hebionis opinione credendus erat. ergo iam dei filius ex patris dei semine, id est spiritu, ut esset et hominis filius caro ei sola erat ex hominis carne sumenda sine viri semine: vacabat enim semen viri apud habentem dei semen. itaque sicut nondum natus ex virgine patrem deum habere potuit sine homine matre, aeque cum de virgine nasceretur potuit matrem habere hominem sine homine patre: sic denique homo cum deo dum caro hominis cum spiritu dei, caro sine semine ex homine, spiritus cum semine ex deo. igitur si fuit dispositio rationis super filium dei ex virgine

33 haec credendo delevit *XB* ista credendo correxit *T Kroy*.
39 eraderet *Rig.* evaderet *TB^{mg}·* redderet *XB*.
18: 1 et *TP Kroy.* ut *MNFRB (quod forsan praestaret)*.
2 ne si *B vulgo* nisi *TX*.
3 ut *Oeh.* et *XB om. T*.
5 caro ei sola erat *scribebam* caro ei (*vel* ea) sola quae erat *XB* caro quae sola erat *T*.
9 hominem *om. X*.

the answer: it is because God by a contrary operation has regained possession of his own image and similitude taken captive by the devil. Into Eve, while still a virgin, had crept the word, constructive of death:[1] into a virgin no less needed to be introduced the Word of God, constructive of life,[2] so that that which through that sex had gone astray into perdition should through the same sex be led back again into salvation. Eve had believed the serpent: Mary believed Gabriel. The sin which the former committed by believing, the latter by believing blotted out. 'But Eve on that occasion conceived nothing in her womb by the devil's word.' Yes, she did. For the devil's word was to her a seed, so that thenceforth she should be abject and obedient, and should bring forth in sorrows:[3] and in fact she did give birth, to the devil, the murderer of his brother.[4] Mary, on the other hand, brought forth him who should sometime bring to salvation his brother according to the flesh, Israel, by whom he himself was slain. So then, God brought down into the womb his own Word, the good brother, that he might erase the memory of the evil brother: for the salvation of man Christ must needs come forth from that organ into which man already under condemnation had entered.

18 Now let us put our case less figuratively. It was not feasible for the Son of God to be born of human seed, lest, if he were wholly the son of man, he should not also be the Son of God, and should be in no sense greater than Solomon or than Jonah, as in Ebion's view we should have to regard him. Therefore, being already the Son of God, of the seed of God the Father (that is, spirit), that he might also be the Son of Man all he needed was to take to him flesh out of human flesh without the action of a man's seed: for a man's seed was uncalled-for in one who had the seed of God. And so, as while not yet born of the Virgin it was possible for him to have God for his father, without a human mother, equally, when being born of the Virgin, it was possible for him to have a human mother without a human father. Thus, in short, is there man with God, when there is man's flesh with God's spirit—

[1] Cf. Gen. 3. 1.   [2] Cf. Luke 1. 35; John 1. 14.
[3] Cf. Gen. 3. 16. [4] Cf. Gen. 4. 1.

proferendum, cur non ex virgine acceperit corpus quod de virgine protulit, quia aliud est quod a deo sumpsit? 'Quoniam, inquiunt, verbum caro factum est.' vox ista quid caro sit factum contestatur et declarat, nec tamen periclitatur quasi statim aliud sit factum caro et non verbum, si ex carne factum est verbum caro: aut si ex semetipso factum est, scriptura dicat. cum scriptura non dicat nisi quod sit factum, non et unde sit factum, ergo ex alio, non ex semetipso, suggerit factum. si non ex semetipso sed ex alio, iam hinc tracta ex quo magis credere congruat carnem factum verbum nisi ex carne in qua et factum est, vel quia ipse dominus sententialiter et definitive pronuntiavit, Quod in carne natum est caro est quia ex carne natum est. sed si de homine tantummodo dixit, non et de semetipso, plane nega hominem Christum et ita defende non et in ipsum competisse. 'Atquin subicit, Et quod de spiritu natum est spiritus est, quia Deus spiritus est, et De deo natus est: hoc utique vel eo magis in ipsum tendit si et in credentes eius.' si ergo et hoc ad ipsum, cur non et illud supra? neque enim dividere potes, hoc ad ipsum, illud supra ad ceteros homines, qui utramque substantiam Christi et carnis et spiritus non negas. ceterum si tam carnem habuit quam spiritum, cum de duarum substantiarum pronuntiat conditione quas in semetipso gestabat non potest videri de spiritu quidem suo de carne vero non sua determinasse. ita cum sit ipse de spiritu dei (et spiritus deus est) ex deo natus, ipse est et ex carne hominis et homo in carne generatus.

14 quia aliud etc. *cum praecedentibus coniunxi.*
15 factum (*priore vice*) TB^{mg}. facta *XB.*
16 et declarat *om. XB (forsan recte).*
17 *post* et non verbum *primus levius distinxit Kroy.*
18, 20 (*bis*) semetipso *TB* semine ipso *X* (*ter*).
23 pronuntiat *T Kroy.*   24 si *om. T Kroy.*
25 nega hominem Christum *XB* nec de homine Christo TB^{mg}.
26 defendes *F Kroy.*
33 pronuntiat conditione *T* conditione pronuntiat *XB*   in semetipso *scribebam* in semet ipse *T* et ipse *XB.*
35 ita cum sit etc. *ita pungebam ex parum certis testimoniis quae vera viderentur indagatis* ita cum sit ipse de spiritu dei et spiritus deus est ex deo natus ipse est et ex carne hominis homo in carne generatus *X* ita cum ipse de spiritu dei spiritus et ex deo natus ipse et ex carne hominis homo in carne generatus *T.*

from man flesh without seed, from God spirit with seed. Therefore if there was an ordinance of reason regarding the need for the Son of God to be brought forth from a virgin, what room is there for doubt that he received from the Virgin that body which he did bring forth from the Virgin, seeing that what he received from God is something else? 'It is', say they, 'because *the Word was made flesh*.'[1] This saying testifies and declares what it was that was made flesh, while yet there is no risk that, in spite of this, something else, and not the Word, was made flesh, if it was out of flesh that the Word was made flesh. Or else, if out of himself he was made flesh, let Scripture say so. Since the Scripture says no more than what the Word was made, and not also from what he was so made, it follows that its suggestion is that he was so made out of something else, and not out of himself. If not out of himself but out of something else, beginning with that admission discuss of what it is more fitting to believe the Word was made flesh, if not of that flesh within which he was made flesh—if for no other reason, because the Lord himself has judicially and categorically stated, *That which is born in the flesh is flesh, because it has been born of flesh*.[2] If he said this of man only, and not also of himself, openly deny that Christ is man, and thus maintain that it did not apply to him. 'Nay, but he adds, *And that which is born of the Spirit is Spirit*,[3] because *God is spirit*,[4] and *He was born of God*:[5] this certainly has him in view, the more so if it has also those who believe in him.' Then if this too applies to him, why not also that other? For you cannot divide them, this to him, the other to the rest of men: for you do not deny the two substances of Christ, that of flesh and that of spirit. But if he possessed flesh no less than spirit, when he makes a statement concerning the condition of the two substances which he bore within himself, he cannot be thought to have made a pronouncement concerning spirit as being his but flesh as not his. Thus, since he was himself by the Spirit of God (and the Spirit is God) born of God, he was also of human flesh and as man conceived and born in the flesh.

[1] John 1. 14.   [2] John 3. 6.   [3] John 3. 6.
[4] John 4. 24.   [5] John 1. 13 (*v.l.*).

64 DE CARNE CHRISTI

19 'Quid est ergo, Non ex sanguine nec ex voluntate carnis nec ex voluntate viri sed ex deo natus est?' hoc quidem capitulo ego potius utar, cum adulteratores eius obduxero: sic enim scriptum esse contendunt, Non ex sanguine nec ex carnis voluntate nec ex
5 viri sed ex deo nati sunt, quasi supradictos credentes in nomine eius designet, ut ostendant esse semen illud arcanum electorum et spiritalium quod sibi imbuunt. quomodo autem ita erit, cum omnes qui credunt in nomine domini pro communi lege generis humani ex sanguine et ex carnis et ex viri voluntate nascantur,
10 etiam Valentinus ipse? adeo singulariter ut de domino scriptum est, Sed ex deo natus est. merito, quia verbum dei, et cum verbo dei spiritus, et in spiritu dei virtus, et quicquid dei est Christus. qua caro autem, non ex sanguine nec ex carnis et viri voluntate, quia ex dei voluntate verbum caro factum est: ad carnem enim,
15 non ad verbum, pertinet negatio formalis nostrae nativitatis, quia caro sic habebat nasci, non verbum. 'Negans autem ex carnis quoque voluntate natum, cur non negavit etiam ex substantia carnis?' neque enim quia ex sanguine negavit substantiam carnis renuit, sed materiam seminis quam constat sanguinis esse calorem
20 ut despumatione mutatum in coagulum sanguinis feminae: nam ex coagulo in caseo eius ⟨vis⟩ est substantiae quam medicando constringit, id est lactis. intellegimus ergo ex concubitu nativitatem domini negatam, quod sapit voluntas viri et carnis, non ex vulvae participatione. et quid utique tam exaggeranter incul-
25 cavit non ex sanguine nec ex carnis aut viri voluntate natum, nisi quia ea erat caro quam ex concubitu natam nemo dubitaret? negans porro ex concubitu non negavit ex carne, immo confirma-

---

19: 1 Quid est etc. *interlocutori assignabam.*
  2 nati sunt *Rig.* (*sed haud opus erat*).
  6 ostendant *T Kroy.* ostendat *XB vulgo*   illud *TB*^{mg}. illius *XB.*
  8 domini *X* eius *TB.*
  16 negans autem etc. *interlocutori assignabam: alioquin* negaverit *scribere possis.*
  19 calorem *XB* colorem *T* colatum humorem *tentavit Kroy.* (*mira felicitate*).
  20–21 sanguinis feminae nam ex coagulo *om. X.*
  21 vis *suppl. Gel.* incaseatio eius est *Kroy.* (*forsan recte*).
  23 voluntas *XB* ex voluntate *T.*
  25 aut viri voluntate *TMPF* voluntate aut viri *PRB vulgo.*

19 'What then is the meaning of, *Was born not of blood nor of the will of the flesh nor of the will of a man, but of God?*'[1] This text will be of more use to me than to them, when I have refuted those who falsify it. For they maintain that it was thus written, *Were born not of blood, nor of the will of the flesh or of a man, but of God*,[2] as though it referred to the above-mentioned believers in his name:[3] and from it they try to prove that there exists that mystic seed of the elect and spiritual which they baptize for themselves. But how can it mean this, when those who believe in the name of the Lord are all of them by the common law of human kind born of blood and of the will of the flesh and of a man, as also is Valentinus himself? Consequently the singular is correct, as referring to the Lord—*was born...of God*. Rightly so, because the Word is God's, and with the Word is God's Spirit, and in the Spirit is God's power, and God's everything that Christ is. As flesh, however, he was not born of blood, nor of the will of the flesh and of a man, because the Word was made flesh by the will of God: for it is to his flesh, not to the Word, that this denial of a nativity after our pattern applies; and the reason is that it was the flesh, not the Word, which might have been expected to be born that way. 'But in denying, among other things, that he was born of the will of the flesh, surely it also denies that he was born of the substance of flesh.' No: because neither does the denial that he was born of blood involve any repudiation of the substance of flesh, but of the material of the seed, which material it is agreed is the heat of the blood, as it were by despumation changed into a coagulator of the woman's blood. For from the coagulator there is in cheese a function of that substance, namely milk, which by chemical action it causes to solidify. We understand, then, a denial that the Lord's nativity was the result of coition (which is the meaning of *the will of a man and of the flesh*), but no denial that it was by a partaking of the womb. And why indeed does the evangelist with such amplification insist that the Lord was born not of blood nor of the will of the flesh or of a man, except that his flesh was such as no one would suspect was not born of coition? Consequently, his denial that it was born of coition involves no

---

[1] John 1. 13 (*v.l.*).   [2] John 1. 13.   [3] Cf. John 1. 12.

vit ex carne, quia non perinde negavit ex carne sicut ex concubitu
negavit. oro vos, si dei spiritus non de vulva carnem participaturus
30 descendit in vulvam, cur descendit in vulvam? potuit enim extra
eam fieri caro spiritalis simplicius multo quam intra vulvam [fieret
extra vulvam]. sine causa eo se intulit unde nihil extulit. sed non
sine causa descendit in vulvam. ergo ex illa accepit, quia si non ex
illa accepit sine causa in illam descendit, maxime eius qualitatis
35 caro futurus quae non erat vulvae, id est spiritalis.

20 Qualis est autem tortuositas vestra, ut ipsam EX syllabam
praepositionis officio adscriptam auferre quaeratis et alia magis uti
quae in hac specie non invenitur penes scripturas sanctas? per
virginem dicitis natum, non ex virgine, et in vulva, non ex vulva,
5 quia et angelus in somnis ad Ioseph—Nam quod in ea natum est,
inquit, de spiritu sancto est—non dixit ex ea. nempe tamen etsi ex
ea dixisset in ea dixerat: in ea enim erat quod ex ea erat. tantundem
ergo et cum dicit in ea, ex ea consonat, quia ex ea erat
quod in ea erat. sed bene quod idem dicit Matthaeus originem
10 domini decurrens ab Abraham usque ad Mariam, Iacob autem
generavit, inquit, Ioseph virum Mariae ex qua nascitur Christus.
sed et Paulus grammaticis istis silentium imponit: Misit, inquit,
deus filium suum factum ex muliere. numquid per mulierem aut
in muliere? hoc quidem impressius, quod factum potius dicit
15 quam natum. simplicius enim enuntiasset natum: factum autem
dicendo, et Verbum caro factum est consignavit et carnis veritatem
ex virgine factae adseveravit. nobis quoque ad hanc
speciem psalmi patrocinabuntur, non quidem apostatae et haeretici

30 cur descendit in vulvam? *om. T Kroy.*
31–2 fieret extra vulvam *om. T.*
32 sed *om. T.*
20: 5–6 *parenthesim indicabam.*
7 quod ex ea erat *om. X.*
14 potius *om. X (forsan recte).*
17 virginis *T Kroy. (contra consuetudinem scriptoris).*

denial that it was born of the flesh, but rather an affirmation that it was born of the flesh, seeing he does not deny 'of flesh' in the same terms in which he denies 'of coition'. I put it to you: if the Spirit of God came down into the womb without the intention of partaking of flesh from the womb, why did he come down into the womb? For he might have been made spiritual flesh outside the womb with far less trouble than within it. To no purpose did he bring himself into a place from whence he took nothing out. But it was not to no purpose that he came down into the womb. Consequently he did receive something from it, because if he did not receive something from it it was to no purpose that he came down into it, the more so if he were going to be flesh of such a character as, being spiritual, had nothing in common with the womb.

20 But what sort of twistiness is yours, that you try to remove that syllable 'of', prefixed in the function of a preposition, and to substitute another, which in this connexion is not found in the holy Scriptures? You allege that he was born 'by the virgin' not 'of the virgin', and 'in the womb' not 'of the womb', on the ground that when the angel in a dream said to Joseph, *For that which is born in her is of the holy Spirit*,[1] he did not say 'of her'. Yet surely, though he had said 'of her' he would have meant 'in her': for that was in her which was of her. Equally then, when he says 'in her', the meaning 'of her' is included, because that which was in her was of her. Also it is in my favour that the same Matthew, when rehearsing the Lord's pedigree from Abraham down to Mary, says *Jacob begat Joseph the husband of Mary of whom Christ is born.*[2] Paul too imposes silence on these teachers of grammar: *God*, he says, *sent his Son, made of a woman.*[3] Does he say 'by a woman' or 'in a woman'? His language is indeed the more accurate in that he says 'made' in preference to 'born'. For it would have been simpler to pronounce that he was born: yet by saying 'made' he has both set his seal on *The Word was made flesh*,[4] and has asserted the verity of the flesh made of the Virgin. We, moreover, shall have in this connexion the support of the Psalms, not indeed those of that apostate and heretic and Platonic

---

[1] Matt. 1. 20. [2] Matt. 1. 16. [3] Gal. 4. 4. [4] John 1. 14.

et platonici Valentini sed sanctissimi et receptissimi prophetae
David: ille apud nos canit Christum, per quem se cecinit ipse
Christus. accipe vicesimum primum et audi dominum patri deo
colloquentem: Quia tu es qui avulsisti me ex utero matris meae:
ecce unum. Et spes mea ab uberibus matris meae, super te sum
proiectus ex vulva: ecce aliud. Et ab utero matris meae deus meus
es tu: ecce aliter. nunc et ad sensus ipsos decertemus. Avulsisti,
inquit, ex utero. quid avellitur nisi quod inhaeret, quod infixum,
quod innexum est ei a quo ut auferatur avellitur? si non adhaesit
utero, quomodo avulsus est? si adhaesit qui avulsus est, quomodo
adhaesisset nisi dum ex utero est per illum nervum umbilicarem
quasi folliculi sui traducem adnexus origini vulvae? etiam cum
quid extraneum extraneo adglutinatur, ita concarnatur et con-
visceratur cum eo cui adglutinatur ut cum avellitur rapiat secum
ex corpore [aliquid] a quo avellitur [quasi] sequelam quandam
abruptae unitatis et producem mutui coitus. ceterum cum et
ubera matris suae nominat—sine dubio quae hausit—respondeant
obstetrices et medici et physici de uberum natura, an aliter manare
soleant sine vulvae genitali passione, suspendentibus inde venis
sentinam illam inferni sanguinis in mamillam et ipsa translatione
decoquentibus in materiam lactis laetiorem: inde adeo fit ut
uberum tempore menses sanguinum vacent. quodsi verbum caro
ex se factum est, non ex vulvae communicatione, nihil operata
vulva, nihil functa, nihil passa, quomodo fontem suum transfudit
in ubera quae nisi *pariendo* non mutat? habere autem sanguinem
non potuit lacti subministrando si non haberet et causas sanguinis
ipsius, avulsionem scilicet suae carnis. quid fuerit novitatis in
Christo ex virgine nascendi palam est: solum hoc scilicet, quod ex

21-2 vicesimum primum...colloquentem *T* et David domino deo patri
eloquentem *XB* (*quod manifesto falsum*) Christum (*pro* David) *B*^{mg}· Oeh.
27 quod (*tertia vice*) *T om. ceteri.*   30 quaero an scribendum adnexus est.
33 aliquid *om. T*   quasi *om. TMNF.*
34 producem *R³B* producis *MPNFR¹* traducis *TB*^{mg}·   cum et *T* et
MNF quae *PRB vulgo* (*quaerendi signo post* nominat *posito*).
35 parenthesim indicavit Kroy.   38 in mamillam *om. TB*^{mg}·
41 communione *T Kroy.* (*manifesto errore*).
43 pariendo *scribere ausus sum* habendo *libri et edd.*
43-4 fontem non potuit *T.*   44 et causas *T om. et ceteri.*

Valentinus, but of the most holy and canonical prophet David. He, in our Church, sings of Christ, because by him Christ sang of himself. Take psalm twenty-one, and hear the Lord conversing with God the Father. *For thou art he that didst rend me out of my mother's womb:*[1] there is one. *And my hope is from my mother's breasts. I have been cast upon thee out of the womb:*[2] there is another. *Thou art my God even from my mother's womb:*[3] there it is in other words. Now let us fight it out in view of the meanings themselves. *Thou didst rend me,* he says, *out of the womb.* What is it that is rent out, except that which inheres, which is fastened in, is entwined with that from which its removal requires it to be rent out? If he did not adhere to the womb, how was he rent out? If he who was rent out did adhere, how could he have adhered, except that while coming out of the womb he was knit by means of that umbilical cord, as it were an offshoot of his caul, to the womb where he originated? Even when something external is cemented to something external, it is so united in flesh and entrails with that to which it is cemented, that when it is rent away it forcibly takes with it [something] out of the body from which it is rent away, [as it were] a sort of corollary of broken unity and an aftermath of mutual coition. Moreover, since he also mentions his mother's breasts—undoubtedly implying that he sucked them —let midwives, physicians, and biologists bear witness concerning the nature of breasts, whether they are wont to flow except at the genital experience of the womb, from which the veins pay over into the teat that cess of the lower blood, and in the course of that transfer distill it into the more congenial material of milk. That is why, during lactation, the monthly periods cease. But if the Word was made flesh out of himself, and not out of what the womb contributed, how did a womb which had wrought nothing, performed nothing, experienced nothing, decant its fountain into those breasts in which it causes change only by the process of giving birth? It cannot have possessed blood for the supply of milk without also having reasons for the blood itself, namely the tearing away of flesh which was its own. What novelty there was in Christ, the novelty of his being born of a virgin, is plain:

[1] Ps. 22. 9.   [2] Ibid.   [3] Ps. 22. 10.

virgine secundum rationem quam edidimus, et uti virgo esset regeneratio nostra spiritaliter, ab omnibus inquinamentis sanctificata per Christum virginem et ipsum etiam carnaliter ut ex
50 virginis carne.

21 Si ergo contendunt hoc competisse novitati ut quemadmodum non ex viri semine ita nec ex virginis carne caro fieret dei verbum, quare non hoc sit tota novitas, ut caro non ex semine nata ex carne ⟨semine nata⟩ processerit? accedant adhuc com-
5 minius ad congressum. Ecce, inquit, virgo concipiet in utero. quidnam? utique dei verbum, non viri semen. certe ut pareret filium: nam Et pariet, inquit, filium. ergo ut ipsius fuit parere, quia ipsius fuit concepisse, ita ipsius est quod peperit, licet non ipsius fuerit quod concepit. contra si verbum ex se caro factum est, iam
10 ipsum se concepit et peperit, et vacat prophetia: non enim virgo concepit neque peperit, si non quod peperit ex verbi conceptu caro ipsius est. sola haec autem prophetae vox evacuabitur? an et angeli conceptum et partum virginis annuntiantis? an et omnis iam scriptura quaecunque matrem pronuntiat Christi? quomodo
15 enim mater nisi quia in utero eius fuit? ⟨ut quid in utero⟩ si nihil ex utero eius accepit quod matrem eam faceret in cuius utero fuit? hoc nomen non debet caro extranea: matris uterum non appellat nisi filia uteri caro; filia porro uteri non est, si sibi nata est. tacebit igitur et Elisabeth, prophetam portans iam domini sui
20 conscium infantem et insuper spiritu sancto adimpleta: sine causa

---

47 et uti *mendosum esse frustra suspicantur edd.*
21: 4 semine nata *supplenda censebam*   accedam *R vulgo*   comminus *T.*
  7 ipsius fuit parere quia *T om. XB vulgo.*
  11 verbi conceptu *T* verbi concepto *MNF* verbo concepto *PRB vulgo.*
  15 ut quid in utero *his suppletis loco difficili mederi tentabam.*
  19 Elisabeth propheta *T Kroy.*

namely, this and nothing else, that he was born of a virgin according to the manner I have expounded, to the further intent that our regeneration should be virginal in a spiritual sense, sanctified from all defilements through Christ, himself virgin even in the flesh, because it was of a virgin's flesh that he was born.

21 If then they claim that novelty required that the Word of God should not be made flesh from the Virgin's flesh, any more than from a man's seed, I ask why the whole novelty should not consist in this, that flesh not born of seed has proceeded forth from flesh ⟨born of seed⟩. Let them meet my attack at an even closer range. *Behold*, he says, *the virgin shall conceive in the womb.*[1] Conceive what? Evidently not a man's seed, but the Word of God. And certainly the intention was that she should bear a son, for it says, *And shall bear a son.*[2] Therefore, as the act of giving birth was hers, because the fact of having conceived was hers, likewise that which she brought to birth is hers, even though that was not hers which she conceived. On the other hand, if the Word was made flesh out of himself, in that case he conceived and bore himself, and the prophecy is pointless. For the Virgin neither conceived anything nor bore anything unless that which she bore as a consequence of the conception of the Word is flesh which was hers. And this utterance of the prophet will not be the only one to be made pointless. What about that of the angel who announced the Virgin's conception and child-bearing?[3] And what about every single scripture which mentions the mother of Christ? For how is she his mother, except that he has been in her womb, ⟨and to what purpose was he in her womb⟩ if he has received from her womb nothing that should confer motherhood upon her in whose womb he was? Flesh from elsewhere has no right to use this name. Only flesh which is the daughter of the womb talks of 'my mother's womb': and certainly it is no daughter of the womb if it was born to itself. Thus Elisabeth too will keep silence, though she not only carries within her that infant who as a prophet is already conscious of his Lord,[4] but herself also is filled with the Holy Spirit: for without reason does she say, *And whence is it to me that*

[1] Isa. 7. 14; Matt. 1. 23.   [2] Ibid.
[3] Cf. Matt. 1. 20; Luke 1. 31.   [4] Cf. Luke 1. 41, 44.

enim dicit, Et unde mihi ut mater domini mei veniat ad me? si
Maria non filium sed hospitem in utero gestabat Iesum, quomodo
dicit, Benedictus fructus uteri tui? quis hic fructus uteri qui non
ex utero germinavit, qui non in utero radicem egit, qui non eius
est cuius est uterus? et qui utique fructus uteri Christus? an quia
ipse est flos de virga profecta ex radice Iesse, radix autem Iesse
genus David, virga ex radice Maria ex David, flos ex virga filius
Mariae qui dicitur Iesus Christus, ipse erit et fructus? flos enim
fructus, quia per florem et ex flore omnis fructus eruditur in fructum. quid ergo? negant et fructui suum florem et flori suam
virgam et virgae suam radicem, quominus suam radix sibi vindicet
per virgam proprietatem eius quod ex virga est, floris et fructus:
siquidem omnis gradus generis ab ultimo ad principalem recensetur, ut iam nunc carnem Christi non tantum Mariae sed et
David per Mariam et Iesse per David sciant adhaerere. adeo hunc
fructum ex lumbis David, id est ex posteritate carnis eius, iurat illi
deus consessurum in throno ipsius. si ex lumbis David, quanto
magis ex lumbis Mariae ob quam in lumbis David.

22 Deleant igitur et testimonia daemonum filium David proclamantia ad Iesum, sed testimonia apostolorum delere non
poterunt, si daemonum indigna sunt. ipse imprimis Matthaeus,
fidelissimus evangelii commentator ut comes domini, non aliam
ob causam quam ut nos originis Christi carnalis compotes faceret
ita exorsus est: Liber generaturae Iesu Christi filii David filii
Abrahae. his originis fontibus genere manante cum gradatim
ordo deducitur ad Christi nativitatem, quid aliud quam caro ipsa

22 gestabat *XB vulgo* portabat *T Kroy.*
25 et qui *XB* ut quid *T.*
35 adeo *T* deo *XB* ideo *Pam.*
38 in *XB* ex *T.*
22: 1-2 proclamantia ad *X* proclamantium *T corr. quaero an legendum* dominum Iesum.
3 poterunt *B* potuerunt *TX.*
6 generaturae *XB vulgo.*
7 *et passim* Abrahae *T* Abraham *ceteri.*

the mother of my Lord should come to me?[1] If Mary was carrying Jesus in her womb not as a son but as a guest, what can Elisabeth mean by *Blessed is the fruit of thy womb?*[2] What sort of fruit of a womb is this, which has neither germinated from the womb, nor struck root in the womb, nor belongs to her whose the womb is? In what sense, really, is Christ the fruit of her womb? Is it not because he is himself the flower from the stem which came forth from the root of Jesse,[3] while the root of Jesse is the house of David, and the stem from the root is Mary, descended from David, that the flower from the stem, the Son of Mary, who is called Jesus Christ, must himself also be the fruit? For flower is fruit, because by means of the flower and from the flower every fruit is perfected into fruit. What then? They deny to the fruit its own flower, to the flower its own stem, and to the stem its own root, so as to preclude the root from laying claim, by means of its own stem, to the ownership of that which is from the stem, namely the flower and the fruit: whereas in fact the whole ladder of descent is counted back from the final to the principal, that now at length these persons may know that the flesh of Christ adheres not only to Mary, but also to David through Mary and to Jesse through David. Thus it is that God swears to David that this fruit out of his loins, that is, out of the posterity of his flesh, will sit upon his throne.[4] If he is out of the loins of David, the more so is he out of the loins of Mary, for on her account he is reckoned as having been in David's loins.

22 Thus even though they delete also the testimony of the devils who cry out to Jesus 'son of David', yet they will not be able to delete the testimony of the apostles, if the devils' testimony is beneath their notice. Matthew himself, to begin with, a most trustworthy compiler of the Gospel, as having been a companion of the Lord, for no other reason than of making us cognisant of Christ's origin according to the flesh begins thus: *The book of the generation of Jesus Christ, the son of David, the son of Abraham.*[5] The fact that, by a descent which flows from these sources of origin, the sequence is brought down step by step to the nativity of

---

[1] Luke 1. 43.   [2] Luke 1. 42.   [3] Cf. Isa. 11. 1.
[4] Cf. Ps. 132. 11; Acts 2. 30.   [5] Matt. 1. 1.

Abrahae et David per singulos traducem sui faciens in virginem
usque describitur inferens Christum—immo ipse Christus prodit
—de virgine? sed et Paulus, utpote eiusdem evangelii et discipulus
et magister et testis, quia eiusdem apostolus Christi, confirmat
Christum ex semine David secundum carnem, utique ipsius. ergo
ex semine David caro Christi. sed secundum Mariae carnem ex
semine David: ergo ex Mariae carne est dum ex semine est David.
quocunque detorseris dictum, aut ex carne est Mariae quod ex
semine est David, aut ex David semine est quod ex carne est
Mariae. totam hanc controversiam dirimit idem apostolus ipsum
definiens esse Abrahae semen: cum Abrahae, utique multo magis
David, quasi recentioris. retexens enim promissionem bene-
dictionis nationum in semine Abrahae, Et in semine tuo bene-
dicentur omnes nationes, Non, inquit, dixit seminibus tanquam
de pluribus, sed semine, de uno, quod est Christus. qui haec
nihilominus legimus et credimus, quam debemus et possumus
agnoscere in Christo carnis qualitatem? utique non aliam quam
Abrahae, siquidem semen Abrahae Christus: nec aliam quam
Iesse, siquidem ex radice Iesse flos Christus: nec aliam quam
David, siquidem fructus ex lumbis David Christus: nec aliam
quam Mariae, siquidem ex Mariae utero Christus: et adhuc
superius nec aliam quam Adae, siquidem secundus Adam
Christus. consequens ergo est ut aut illos spiritalem carnem
habuisse contendant, quo eadem conditio substantiae deducatur in
Christum, aut concedant carnem Christi spiritalem non fuisse,
quae non de spiritali stirpe censetur.

23 Sed agnoscimus adimpleri propheticam vocem Simeonis
super adhuc recentem infantem dominum pronuntiatam, Ecce hic
positus est in ruinam et suscitationem multorum in Israel et in

---

10-11 *parenthesim indicabam* prodit *scribebam* producitur *TB*^{*mg*}. proditur *XB*.
21 semine (*priore vice*) *TB*^{*mg*}. nomine *XB vulgo*.
24 nihilominus *T om. XB*.
29 quam Mariae *scribebam* quam ex Mariae utero *T* quam ex Maria *XB*.
30 Adae *T* Adam *ceteri*.
32-3 in Christum *T* in Christo *X*.

Christ, can only mean that the very flesh of Abraham and David is registered as making an offshoot of itself through each several ancestor right down to the Virgin, and as bringing in Christ—nay rather, Christ himself comes forth—from the Virgin. Paul also, being a disciple and teacher and witness of the same Gospel, because he is an apostle of the self-same Christ, attests that Christ is *of the seed of David according to the flesh*[1]—evidently Christ's own flesh. Consequently Christ's flesh is of the seed of David. But it is of the seed of David in consequence of the flesh of Mary, and therefore it is of Mary's flesh, seeing it is of the seed of David. In whatever direction you twist the expression, either his flesh is of Mary's flesh because it is of David's seed, or else it is of David's seed because it is of Mary's flesh. The same apostle resolves this whole controversy by defining Christ himself to be Abraham's seed: and since he is Abraham's, evidently much more is he David's, who is the more recent. For when tracing back the promise of the blessing of the nations in the seed of Abraham— *And in thy seed shall all the nations be blessed*[2]—he says, *He said not seeds, as of many, but seed, of one, which is Christ.*[3] What quality of flesh must and can we, who (in spite of our opponents' objections) read and believe this, acknowledge in Christ? Evidently no other than Abraham's, in that Christ is the seed of Abraham: nor other than Jesse's, in that Christ is the flower out of the root of Jesse:[4] nor other than David's, in that Christ is the fruit out of the loins of David:[5] nor other than Mary's, in that Christ is from Mary's womb: and, still higher up, no other than Adam's, in that Christ is the second Adam.[6] It follows, therefore, that they must either claim that those others had flesh composed of spirit, so that the same quality of substance may be brought down into Christ, or else admit that Christ's flesh was not composed of spirit, since its descent is not recounted from a spiritual stock.

23 We recognize here the fulfilment of the prophetic word of Simeon which he pronounced over the still new-born infant Lord: *Behold, this child is set for the ruin and raising up of many in*

---

[1] Rom. 1. 3; cf. 2 Tim. 2. 8. [2] Gen. 22. 18.
[3] Gal. 3. 16. [4] Cf. Isa. 11. 1.
[5] Cf. Ps. 132. 11. [6] 1 Cor. 15. 45.

signum quod contradicitur. signum enim nativitatis Christi secundum Esaiam: Propterea dabit vobis dominus ipse signum: ecce virgo concipiet in utero et pariet filium. agnoscimus ergo signum contradicibile conceptum et partum virginis Mariae, de quo Academici isti, 'Peperit et non peperit virgo et non virgo.' quasi non, et si ita dicendum esset, a nobis magis dici conveniret: peperit enim quae ex sua carne, et non peperit quae non ex viri semine, et virgo quantum a viro, non virgo quantum a partu— non tamen, ut ideo non pepererit quae peperit quia non ex sua carne, et ideo virgo quae non virgo quia non de visceribus suis mater. sed apud nos nihil dubium, nec retortum in ancipitem defensionem: lux lux et tenebrae tenebrae et est est et non non: quod amplius hoc a malo est. peperit quae peperit, et si virgo concepit in partu suo nupsit: nam nupsit ipsa patefacti corporis lege, in quo nihil interfuit de vi masculi admissi an emissi: idem illud sexus resignavit. haec denique vulva est propter quam et de aliis scriptum est, Omne masculinum adaperiens vulvam sanctum vocabitur domino. quis vere sanctus quam sanctus ille dei filius? quis proprie vulvam adaperuit quam qui clausam patefecit? ceteris omnibus nuptiae patefaciunt. itaque magis patefacta est quia magis erat clausa. utique magis non virgo dicenda est quam virgo, saltu quodam mater antequam nupta. et quid ultra de hoc retractandum est? cum hac ratione apostolus non ex virgine sed ex muliere editum filium dei pronuntiavit agnovit adapertae vulvae nuptialem passionem. legimus quidem apud Ezechielem de vacca illa quae peperit et non peperit: sed videte ne vos iam tunc pro-

23: 4 quod contradicitur *PR*[1] quod contradicetur *MNFR*[3]*B* contradicibile *T*.
12 pepererit *scribebam* peperit *libri*   quae peperit quia non ex sua carne *T* om. *ceteri*.
21 sanctus ille dei filius *scribebam* sanctus ille *T* sancti filius *FR*[mg.] dei filius *MPNRB*.
23 ceteris *iampridem scribebam, assentitur Kroy.* ceterum *libri*.
23–24 pro itaque...quia...utique *scribere velim* utique...quae...itaque.
29 tunc *T* nunc *XB*.

Israel, and for a sign that is being spoken against.[1] The sign is that of the nativity of Christ, according to Isaiah: *Therefore the Lord himself shall give you a sign: behold, a virgin shall conceive in the womb and shall bear a son.*[2] Consequently we recognize as a sign capable of being spoken against the conception and child-bearing of Mary the virgin, concerning which these Academics say, 'She bare and bare not, virgin and no virgin.' And yet, even though this expression were tolerable, it would be one more suitable for us to use: for she bare, seeing she did so of her own flesh, and she bare not, seeing she did so not of a man's seed, a virgin as regards her husband, not a virgin as regards child-bearing: not however that the expression 'bare and bare not' implies that it was not of her flesh, or that 'virgin and not virgin' means that she was not from her own bowels a mother. With us, however, there is nothing doubtful, or that is twisted back into a plea that can recoil upon those who make it: light is light and darkness is darkness,[3] and yea is yea and nay is nay, and what is more than this is on the side of evil.[4] She bore which did bear: and if as a virgin she conceived, in her child-bearing she became a wife. For she became a wife by that same law of the opened body, in which it made no difference whether the violence was of the male let in or let out: the same sex performed that unsealing. This in fact is the womb by virtue of which it is written also concerning other wombs: *Everything male that openeth the womb shall be called holy to the Lord.*[5] Who is truly holy, except that holy Son of God? Who in a strict sense has opened a womb, except him who opened this that was shut? For all other women marriage opens it. Consequently, hers was the more truly opened in that it was the more shut. Indeed she is rather to be called not-virgin than virgin, having become a mother by a sort of leap, before she was a bride. Why need we discuss this any further? In stating, on these considerations, not that the Son of God was born of a virgin, but of a woman,[6] the apostle acknowledges the nuptial experience of the opened womb. We read indeed in Ezekiel of that heifer which bare and bare not:[7] but it is more than likely that by this expres-

[1] Luke 2. 34.   [2] Isa. 7. 14.   [3] Cf. Isa. 5. 20.   [4] Cf. Matt. 5. 37.
[5] Ex. 13. 2; Luke 2. 23.   [6] Cf. Gal. 4. 4.   [7] Not in Ezekiel.

30 videns spiritus sanctus notarit hac voce disceptaturos super uterum
Mariae. ceterum non contra illam suam simplicitatem pronuntiasset dubitative, Esaia dicente Concipiet et pariet.

24 Quod enim et alias [Esaias] iaculatur in suggillatione haereticorum ipsorum, et imprimis Vae qui faciunt dulce amarum et tenebras lucem, istos scilicet notat qui nec vocabula ipsa in luce proprietatum suarum conservant ut anima non alia sit quam quae
5 vocatur et caro non alia quam quae videtur et deus non alius quam qui praedicatur. ideo etiam Marcionem prospiciens, Ego sum, inquit, deus, et alius absque me non est. et cum alio idipsum modo dicit, Ante me deus non fuit, nescioquas illas Valentinianorum aeonum genealogias pulsat. et Non ex sanguine neque ex
10 carnis aut viri voluntate sed ex deo natus est, Hebioni respondit. aeque Etiamsi angelus de caelis aliter evangelizaverit vobis quam nos anathema sit, ad energema Apelleiacae virginis Philumenes [filium] dirigit. certe Qui negat Christum in carne venisse hic antichristus est, nudam et absolutam et simplici nomine naturae
15 suae pronuntians carnem, omnes disceptatores eius ferit, sicut et definiens ipsum quoque Christum unum multiformis Christi argumentatores quatit, qui alium faciunt Christum alium Iesum, alium elapsum de mediis turbis alium detentum, alium in secessu montis in ambitu nubis sub tribus arbitris clarum alium ceteris
20 passivum, ⟨alium nobilem alium⟩ ignobilem, alium magnanimum alium vero trepidantem, novissime alium passum alium resuscitatum, per quod suam quoque in aliam carnem resurrectionem adseverant. sed bene quod idem veniet de caelis qui est passus, idem omnibus apparebit qui est resuscitatus, et videbunt et

32 ut dubitativae *T*.

24: 1 Esaias *om. T*.

    2–3 dulce amarum et tenebras *XB vulgo* de luce tenebras de tenebris *T Kroy*.

    3 ipsa *T* ista *ceteri*.

    7 alio idipsum modo *scribebam* alio eodem ipso modo *T* alio idipsum eodem modo *XB*.   10 aut *TKroy.* et *ceteri*.

    13 filium *seclusi* filium filumenen *MPN alia alii*.

    20 alium nobilem alium *supplenda censebam, nisi forte totum locum ita rescribere malis,*...sub tribus arbitris ⟨secretum⟩, alium ceteris (*sc. ix apostolis*) passivum, ⟨alium⟩ clarum ⟨alium⟩ ignobilem.

    22 aliam carnem *T Kroy*. alia carne *ceteri*.

sion the Holy Spirit, even then having you in mind, censured such as should argue about Mary's womb. Otherwise he[1] would not, with the opposite of his usual clarity, have made a hesitating statement: for Isaiah says, *Shall conceive and bear*.[2]

24 For by the weapons he[1] hurls in other places also for the bruising of the heretics' persons (not to speak of their opinions), and in the first place, *Woe unto them that make sweet bitter and darkness light*,[3] he censures of course these who fail to keep even words in the clarity of their proper meaning, that soul should be no other than the soul which is so called, and flesh no other than the flesh which is visible, and God no other than he who is preached. Consequently, this time with an eye to Marcion, he says, *I am God, and other apart from me there is not*.[4] And when he repeats this in other terms, *Before me there was no god*,[5] he is having a knock at those I know not what genealogies of aeons, of the Valentinians. And, *Was born not of blood nor of the will of the flesh or of a man, but of God*,[6] was his answer to Ebion. No less, *Even if an angel from heaven preach the gospel to you otherwise than we, let him be anathema*,[7] is directed against the energeme of Apelles' virgin Philumena. Certainly, *Whoso denies that Christ is come in the flesh, this same is antichrist*,[8] using the word 'flesh' unadorned and unqualified and in the straightforward sense of its own nature, strikes a blow at all who initiate discussions about it: as also when he defines that Christ himself is one,[9] he overthrows these arguers for a multiform Christ, who make Christ one and Jesus another; one who slipped away from the midst of the multitude, another who was arrested; one who having withdrawn to the mountain was glorious in the midst of a cloud in the sight of three witnesses, another who was commonly visible to the rest; ⟨one well known, another⟩ unknown; one courageous, but another anxious; and, at the last, one who suffered, and another who was raised again, whereby they affirm also their own resurrection into other flesh. But it is in my favour that the same will come from heaven as did suffer, the same will be evident to all as was raised up again,[10]

---

[1] he—i.e. the Holy Spirit. [2] Isa. 7. 14. [3] Isa. 5. 20.
[4] Isa. 45. 5, 6. [5] Isa. 43. 10. [6] John 1. 14. [7] Gal. 1. 8.
[8] 1 John 4. 3. [9] Cf. 1 Cor. 8. 6. [10] Cf. Acts 1. 11.

agnoscent qui eum confixerunt, utique ipsam carnem in quam saevierunt, sine qua nec ipse esse poterit nec agnosci: ut et illi erubescant qui adfirmant carnem in caelis vacuam sensu ut vaginam exempto Christo sedere, aut qui carnem et animam tantundem, aut tantummodo animam carnem vero non iam.

25   Sed hactenus de materia praesenti. satis iam enim arbitror instructam esse carnis in Christo et ex virgine natae et humanae probationem. quod et solum discussum sufficere potuisset—citra singularum ex diverso opinionum congressionem quam et argumentationibus earum et scripturis quibus utuntur provocavimus ex abundanti—uti cum eo quod probavimus quid et unde fuerit Christi caro, quid non fuerit adversus omnes praeiudicaverimus. ut autem clausula de praefatione commonefaciat, resurrectio nostrae carnis alio libello defendenda hic habebit praestructionem, manifesto iam inde quale fuerit quod in Christo resurrexerit.

25: 3–6 *parenthesim indicabam.*
    6 cum *T   om.* XB *vulgo* (*forsan recte*).
    8 clausula *TMPNRB* clausulam *F*   commonefaciat *Kroy.* (*mira felicitate*) communem faciat *T*   communi faciat *XB vulgo.*
    10 manifestato *T*   resurrexerit *TMPNR³* resurrexit *FR¹B* (*forsan recte*).

and that those who pierced him will look upon him and recognize him,[1] without doubt the same flesh upon which they wrought their savagery, for without it he can neither be nor be recognized as himself: so that those also may be put to confusion who affirm that his flesh is seated in heaven void of perception, like a scabbard with Christ withdrawn, or that his flesh and soul are indistinguishable, or that there exists only soul, but flesh no longer.

25 But enough of the present subject. For I think I have now furnished sufficient proof that the flesh of Christ was both born of the Virgin and was human. The discussion of this in itself ought to have been sufficient, without that tackling of individual hostile opinions to which, beyond the requirements of my case, I have challenged them in terms both of their own arguments and of the texts of Scripture which they employ: and thus not only have I proved what Christ's flesh was and whence it came, but I shall be found also to have established a previous judgement against them all as to what it was not. But, that the conclusion of my argument may recall its preamble, the resurrection of our flesh, which I shall have to defend under a different brief, will here be found to have had its foundation laid, it being manifest now, if not before, what sort of thing that was which rose again in Christ.

[1] Cf. Zech. 12. 10; John 19. 37.

NOTES AND COMMENTARY

TITLE

In modern English 'flesh' has a more materialistic sound than 'body'. In Greek and in Latin the opposite is the case. Σῶμα hardly ever seems to forget its Homeric meaning 'dead body', and though both σῶμα and *corpus* come to signify the bodies of living men and animals, they can also refer to the 'mass' of an inanimate object. On the other hand σάρξ, *caro*, can only refer to flesh actually or potentially alive: it denotes the material of which the animate body consists, and in the case of actually living bodies is understood to involve the soul, *anima*, that principle or entity or ratio (differently conceived of by different philosophers, and differently again by Christian theologians) which gives to the material elements of the body their unity, life, and cohesion. The subject of the present treatise is not the Body of Christ in either the natural or the mystical or the sacramental sense of that phrase, but his Flesh: that is, the substance, nature, attributes, and origin of the whole of that human nature which the divine Word assumed at the Incarnation. The question under discussion is one of substance, even of material: not of body as the organized vehicle and instrument of human life, but of the verity of the whole human nature of Christ as involved in the statement that his flesh is truly flesh and his soul is truly soul, both the one and the other derived by natural descent from the progenitors of all mankind.

CHAPTER I

Those who interpret 'resurrection of the dead' in such a sense as to exclude the flesh are also disposed to make difficulties as to the truth of Christ's incarnation: logically so, for if Christ's body which rose again was of flesh such as ours, this constitutes a presumption that our bodies also will rise again. So we have to build up our case from the point at which these break it down, and the purpose of the present discourse is to lay foundations for that which will follow. Our subject here is the flesh of Christ, its existence, its provenance, and its quality. The verdict in this case will serve as precedent for the proof of our own resurrection. Our adversaries are Marcion who denied Christ's flesh and his nativity, Apelles who admitted the flesh while denying the nativity, and the Valentinians and others, who profess to acknowledge both, but in a non-natural sense. Actually Marcion, who alleged that the flesh was 'putative', might just as well have acknowledged a putative nativity and a putative growth to maturity.

1   **istos Sadducaeorum propinquos.** Tertullian supposes himself in court and refers to his adversaries as though they were present. The Sadducees said there was no resurrection, neither angel, nor spirit: Acts 23. 8.

2   **moratam.** This, followed by *ita* (Rigaltius), is undoubtedly the right reading. Rhenanus, in the note quoted by Oehler, seems to read the word as *mōratam* (*stabilem et firmam et inconcussam*): so also Oehler, whose index does not distinguish between the present instance and *De Pat.* 4, *moratus secundum dominum*: *De Anima* 33, *integre morati*: *Adv. Marc.* IV. 15, *aliquid et cum creatore moratus nec in totum Epicuri deus* (which last is rightly interpreted in a note by Rigaltius, Oehler *ad loc.*). Here however we must surely read *mŏratam*; cf. Juvenal VI. 1 *Pudicitiam Saturno rege moratam in terris visamque diu*, where the word stands for the non-existent past participle of *manere*.

3   **merito**: logically, with good reason (as far as they are concerned). Cf. §4, *si Christus creatoris est, suum merito amavit*: §17, *si primus Adam ita traditur, merito sequens*: and frequently. Cf. also Novatian, *De Trin.* 10, quoted below on §2.

4   **distrahunt.** So all the MSS. except *A* (the oldest) which has *distruunt* (an impossible word), on the strength of which Mercer, followed by Kroymann, reads *destruunt*, which they observe occurs in the following sentence. This would be good enough stylistic reason for it not to occur here, and in any case the sentences are not parallel. Here the point is that the flesh of Christ is pulled asunder with inquisitions, like a body on the rack:

for *quaestio* can mean either a judicial inquiry (as in the republican *quaestiones perpetuae*) or the examination of slave witnesses by torture: e.g. Cicero, *pro Milone* 21. 57, *facti enim in eculeo quaestio est, iuris in iudicio*. In the following sentence there is a change of metaphor: Tertullian supposes that the aspirations of the flesh for eternal life (*carnis vota*) are being pulled down or dismantled (*destruunt*), and that it is his business to lay again their foundations (*praestruere*) by establishing the verity of Christ's flesh and of its resurrection. For the metaphor from building-works cf. *Adv. Marc.* II. 1, *aliud subruere necesse habuit ut quae vellet exstrueret: sic aedificat qui propria paratura caret*: and *De Res. Carnis* 4, *statim incipiunt et inde praestruunt, dehinc interstruunt*.

4 tanquam aut nullam omnino. This was the view of Marcion, who regarded everything material as the work of the creator, the enemy of the good god, and therefore evil. Consequently in his view Christ, the representative of the good god, could not have been in possession of a real body, and that which he seemed to have was none at all. Cf. *Adv. Marc.* v. 20 for the Marcionite comment on Philippians 2. 6, *plane de substantia Christi putant et hic Marcionitae suffragari apostolum sibi quod phantasma carnis fuerit in Christo, cum dicit quod in effigie dei constitutus non rapinam existimavit pariari deo sed exhausit semetipsum accepta effigie servi, non veritate, et in similitudine hominis, non in homine, et figura inventus homo, non substantia, id est non carne*. Tertullian in reply quotes Colossians 1. 15, 'image of the invisible God', and remarks that if the Philippians text means that Christ is not truly Man, then the Colossians text must mean that he is not truly God.

4 aut quoquo modo aliam. Marcion's disciples apparently so far improved on their master's teaching as to admit that there is a certain celestial matter or substance which is not evil, and suggested that Christ's flesh was of stellar origin: cf. §6, *de sideribus, inquiunt, et de substantiis superioris mundi mutuatus est carnem*. Others, apparently not Marcionites but Valentinians, were of opinion that Christ's flesh was constituted of condensed (or otherwise transmuted) soul. Marcion's view is discussed §§1–5, his disciples' §§6–9, the others' §§10–16. *Quoquo modo* would

naturally mean 'in any and every way', 'at all events', as in
§ 12 (twice) and *Adv. Marc.* II. 9, *quoquo tamen, inquis, modo substantia creatoris delicti capax invenitur cum afflatus dei, id est anima, in homine deliquit*: it is echoed here by *omni modo*, 'in every way', 'at all events', later in the sentence. But conceivably Tertullian could have written *quoquo* when he meant *aliquo*, 'in some way or other', and that may be his meaning here.

7 carnis vota. Oehler compares *De Res. Carnis* 4, *nimirum haec erunt vota carnis recuperandae, iterum cupere de ea evadere*. But the sentences are not parallel. Here *carnis vota* (a subjective genitive) are the hope of the flesh concerning its own future: *vota carnis recuperandae* (an objective genitive) are the soul's hope that it will be again united to the flesh from which death has separated it.

8 examinemus...certum est. Tertullian perhaps had in mind Quintilian, *Inst. Orat.* XII. 3. 6, *omne ius quod est certum aut scripto aut moribus constat: dubium aequitatis regula examinandum est*: where Lewis and Short (*s.v.* examino, *ad fin.*) are wrong in saying that the reference is to judicial examination: rather it is to the advocate preparing his case, and *examinare* (as in Tertullian) has not lost its primary sense of 'weigh', 'estimate the value of'.

9 caro quaeritur etc. This reading, with the common punctuation of these sentences, is almost certainly right. The second hand of *T*, and Mesnart, have *carnis* (dependent on *veritas*), which makes sense, though not the best sense. It is not true that the verity of Christ's flesh was being sought for, but that the flesh itself was the subject of a judicial inquiry (*quaestio*). The subject of the present treatise (*retractatur*) is its verity (*an fuerit*) and its quality, which last involves the two further questions of its origin (*unde fuerit*) and its attributes (*cuiusmodi fuerit*). Kroymann's punctuation, with a semicolon after *eius*, spoils the rhythm of the sentence without affecting the meaning. *Qualitas* is practically the same as *natura*, the essential attributes by which an object is what it is, but with a further suggestion of the worth or dignity attendant upon that: see a note on § 3 *periculum enim status sui*.

11 renuntiatio eius. Kroymann wrongly observes, *hoc est responsio carnis*. *Renuntiatio* cannot mean a speech in reply to an accusation or in support of a plea: it means the official declaration either of the result of an election or (as here) of the judicial verdict. *Eius* is an objective genitive, standing not for *carnis* but for *veritatis*. Cf. Cicero, *Pro Murena* 8. 18, *non eundem esse ordinem dignitatis et renuntiationis, propterea quod renuntiatio gradus habeat, dignitas autem sit persaepe eadem omnium*. The verdict passed concerning the verity of Christ's flesh will constitute a leading case (*dabit legem*) concerning our own resurrection: for (as already observed) it is really our resurrection which these people wish to impugn when they deny that Christ's flesh is of the same origin and quality as ours.

13 invicem sibi testimonium responderent (*A*), the superficially more difficult reading, looks like the original: it is perfectly good Latin, of Tertullian's kind, though sufficiently unusual to have provoked variants. *Testimonium redderent* (*T*) has the appearance of an attempt at interpretation. The other readings are evident conflations, and serve merely to show that both the older variants were known to the copyists of *M* and *P*. Kroymann's *invicem sibi responderent* hardly meets the case, for it means no more than 'correspond' or 'form the counterpart of one another'. What is required is not mutual correspondence but mutual testimony, and that is what *A* gives us. For other senses of *respondere* cf. *Apol.* 9, *cum propriis filiis Saturnus non pepercit, extraneis utique non parcendo perseverabat, quos quidem ipsi parentes sui offerebant et libentes respondebant* (either 'acceded to his demand' or, more probably, 'answered in the affirmative the priest's challenge as to whether they were making a willing gift'): *De Corona* 11, *credimusne humanum sacramentum divino superduci licere et in alium dominum respondere post Christum*, a reference to the *responsio fidei* at baptism.

15 licentia often retains its natural sense of 'permission': e.g. *De Exhort. Cast.* 8, *multum existimo esse inter licentiam et salutem: de bono non dicitur 'licet', quia bonum permitti non expectat sed assumi*: so also *Ad Uxorem* 1. 2, *per licentiam tunc passivam materiae subsequentium emendationum praeministrabantur*, 'general permission', and *Adv. Marc.* 1. 29, *vacat enim abstinentiae testimonium cum licentia* *eripitur*. But there are places where it means a permission assumed rather than granted, something of the nature of presumption, as seems to be the case here, and at *Adv. Marc.* I. 3, *an duos deos liceat induci poetica et pictoria licentia, et tertia iam haeretica*.

16 Apelles, according to Hippolytus, *Philos.* VII. 38, said that Christ οὐκ ἐκ παρθένου γεγενῆσθαι, οὐδὲ ἄσαρκον εἶναι...ἀλλ᾽ ἐκ τῆς τοῦ παντὸς οὐσίας μεταλαβόντα μερῶν σῶμα πεποιηκέναι, τουτέστι θερμοῦ καὶ ψυχροῦ καὶ ὑγροῦ καὶ ξηροῦ. For his relation to Marcion see *De Praescr. Haer.* 30.

18 confessus, the reading of most MSS., should probably be retained. *Professus* (*T Kroy*.) is the wrong word in this context. Its correct use is of things personal to the professor, e.g. *artem aliquam, philosophiam*, etc. Its appearance here will be due to editing by *T* or his archetype, on the ground that *confessus* is too good a word for the supposedly insincere admission of a truth: hence the substitution of *professus* in its medieval sense 'pretend to acknowledge'. For *confiteri* in this sense cf. *Adv. Marc.* I. 6, *deum vero confessus utrumque* (sc. *et potiorem et quem credit minorem*) *duo summa magna confessus est*.

18 aliter illas interpretari: so *A TB^{mg.}*: *illis* of the other MSS. makes no evident sense. According to Irenaeus, whose account of the matter is adopted by Tertullian and Hippolytus, the Valentinian doctrine was briefly this: There are two Christs, both of them distinct from (though one of them comes into a loose association with) Jesus. The superior Christ, who is, and must remain, totally unknown to any except his four superiors in the pleroma, is the last-born fruit of the pleroma. Along with his consort Holy Spirit he was emitted by Mind, after the expulsion of Achamoth, with the function of teaching the æons that Abyss and Silence, the primary æons, are forever unknowable and incomprehensible. This gospel of the unknowable so delighted the æons that each of them contributed the best it possessed, and the combination of all their gifts produced Jesus, the perfect fruit of the pleroma. The lower Christ is in no way connected with the above. He was fabricated by Craftsman, the non-divine creator of the world, and (like his maker) is of 'spiritual' (i.e. non-divine) constitution. This Christ appeared on earth in an 'animal' body, i.e., a body constructed of soul (*anima*), being born 'through' (not 'of') a virgin. At his baptism in Jordan he was taken possession of by that composite almost-divine Jesus-Saviour. In this manner the Valentinians, admitting Christ's flesh, 'otherwise interpreted it' as being constructed of soul: and, admitting his nativity, they could explain it in any or all of four ways—as confection by all the æons, as fabrication by Craftsman, as birth through a virgin, or as possession by Jesus-Saviour descending in the form of a dove. The third of these, birth through a virgin, in a body constructed of soul, is chiefly in Tertullian's mind here and in §§ 10–16. The above description is condensed from Tertullian, *Adv. Valentinianos*, Irenaeus, *Haer.* I, Hippolytus, *Philos.* VI.

19 sed et must be retained. Kroymann, without MS. authority, writes *scilicet*, which is out of place in introducing an author's explanation of his own remarks, its proper function being to indicate his deductions (with which he suspects the other will not agree) from the theories or expressions of his adversary. The sentence refers to Marcion, who denied the flesh of Christ by alleging it to be merely putative, and (removing all Matthew and the beginning of Luke from the Gospel) denied the nativity altogether, suggesting that Christ appeared on earth full-grown, without antecedents, by the bank of Jordan in the fifteenth year of Tiberius Caesar, in a form which was not flesh, but merely looked like it. Tertullian retorts that he might just as well have retained the nativity, arguing that it was only a phantasm of a nativity in the same way as what had all the appearance of flesh was merely putative flesh. Cf. *Adv. Marc.* III. 8, *phantasma vindicans Christum*; and below, *iam nunc cum mendacium deprehenditur Christus caro, sequitur ut et omnia quae per carnem Christi gesta sunt mendacio gesta sint, congressus, contactus, convictus, ipsae quoque virtutes*: and again, *sic nec passiones Christi eius* (sc. *Marcionis*) *fidem merebuntur: nihil enim passus est qui non vere est passus: vere autem pati phantasma non potuit.*

20 nativitatem (*A Oeh. Kroy.*) receives support from *mendacium Christus caro* in the previous quotation: all the other MSS., with

Rhenanus and Mesnart, have *nativitatis*, which makes no difference to the general sense, but runs better with *phantasma confingere* and may be what Tertullian wrote.

21 infantis ordo, 'birth and growth of the Child': cf. *Adv. Marc.* IV. 21, where *ordo* appears in the same connexion: *quando nec confusionis materia conveniat nisi meo Christo, cuius ordo magis pudendus ut etiam haereticorum conviciis pateat, omnem nativitatis et educationis foeditatem et ipsius etiam carnis indignitatem quanta amaritudine possunt perorantibus*. Oehler, in a note to *De Pud.* 9, *ordinem filii prodigi*, suggests that *ordo* means 'narrative', which in some cases is possible, but not at *Adv. Marc.* IV. 7, *reliquum ordinem descensionis expostulo*, 'the concomitants of that alleged descent'.

22 τῷ δοκεῖν haberentur. Kroymann marks a lacuna here, which he suggests should be filled out with *magis esse quam haberent ut eosdem etc.* If this meant what it is supposed to mean, it would indicate that Tertullian was a partial, but not a thoroughgoing, docetist: which is not the case. Also it would throw *fefellissent* into the wrong tense. The sentence is perfectly clear, and no alteration is called for.

23 elusit, *T* (and, by implication, *A*) *Rig. Oeh. Kroy.*: the other authorities have *illusit*. The sense required is apparently 'mocked at', 'played tricks with', which would be *illusit* (which would require a dative object, as at Tacitus, *Ann.* XVI. 1): *eludere* more commonly means 'escape by guile', as at Petronius 97, *scrutantium eluderet manus* (like Ulysses escaping from the Cyclops), but it can approach to the sense here required, as at Tacitus, *Hist.* I. 26 *quaedam apud Galbae aures praefectus Laco elusit*. For the general sense cf. *Adv. Marc.* V. 20 (commenting on Philippians 2. 8) *et mortem crucis: non enim exaggeraret atrocitatem extollendo virtutem subiectionis quam imaginariam phantasmate scisset, frustrato potius eam quam experto, nec virtute functo in passione sed lusu*.

CHAPTER II

Marcion repudiates the prophecies, and deletes from his gospel the narratives, of Christ's conception, birth, and childhood. We can guess his reasons for this, while denying his authority to do it.

If he is a Christian he ought to believe the Christian tradition. But he is not a Christian: his own action in denying the Christian belief he once held at once shows this and proves that that former belief is older than the heresy he has invented, and is therefore the original belief, and is the truth. This appeal to antiquity is my standing refutation of all heresies, and would of itself be sufficient in the present case: yet, to fortify my argument still further, I proceed to examine the reasons he alleges.

1 **quid illi etc.** Cf. *Adv. Marc.* v. 6, *quid illi cum exemplis dei nostri?* Similar phrases frequently occur. On the rejection of the Old Testament cf. *Adv. Marc.* I. 19, *separatio legis et evangelii proprium et principale opus est Marcionis*. *Gabriel*, though mentioned in the Gospel (but in those chapters which Marcion rejected), belongs to the original creation and not (Marcion would say) to the father of Marcion's Christ. *Adnuntiatur*, in the language of the public spectacles, would refer to the (spoken) programme: *inducitur* to entrance on the scene: but the theatrical metaphor is so remote as to be almost out of view.

2 **et in virginis utero etc.** *Utero* (*TB*) (since *inducitur* follows) is more likely to have been altered to *uterum* than conversely. *Conceptus*, balancing *nativitas*, will be the substantive, not the participle: there is no question of the child conceived being introduced into the womb, but rather of Isaiah's prophecy concerning conception in a virgin's womb bringing that fact to public notice.

2 **cum [Esaia] propheta creatoris?** *Esaia* (*XR*) may be a marginal note on *propheta*. *A* reads *cum esset a propheta creatoris*, which is meaningless. For *esset a TB* (followed by Kroymann) have *essentia* (omitting *propheta*), which is almost as meaningless, for what has the essence of the Creator to do with the present subject? The passages of Quintilian referred to by Kroymann simply state that *essentia* was a word newly invented by Sergius Flavius or by Plautus the Stoic: they have no relevance to the present passage. Evidently Tertullian's point is that though we refer to Gabriel and Isaiah for testimony to the reality of the nativity and conception, Marcion repudiates both, as belonging to the older dispensation: for according to him the new dispensa-

tion began, not with any annunciation, but with the unheralded appearance of Christ at the baptism in Jordan. Cf. *Adv. Marc.* I. 15, *at nunc quale est ut dominus anno xii Tiberii Caesaris revelatus sit?* and ibid. 19, *anno xv Tiberii Christus Iesus de caelo manare dignatus est, spiritus salutaris.* This discrepancy in the dates is explained by referring *xii* to the beginning of the ministry, *xv* to Pentecost: but Luke 3. 1 has 'fifteenth year' for the former (unless perhaps Marcion altered it to 'twelfth'). See also *Adv. Marc.* IV. 7 (quoted in the following note).

3 **qui subito etc.** Cf. *Adv. Marc.* III. 2, *atquin nihil putem a deo subitum, quia nihil a deo non dispositum.* Novatian, *De Trin.* 10, *ut merito haereticorum istorum testamenti veteris auctoritatem respuentium nescio cui commenticio et ex fabulis anilibus ficto Christo atque fucato possim vere et constanter dicere, Quis es? unde es? a quo missus es? quare nunc venire voluisti? quare talis? vel qua venire potuisti? vel quare non ad tuos abisti, nisi quod probasti* [leg. *probas te*] *tuos non habere dum ad alienos venis? etc.* Novatian's argument is that the Incarnation was the climax of a long preparation and the fulfilment of many prophecies: like Tertullian, he observes that Marcion's Christ comes without preparation (*subito*) and as a trespasser upon another's property. Cf. *Adv. Marc.* I (*passim*) and IV. 7, *anno xv principatus Tiberiani proponit eum descendisse in civitatem Galilaeae Capharnaum, utique de caelo creatoris in quod de suo ante descenderat... apparere subitum ex inopinato sapit conspectum qui semel impegerit oculos in id quod sine mora apparuit... quid autem illi cum Galilaea, etc.?*

4 **aufer hinc, inquit, etc.** These will not be supposed to be Marcion's actual words: it is a common enough rhetorical trick to put words into one's opponent's mouth which may reasonably be supposed to express the consequences of his thought.

6 **deum suum etc.** As the angels belonged to the Creator's dispensation it would have been their own God whom they praised if Luke 2. 14 had been included in Marcion's gospel. *Viderit etc.* seems to mean: 'What they meant by this, and what particular bearing it has on nativity, is their own concern, and I, Marcion, refrain from inquiring into it.' *AF*, followed by *Oeh.*,

Kroy., read *dominum*: Tertullian usually, but not invariably, says *deus* for the Father and *dominus* for the Son: by this rule, in view of Luke 2. 14 *deum* would be correct, unless perchance *honorans* refers not to the angels' song in particular, but to their presence in honour of the new birth. *Noctibus* = *noctu*, as Kroymann observes: but *De Cor.* 11 is not in point, as the sense there is distributive.

8 glorietur, i.e. at having his prophecy fulfilled: Jer. 31. 15, quoted at Matt. 2. 17.

10 oblationis. I have adopted this reading of *TB* with some hesitation: it is an obvious correction for anyone to make who found *obligationis* in his text, whereas there seems no reason for a change in the other direction. *Sumptu obligationis* would mean 'the expense to which the Law bound them', with a reference to the thrice repeated 'Law of the Lord' in Luke 2. 22–24.

11 senem moriturum...contristet has the more abundant MS. testimony. Tertullian makes Marcion misunderstand the text. Simeon was not sad at the approach of death, but relieved at the prospect of departure.

12 ne fascinet puerum. According to the superstition (still current on the continent, and not unknown in parts of England) the evil eye is put upon children by their having kind words addressed to them by strangers, especially old women. Cf. *De Virg. Vel.* 15 (quoted in part by Oehler): *nam est aliquid etiam apud ethnicos metuendum, quod fascinum vocant, infeliciorem laudis et gloriae enormioris eventum: hoc nos interdum diabolo interpretamur, ipsius est enim boni odium: interdum deo deputamus, illius est enim superbiae iudicium, extollentis humiles et deprimentis elatos.* The latter, however, is not 'evil eye', but more akin to what Homer calls νέμεσις.

12 originalia instrumenta. *Instrumentum* means documentary authority: Lewis and Short give examples of this sense from Quintilian and Suetonius: so also *Apol.* 18, *instrumentum litteraturae*, 'literary evidence', i.e. the Old Testament (where Oehler gives a number of parallels). For *originalia* cf. *De Praesc. Haer.* 21, *ecclesiis apostolicis matricibus et originalibus fidei*, 'seedbeds and nurseries of the faith': *De Monog.* 7, *vetera exempla originalium personarum*, referring back to ibid. 6, *sed adhuc nobis quaeramus aliquos originis* *principes*, 'our spiritual fathers from whom we trace our origin', e.g. Adam, Noah, St Paul, Abraham in respect of faith, not of polygamy, Joseph, Moses, Aaron: *Apol.* 21, *dudum Iudaeis erat apud deum gratia ubi et insignis iustitia et fides originalium auctorum*, 'in so far as they continued in the notable righteousness and faith of the patriarchs from whom they took their origin': *Adv. Marc.* II. 9, *nec potest* ⟨*inquis*⟩ *non ad originalem summam referri corruptio portionis*—in Marcion's view, the fall of man, resulting from the corruption of that breath of life, the soul, which the Creator breathed into Adam, proves that the *originalis summa*, the original account on which (so to speak) the cheque was drawn, i.e. the substance of the Creator, is *delicti capax* (which to Tertullian is blasphemy): *Adv. Hermog.* 19, *ad originale instrumentum Moysi provocabo*, 'Moses' narrative of the creation'. So here *originalia instrumenta* are the documents which testify to Christ's origin, the nativity stories of the Gospel, which are as it were his birth-certificate, and which Marcion has presumed to suppress. At *De Anima* 3, by *argumentationes originales, id est philosophicas*, we must understand not (as Junius suggests) theories drawn from natural principles, but theories which the philosophers have constructed concerning the origins of things.

14 ex quo, oro te: etc. Oehler's correction of *A* (*quo* for *qua*) is apparently intended to mean, 'Since how long ago, pray?', and gives a good sense in conformity with Tertullian's general criticism of the recent emergence of the heresies: cf. e.g. *De Praesc. Haer.* 30, where however we have *ostendant mihi ex qua auctoritate prodierint*. Kroymann, with more than his usual felicity, takes the reading of *TX*, adding *exhibe* from *A*, *ex qua oro te auctoritate? exhibe*, which could find parallels in Cicero, e.g. *Pro Flacco* 32. 78, *litteras...quas ea de muliere ad me datas...requisivit: recita* (though here *recita* is addressed to the clerk of the court). For the general sense of the passage cf. *Adv. Marc.* I. 21, *exhibe ergo aliquam* (sc. *ecclesiam*) *ex tuis apostolici census et obduxeris...non esse credendum deum quem homo de suis sensibus composuerit, nisi plane prophetes, id est non de suis sensibus: quod si Marcion poterit dici, debebit etiam probari*.

15 **si apostolicus.** Cf. *De Praesc. Haer.* 32, 33, where the following phrases occur, in this order: *aetas apostolica: ecclesiae apostolicae* (plural): *ab apostolis in episcopatum constitutos apostolici seminis traduces: apostolica doctrina: apostolicus* (sc. *vir*): *apostolici* (*viri*). Also *Adv. Marc.* I. 21, *apostolica traditio: apostolici census ecclesiam*: ibid. IV. 2, *apostolicos* (Mark and Luke, as distinguished from Matthew and John): ibid. V. 2, *scriptura Apostolicorum* (the Acts). Also *De Pud.* 21, *exhibe igitur et nunc mihi, apostolice, prophetica exempla, ut agnoscam divinitatem*, addressed to the Roman pontiff, with whose policy concerning second marriages Tertullian does not agree: apparently the pope described himself as *apostolicus*: possibly so also did Marcion, with less justification.

16 **si tantum Christianus es,** for *dummodo Christianus sis*, seems somewhat lame, but is not impossible: *si autem* (T) and *si tantummodo* (F) seem to be editorial attempts at improvement.

20 **rescindendo quod retro credidisti:** cf. *Adv. Marc.* I. 1, *non negabunt discipuli eius primam illius fidem nobiscum fuisse...ut hinc iam destinari possit haereticus qui deserto quod prius fuerat id postea sibi elegerit quod retro non erat*: ibid. IV. 4, *adeo antiquius Marcione est quod est secundum nos, ut et ipse illi Marcion aliquando crediderit.* To the same effect *De Praesc. Haer.* 30, with a brief history of the various sects.

Retro is Tertullian's regular word for *antea*: he even says *retrosiores* for *aetate priores* (*Apol.* 19). There is precedent for it in Horace, *Carm.* III. 29. 46, *non tamen irritum | quodcunque retro est efficiet, neque | diffinget infectumque reddet | quod fugiens semel hora vexit.* But there may be a Christian reason for Tertullian's practice. The ancients, facing with hopeless longing towards a vanished golden age, regarded the past as in front of them (ἔμπροσθεν, *antea*) and the future as behind them (ὄπισθεν, *postea*). The Christian, looking for the resurrection of the dead and the life of the world to come, takes the opposite view: and, in spite of the inveterate usage of the Latin language, the change of thought is reflected in Tertullian's vocabulary. Philippians 3. 13 τὰ μὲν ὀπίσω ἐπιλανθανόμενος τοῖς δὲ ἔμπροσθεν ἐπεκτεινόμενος (a metaphor from running a race) may have influenced Tertullian to the regular use of a word which Horace used in this sense only once. But I am not aware that other Christian writers copied him: nor, for that matter, does modern English.

21 et nostri probant: wrongly omitted by Kroymann: what he means by saying that they break the rule of the clausula is not clear: they have precisely the same rhythm as those he leaves by removing them. The circumstances are those referred to *Adv. Marc.* I. I, *non negabunt discipuli eius primam illius fidem nobiscum fuisse, ipsius litteris testibus*: cf. ibid. IV. 4, *quid nunc si negaverint Marcionitae primam apud nos fidem eius adversus epistulam quoque ipsius? quid si nec epistulam agnoverint? certe Antitheses non modo fatentur Marcionis sed et praeferunt: ex his mihi probatio sufficit.* It is not clear what this letter was. It can hardly have been a profession of faith exacted by the Roman church on Marcion's arrival from Pontus: there is no evidence that at that date or for centuries later any church exacted such written professions, even from the clergy. It appears from the second quotation (above) that the Marcionites denied the authenticity of the letter, so that Tertullian is prepared to waive it and prove his point from the *Antitheses* alone.

24 aliter fuisse is intelligible, though somewhat concise, and need not be altered. Kroymann inserts *creditum tibi*, meaning presumably *abs te creditum*: there is no need for it. Cf. *De Praesc. Haer.* 38, *ex illis* (sc. *scripturis*) *sumus antequam aliter fuit, antequam a vobis interpolarentur*, where the text is doubtful: ibid. 30, *quidquid emendat ut mendosum retro alterius fuisse demonstrat*, where Ursinus' suggestion of *anterius* would simply duplicate *retro*, so probably read and punctuate *ut mendosum, retro aliter fuisse etc.*: ibid. 32, *nisi illi qui ab apostolis didicerunt aliter praedicaverunt*.

29 ex abundanti retractamus. The general rejection of all heresies on the ground of their recent emergence would have been sufficient to cover this present case: but, offering more proof than our cause strictly requires, we proceed to discuss Marcion's reasons for denying Christ's nativity. Tertullian dislikes argumentation, but he will use it under protest to prepare the way for scriptural exposition: cf. *Adv. Marc.* I. 16, *nunc enim communibus* *plurimum sensibus et argumentationibus iustis secuturae scripturarum quoque advocationi fidem sternimus.* Cf. Quintilian, *Inst. Orat.* IV. 5. 15, *egregie vero Cicero pro Milone insidiatorem primum Clodium ostendit, tum addidit ex abundanti, etiam si id non fuisset, talem tamen civem cum summa virtute interfectoris et gloria necari potuisse*: ibid. v. 6. 2, the wise litigant will not rest his case on his own affidavit, nor will he challenge his adversary to that course, but will prove his case on argument or testimony and will introduce the affidavit, if at all, *ex abundanti*.

CHAPTER III

Marcion's reasons for denying Christ's nativity can only be either that to God such a birth is impossible or else that it does not beseem him. We discuss first the question of impossibility, on which we observe: (1) That to God nothing is impossible except that which is not his will, and thus we have to inquire whether this was his will. We submit that if it had not been his will to be born he would have abstained from showing himself in human form and thus giving the impression of having been born: for this would have been a false impression, unworthy of God. (2) There is no force in the objection that it was enough that Christ should know the truth about himself, and that it was men's own fault if they received a false impression of him: the fact would remain that he had forfeited our confidence by giving the false impression. (3) Ill-founded also is the suggestion that if he had really been born and had truly taken manhood upon him, that is, if God had really been changed into man, he would have ceased to be God. In ordinary cases, we admit, by changing into something else a thing ceases to be what it was. But God, being unchangeable, is not subject to this law, and it is in his power to change into man without ceasing to be God. (4) We add that angels are reported to have assumed real human bodies and yet remained angels: if angels have this power (and they, according to Marcion, belong to an inferior God), *a fortiori* Marcion's superior god must have it. And Marcion dare not say that these angels had only a phantasm of a body: for this would put the Creator's angels on a level with Marcion's Christ. (5) Similar was the case of the Holy Spirit descending in bodily form as a dove—except that this is not in Marcion's gospel. If asked what afterwards became of those bodies, we answer that they were withdrawn into the nothingness from which they had been brought into being: and, in any case, what the Scripture says must be true.

1 **quatenus** stands for *quandoquidem*: cf. *Apol.* 19, *habetis quod sciam, et vos sibyllam, quatenus appellatio ista verae vatis veri dei passim super ceteros qui vaticinari videbantur usurpata est*. *Hoc*, the judgement which Marcion considered himself competent to make, *non natum esse Christum*. *Arbitrium* is strictly speaking a judgement in equity concerning not the fact of obligation but the amount: cf. Cicero, *Pro Rosc. Com.* 4. 10, *iudicium est pecuniae certae, arbitrium incertae*. It is from the other (also classical) sense of *arbitrium*, 'power', 'authority' (e.g. Tacitus, *Ann.* VI. 51, *rei Romanae arbitrium*, the imperial power), that we obtain the expression *liberum arbitrium*, 'freedom of choice'.

3 **voluerit** is the reading of all the MSS. Ursinus, followed by Kroymann, reads *noluerit*, wrongly. The catch is in the particle *an*. Tertullian uses these interrogative particles in ways peculiar to himself: e.g. *Apol.* 1 (Hoppe, line 15), *an* = *nonne*: ibid. 9 (line 37), *necubi* = *annon alicubi*: ibid. 19 (line 65) and frequently, *non* = *nonne*: ibid. 35 (line 24), *ne forte* = *an forte*. Here *an* stands for *annon*, and no alteration is called for.

4 **compendium** may prossibly be used here in its original sense of weighing two things in the same balance: Lewis and Short give several examples. The two questions, whether God was incompetent, and whether it was unseemly, could be treated as one. God did consent to give the impression of manhood, and consequently of having been born. That establishes the seemliness of it: and as God's veracity requires that the impression given should correspond with the truth, we have also the answer to the question of fact, and therefore of competence as well as seemliness. But the question of seemliness is pursued further in the following chapter. It appears then more likely that *compendium* here means a short cut: cf. *Adv. Marc.* I. 1, *nunc quatenus admittenda congressio est, interdum ne compendium praescriptionis ubique advocatum diffidentiae*

deputetur, regulam adversarii prius retexam, ne cui lateat in qua principalis quaestio dimicatura est: ibid. II. 29, *quodsi utraque pars bonitatis atque iustitiae dignam plenitudinem divinitatis efficiunt omnia potentis, compendio interim possum Antitheses retudisse.*

10 illud is in all MSS. except *A*, and should no doubt be restored. Kroymann rightly indicates that it is the object of *patiatur*, not the subject of *interest*: but his reading *falsam* (sc. *opinionem*) is unnecessary and unjustified. On the sentence as a whole cf. *Adv. Marc.* I. 11, *quid ergo tantopere notitiam sui procuravit, ut in dedecore carnis exhiberetur, et quidem maiore si falsae? nam hoc turpius, si et mentitus est substantiam carnis.*

11 conscientia in common Latin usage is either (*a*) joint knowledge, knowledge shared with others, or (*b*) consciousness, or (*c*) a good or bad conscience (not necessarily with *bona* or *mala*). In Tertullian it seems to take its meaning from the Pauline text (1 Cor. 4. 4) οὐδὲν γὰρ ἐμαυτῷ σύνοιδα, and to indicate that which one is conscious of in one's own judgement of oneself, though it may not of necessity be within the cognisance of others. Cf. *Adv. Prax.* 13, *ceterum si ex conscientia* ('that private Christian knowledge') *qua scimus dei nomen et domini et patri et filio et spiritui sancto convenire deos et dominos nominaremus etc.* The word appears again at the end of the following sentence almost in its modern sense of 'conscience'.

15 quantum ad fiduciam etc. This reading of *A* is apparently correct. *Quam tu*, of the other authorities, is somewhat lame, and *tu* is redundant. *Fiducia* apparently means our confidence or trust in Christ: 'If his birth and his manhood were an acted lie, how could we trust him in anything?' From *Apol.* 39, *fidem sanctis vocibus pascimus, spem erigimus, fiduciam figimus*, it seems likely that *fides* refers to the formal content of the faith, while *fiducia* is the Christian's personal trust in Christ.

19 hominem vere induisset. *Homo* is Tertullian's regular word (and in this he is followed by the other Latin fathers, including St Augustine) for Christ's human nature, with nowhere any suggestion that the use of this term might be mistaken (in a

Nestorian sense) to indicate a distinct human person. Cf. *Adv. Prax.* 30, *hominem eius*, and my note.

20 periculum enim status sui etc. Cf. *Adv. Marc.* I. 6, *non est autem dei desinere de statu suo, id est de summo magno*. Status, I have suggested elsewhere (*Adv. Prax.*, Introduction, pages 50–53), represents the copulative verb in so far as it introduces attributes which are essential and permanent, and constitute the *natura* of an object: in that case, it also involves the idea of stability. And as *substantia* represents the existential verb, being the thing as it is in itself, in the case of God both *substantia* and *status* are *ex hypothesi* indestructible and eternal: and as *status* represents the sum total of the necessary attributes, the properties, the meaning here is that whatever it is that God does with himself there is no danger of his losing all or any of those properties (of eternity, immortality, etc.) by which as God he is distinguished from all that is not God: if there were, it would be conceivable that he could *amittere quod erat dum fit quod non erat*.

21 conversum. Cf. *Adv. Prax.* 27, *quaerendum quomodo sermo caro sit factus, utrum quasi transfiguratus in carne an indutus carnem*, and the answer to this question there given. On the term *conversum* and its subsequent rejection I venture to refer to my note on the above passage (page 320) and to my Introduction, pages 72, 73: to which I would now add that it seems possible that it was Marcion who said *conversum*, and that Tertullian, to avoid complicating the argument, accepts the word without protest and (for the moment) argues from it without remarking on its unsuitability.

24 non competit ergo etc. *A* alone has *eius cui* (*T* is here defective). Kroymann's (inexact) quotation from *Ad Nat.* I. 5 is apparently intended to show that *competere* can be used absolutely, to mean 'is possible'—which is true enough, though the clause quoted does not exemplify this.

25 ea lege est is conceivably equivalent to a verb of commanding, and so is followed by *ne* instead of the more correct *ut non*: cf. *Adv. Marc.* I. 3, *conditione et ut ita dixerim lege quae summo magno nihil sinit adaequari*.

27 nihil deo par est literally means that nothing is on a level with God: from which it follows that there is nothing which can be used as an analogy to suggest that what happens to it in certain circumstances will happen to God in like circumstances: cf. *Adv. Marc.* I. 4, *de deo agitur, cuius hoc principaliter proprium est, nullius exempli capere comparationem*, quoting Isaiah 40. 18, 25, and adding, *divinis forsitan comparabuntur humana, deo non ita: aliud enim deus, aliud quae dei.*

27 ab omnium rerum conditione: so *ATP*, the others having *condicione*. The words are often confused, not by Tertullian, but by his copyists. See a separate note, p. xxxix, in which it is suggested that *conditio* (when it does not mean the act or process of creation, or the created world or *rerum natura*) refers to those natural attributes or relationships which accrue to an object by virtue of its *natura*, but looking outward rather than inward: whereas *condicio* refers also to outward relationships, but of a more fortuitous or transitory character. Here apparently *conditione* is correct, (*a*) as contrasting the natural attributes of things with the essential attributes of God, and (*b*) as suggesting that, being created things, they will necessarily be subject to influences to which the Creator is not subject.

30 diversitas means more than 'difference': in many cases 'opposition' will not be too strong, as in the common expression *diversa pars*, 'my opponents'. Here the suggestion is that just because created things are in this way affected by change, the opposite must be the case with God, and that he cannot be affected, even by change.

33 quorum utique etc. In the clause as usually punctuated *ut* (added by Kroymann before *in omnibus*) seems necessary, unless (as is very unlikely) *utique* can stand for *sicut*. But this makes a very ugly sentence, and probably the easiest way out is to correct the punctuation, placing a colon after *non est*.

34 angelos creatoris etc. The narrative of Genesis 18 and 19, if carefully read, indicates that the Lord appeared to Abraham accompanied by two angels: that after Abraham's hospitality and the conversation with Sarah the two angels went away to

Sodom while the Lord remained behind in conversation with Abraham: that the angels alone entered into Sodom and rescued Lot: and that when they had come out of the city the Lord rained fire and brimstone from the Lord out of heaven and destroyed it. It was assumed by Tertullian (as by Justin and by practically all commentators until the fourth century) that the Lord here is God the Son—a point however upon which Tertullian does not insist in the present context, being concerned only to refute the Marcionite suggestion about the angels. His observations here are a summary of what he writes *Adv. Marc.* III. 9, where his argument is as follows: Marcion's suggestion that the flesh of Christ can be taken to have been putative because the angels appeared to Abraham and to Lot *in phantasmate, putativae utique carnis*, must be rejected, because (1) *non admitteris ad eius dei exempla quem destruis*, for, the better and more perfect you suppose your god to be, the less do the Creator's precedents apply to him: (2) The angels' flesh was not putative, it being just as easy for God to provide *veram substantiam carnis* as to exhibit real sensations and actions in putative flesh: (3) Marcion's god, who has created no flesh (nor anything else), might perhaps be allowed a phantasm of flesh, whereas our God, who had made flesh out of clay, would have been able to make for the angels flesh out of any material he wished: for it was much easier for him to do this than to make the world out of nothing, by his mere word: (4) The God whom Marcion acknowledges promises to men *veram substantiam angelorum* (Luke 20. 36): why then shall not our God have given to the angels *veram substantiam hominum, undeunde sumptam*? (5) The verity of their flesh is attested by three witnesses, sight, touch, and hearing: and it is more difficult for God to deceive than to produce true flesh, *undeunde*: (6) Other heretics allege that the angels' flesh ought to have been born of flesh: we reply that their flesh had to be human for purposes of human converse, but needed not to be born because the reason for their appearance was not (as Christ's was) to reform our nativity by nativity and to destroy our death by resurrection: for which reason Christ himself appeared to Abraham *in veritate quidem carnis, sed nondum natae quia nondum moriturae, sed et discentis iam inter homines conversari*: (7) Since 'he maketh his angels spirits (breaths or winds) and his apparitors a flaming fire', truly winds and truly fire, he also made them truly flesh.

38 adeo detinebatur. It does not appear from Oehler's or Kroymann's data who was responsible for this obvious correction of the MSS. *a deo.* *T*'s reading is easy to explain, and may safely be disregarded.

39 inferioris dei...potentiori deo. It is necessary (though, in view of his language, not always easy) to remember that Tertullian's God, the God of Christians, is the Creator of the world, the God of the Old Testament as well as of the New. Expressions such as the present (which are sufficiently frequent) are therefore ironical, arguing against Marcion on Marcion's own ground. Cf. *Adv. Marc.* I. 11, *nam et quale est ut creator quidem ignorans esse alium super se deum...tantis operibus notitiam sui armaverit...ille autem sublimior sciens inferiorem deum tam instructum nullam sibi prospexerit agnoscendo paraturam?* Also ibid. II. 1, *nam qui in inferiorem deum caecutis, quid in sublimiorem?* and ibid. II. 27, *si enim deus, et quidem sublimior, tanta humilitate fastigium maiestatis suae stravit ut etiam morti subiceret, et morti crucis, cur non putetis nostro quoque deo aliquas pusillitates congruisse?* The above reading (of *A* alone) is therefore undoubtedly correct.

42 hominem indutus: see above, *hominem induisset.*

43 sed non audebis etc. Precisely because Marcion has ascribed to Christ a phantasm of flesh, he is bound to maintain that the flesh assumed by the angels was real: otherwise there will be parallel action between the New Testament and the Old, and it will follow that the same God is responsible for both—which Marcion would not care to admit. A specious argument, but hardly convincing.

48 qui spiritus cum esset. *Hoc* is without meaning, and must be removed, as Mesnart suggested. *Spiritus* here is a general term, the predicate of the sentence, 'and though he was spirit'. From John 4. 24, *deus spiritus est*, Tertullian deduces that 'spirit' is a generic term descriptive of the divine being, the kind of 'substance' God is. The meaning here is that although (or because) the Holy Spirit who descended upon Jesus was God, he was no less truly a dove than he was God, yet his assumption of that new thing which he had not previously been, involved no destruction of that divine Thing which is unalterably himself. Cf. *Adv. Prax.* 26.

55 corporis soliditas. Cf. Cicero, *De Nat. Deorum* I. 19. 49, who says that according to Epicurus the gods are perceived *non sensu sed mente, nec soliditate quadam nec ad numerum ut ea quae ille propter firmitatem* στερέμνια *appellat, sed imaginibus similitudine et transitione perceptis.* This is probably the sense Tertullian has in mind here. For other meanings of *solidus* see a note on § 6.

CHAPTER IV

Having disposed of the suggestion of impossibility, we turn to the complaint of unseemliness. It is possible to make great play with the inconveniences, even the sordidness, of conception, pregnancy, childbearing, and infancy. These are really sacred things, the concern of all men alike, and those who think ill of them despise our common humanity—which indeed Christ did not despise, but loved it, redeeming it at great cost. In loving our humanity he loved all that appertains to it, nativity and flesh included, for these are inseparable from it. During his ministry he cleansed the flesh from all manner of diseases, and finally from death itself. If he had appeared among men in a form lower than human, this in our human judgement might have been accounted foolish. But 'God hath chosen the foolish things of the world'—and what is it that the world counts as foolish? Not, surely, the conversion of mankind from idolatry and their instruction in all virtues, but that God should be born, born of a virgin, born in human fashion with all its inconveniences. In spite of the fables of its mythology the world can imagine no greater foolishness than this.

2 corporatio seems to be a new coinage. Σωμάτωσις is used by Hermes Trismegistus (*apud Stobaeum, Eclog.* I, page 730) for the eternal fact or process by which bodies are brought into existence so as to be the object or instrument of the eternal operations of science and art: for since science and art are eternal there must eternally exist, or be coming into existence, in the transcendental sphere, bodies for them to work on. This is certainly not what Tertullian means by the word: the whole tenor of his argument shows that by *corporatio* he means not the genesis of a body but the assumption of one, either fabricated for the purpose, as in the Theophanies, or drawn from the stock of Adam, as in the Incarnation. The word in this sense is a synonym of *incarnatio*, and by implication scriptural: though it remains conceivable that in the present context it is due not to Tertullian but to Marcion, who may have wished to becloud the Incarnation by the use of a term borrowed from an alien philosophy.

3 **perora, age iam** etc. Cf. *Adv. Marc.* III. 11, *age iam, perora, in illa sanctissima et reverenda opera naturae, invehere in totum quod es*. Tertullian is an inveterate plagiarizer from himself. Cf. *Adv. Marc.* IV. 20, where it is objected that Marcion's Christ, being incapable of these *indignitates*, must also be incapable of *confusio*, quoting Luke 9. 26, 'Of him shall the Son of man be ashamed.'

5 **coagula** etc. The punctuation used in the text seems to be the best: Kroymann's is ingenious, but breaks the flow of the sentence. All difficulty would disappear if we could insert *sordes* after *carnis*.

6 **in diem** (*TB*) should perhaps be restored, if only on the principle that the longer text is usually the correct one.

9 **honorandum** is almost certainly correct: cf. *infra, hanc venerationem naturae*, and *Adv. Marc.* III. 11, quoted above. *Horrendum* (*T*) gives exactly the wrong sense, as *horres*, in the next sentence, shows.

10 **utique et oblitum. dedignaris quod** etc. So I read, and punctuate, following exactly neither set of authorities. *Ablutum* would also make sense, 'even when he has been washed you despise him because he is straightened out etc.' But the more forcible word is better: Tertullian is making Marcion insist to the full on the unseemliness of the process.

16 **certe Christus dilexit** etc. Cf. *Adv. Marc.* I. 14, *postremo te tibi circumfer, intus ac foris considera hominem: placebit tibi vel hoc*

opus dei nostri quod tuus dominus, ille deus melior, adamavit, propter quem in haec paupertina elementa de tertio caelo descendere laboravit, cuius causa in hac cellula creatoris etiam crucifixus est: and ibid. 1. 29 (of Marcion's god, who forbids marriage), *quomodo diligit cuius originem non amat?*

20 magno redemit, from 1 Cor. 6. 20, ἠγοράσθητε γὰρ τιμῆς, where Lat. vg. has *pretio magno*: cf. ibid. 7. 23, τιμῆς ἠγοράσθητε (Lat. vg. *pretio empti estis*).

26 qui redemit. *Qui*, my own correction of what I took to be a misprint in Oehler, seems also to have occurred to the corrector of *T*.

31 si revera etc. This piece of bad taste is not without parallel: it neither can nor need be excused. *Opinor* is commonly used ironically, of an opinion attributed to the adversary, but with which the writer does not agree: here the suggestion is the writer's, and neither party ought to have entertained such an idea.

34 de nostro sensu etc. So I read, following *A*. We have a perfect right, even a duty, to judge according to our own best mind concerning things it is suggested that God might have done. If any alteration is needed, it is the substitution of *est* for *si* or *sit* before *plane stultum*.

35 si tamen non delesti. Marcion retained this text, 1 Corinthians 1. 27, 28. Cf. *Adv. Marc.* v. 5, *etiam Marcion servat. quid est autem stultum dei sapientius hominibus nisi crux et mors Christi? quid infirmum dei fortius homine nisi nativitas et caro dei? ceterum si nec natus ex virgine Christus nec carne constructus, ac per hoc neque crucem neque mortem vere perpessus est, nihil in illo fuit stultum et infirmum, nec iam stulta mundi elegit deus ut confundat sapientiam etc.* Tertullian often quotes this text: e.g. *De Praesc. Haer.* 7, *de ingenio sapientiae saecularis quam dominus stultitiam vocans stulta mundi in confusionem etiam philosophiae ipsius elegit.*

45 apud. For the practical equivalence of *apud* and *penes*, cf. *De Anima* 14 and Waszink's note. At *Apol.* 17, *desinunt tamen Christiani haberi penes nos*, it appears that *penes* has quite lost its 'internal' significance.

CHAPTER V

Since we are speaking of 'foolish things', things supposedly unworthy of God, are not the passion of Christ, and its accompaniments, more foolish in appearance even than his birth and incarnation? Why does not Marcion excise these? Possibly because, as a phantasm, Christ can have had no sensation of them. Therefore we have to ask, was Christ really crucified, and did he really die? If not, the apostle was at fault in claiming to know nothing save Jesus Christ, and him crucified, and in insisting that he was buried and that he rose again. In such a case our faith also is false and our hope in Christ is a phantasm: also Christ's murderers will be excusable, for they will be found not to have really killed him. But all this is simply to deny the world's only hope. Our faith has to have something for men to be ashamed of—else why did our Lord warn us of the consequences of being ashamed of him? It is precisely these things that can be considered a matter of shame: yet how can they have been real in him, unless he was real in himself, having real flesh like ours? This in fact was the reason for his becoming the Son of Man, that he might have wherewith to suffer these indignities: and he cannot have been man without flesh, or have possessed flesh without birth from a human parent, any more than he can have been God without the divine substance, begotten of God as Father. This is how he is presented to us, at the same time God with divine powers and man subject to human weaknesses, his miracles showing the one, his passion showing the other. It is not permissible to make out that Christ was half a lie, for he is wholly the Truth: his manhood must be as real as his godhead, and manhood involves human birth and the possession of a body like ours. On his own testimony we may not think of him as a phantasm, either before his resurrection or after: and Marcion in particular has no right to think so, for he derives his Christ from a god wholly good and candid and veracious. But Marcion's Christ ought not to have come down from heaven, but out of a troupe of wonder-working magicians—except that, even so, he would have been a real man.

[This is one of the most lucid sections of Tertullian's work, in which his Latin flows with unwonted ease and perspicuity. There was therefore the less reason for Kroymann to have disturbed the text with a multitude of alterations of words and punctuation. The text printed is that commonly received, with perhaps one or two minor improvements.]

7 **sed non eris...credendo.** This sentence, as Kroymann remarks, is not necessary to the argument. But it is precisely the kind of aside which would have been interpolated by a pleader making a speech with his adversary present: and this is what Tertullian is pretending to do.

8 **passiones...non rescidisti.** Marcion retained St Luke's narrative of the passion, though he excised the parting of the garments so as to avoid the acknowledgement of Psalm 22. See *Adv. Marc.* IV. 40–42 for Tertullian's comments which (except for the tone of voice in which they are made) seem entirely justified. Apparently Marcion said that 'the Christ' deserted the phantasm of a body at the supposed moment of death, and returned to heaven: he omitted to consider what it was that was left behind, or what it was for which Joseph provided burial—though this too, with the narrative of the Easter appearances, was retained in his gospel.

9 **diximus retro,** i.e. in § 1.

10 **nativitatis...imaginariae.** *Imaginarius* apparently in this connexion means no more than 'unreal': cf. *De Corona* 13, *omnia imaginaria in saeculo et nihil veri*: so *Adv. Marc.* III. 8, 11 *caro imaginaria*. But there are places where it (still meaning 'unreal') refers to the imaginary (supposedly real) entities of the gnostic ideal worlds; e.g. *Adv. Val.* 27, *ita omnia in imagines urgent, plane et ipsi imaginarii Christiani*: and other places where it seems to mean imaginative (if I understand these two passages aright) in a reprehensible sense, as at *De Monog.* 10, the widow *habet secum animi licentiam, qui omnia homini quae non habet imaginario fructu repraesentat*, and *Adv. Val.* 17, of the conceptual effects of Achamoth's imagination.

11 interfector may conceivably have the sense assigned to it by Tertullian's compatriot Appuleius, in the phrase *interfectae virginitatis*.

11 crucifixus est deus: so all the MSS. except *T*, which has *dominus*: but cf. *passiones dei, deum crucifixum*, above. The whole context requires *deus*.

15 igitur means 'in that case', and there is no need to make the present sentence into a question. It is the necessary deduction from an affirmative answer to the questions preceding.

20 qui me confusus fuerit: Mark 8. 38, Luke 9. 26, conflated with Matthew 10. 32. Cf. *Apol.* 4, *bonorum adhibita proscriptio suffundere maluit hominis sanguinem quam effundere*, 'is more a matter of exaction than of execution'. *Confusus*, for *pudore suffusus*, unknown in classical and pagan Latin, appears first in the versions of the above texts. As appears from Irenaeus, *Haer.* III. 19. 4, the verb can be active, or deponent (with an accusative object), or passive: *et confusurum qui confundentur confessionem eius ...a Christo confundentur*. It belongs to that class of expressions which developed in the popular speech which lies behind the biblical versions, and is older than Christian Latin literature, having become necessary in view of the new Christian attitude towards certain moral acts or experiences. The Roman was incapable of personal shame or personal repentance: the most he could arrive at was the impersonal *pudet me, poenitet me*. Christians found that impersonality was not good enough, and developed expressions like *confusus sum, poenitentiam ago* (which does not mean 'do penance') to describe what was to them a personal act. Rigaltius, and subsequent editors, altered *me* of the MSS. to *mei*, apparently to balance *eius* in the following clause: the versions of the Gospel all read *confusus me fuerit...confundetur eum*: Rönsch, *Itala und Vulgata*, p. 354, makes no mention of genitive government.

23 bene impudentem. On first reading this (in Oehler's text) I thought there was possibly a misprint for *bene imprudentem*, which would balance better with *feliciter stultum*: but cf. *non pudet etc.*, below. *Imprudens* and *impudens* were often confused by the copyists: cf. e.g. Cicero, *De Lege Agraria* II. 17. 46, *an is impudenter populo Romano per legis fraudem surripiatur*, where Lauredanus rightly suggests *imprudente*: ibid. III. 2. 5, *multo impudentior*, where one group of MSS. have (wrongly) *imprudentior*: ibid. III. 2. 8, *nemo est tam impudens istorum*, where all the MSS. have *imprudens* (corrected by Naugerius).

30 novit, almost equivalent to *potest*, is unusual in Latin, especially with a non-personal subject. Tertullian may have been copying the Greek idiom, e.g. Demosthenes, *Phil.* I. 40, προβάλλεσθαι δ' ἢ βλέπειν ἐναντίον οὔτ' οἶδεν οὔτ' ἐθέλει. *Posse* to Tertullian is a matter of power: whereas being born, and dying, are in a sense a restraint of power, for which *nosse* is more suitable. See the critical note for a possible difference of reading and punctuation.

33 nisi si aut aliud etc. The sequence of thought is perfectly clear, and no alteration is called for. It is admitted that Christ is 'man' and 'son of man', for so it is written in St Luke's Gospel. If then, as Marcion demands, we deny the obvious deduction from this, that Christ was possessed of human flesh, we need to find some other means of justifying those expressions: which can only be either (*a*) that 'man' signifies not human flesh but something else, or (*b*) that human flesh can have some origin other than human birth, or (*c*) that Christ's mother is not human, or (*d*) that the father of Marcion's Christ, Marcion's 'good god', is human. The second and third suggestions are hardly in point here: but they fill out a good rhetorical sequence, and there is no reason for thinking that Tertullian did not write them.

37 nec deus sine spiritu dei. 'Spirit', once more, means the divine substance: see above on § 3, *qui spiritus cum esset*.

38 utriusque substantiae census, a pregnant expression, very difficult to translate. *Census* means both origin, and the rank or quality which depends upon origin. Perhaps 'the rank (or quality) deriving from the two substances'.

40 quae proprietas conditionum etc. Cf. *Adv. Prax.* 27, *secundum utramque substantiam in sua proprietate distantem...et adeo* *salva est utriusque proprietas substantiae ut spiritus res suas egerit in illo...et caro passiones suas functa sit*, where Tertullian's argument is that the facts of the case, recorded in the Gospel and referred to by St Paul, preclude us from thinking that the Incarnation involved such a confusion or mixture of godhead and manhood as would have produced neither the one nor the other but something in between. *Proprietas* does not mean 'property' in any sense involving possession, but the fact that each of the substances, and the *conditiones*, is what it is and is not the other. On *conditio* see a note on page xxxix.

44 perinde is the reading of *A*: the other authorities have *proinde*. There are indications that, either by second-century writers or by their medieval copyists, the two words were either confused or treated as equivalent, as in several places in this treatise. In the Medicean codex of Tacitus *proinde* occurs several times in the sense of *perinde*: e.g. *Hist.* II. 27, *haud proinde id damnum Vitellianos in metum compulit quam ad modestiam composuit*: ibid. II. 39 and 97, where Rhenanus in the *editio princeps* substituted *perinde*.

46 maluit, credo, nasci etc. Cf. *Adv. Prax.* 11 (with C. H. Turner's brilliant emendation), *unum tamen veritus est, mentiri veritatis auctorem semetipsum et suam veritatem*. I have ventured to write *credo* for the MSS. *crede* or *credi* (the latter is certainly wrong): though with some hesitation, for in Latin oratory this interjected *credo* seems to be usually ironical, and not to express the speaker's real opinion: e.g. Cicero, *Phil.* x. 7. 15, *qui autem hos exercitus ducunt? ei credo qui C. Caesaris res actas everti, qui causam veteranorum prodi volunt*: and ibid. 9. 18, *non sunt enim credo innumerabiles qui pro communi libertate arma capiant*.

57 ecce fallit etc. This theme is developed more fully *Adv. Marc.* III. 8, especially: *et ideo Christus eius, ne mentiretur, ne falleret, et hoc modo creatoris forsitan deputaretur, non erat quod videbatur et quod erat mentiebatur, caro nec caro, homo nec homo, proinde deus Christus nec deus: cur enim non etiam dei phantasma portaverit?... quomodo verax habebitur in occulto tam fallax repertus in aperto?... iam nunc cum mendacium deprehenditur Christus caro, sequitur ut et* *omnia quae per carnem Christi gesta sunt mendacio gesta sint, congressus, contactus, convictus, ipsae quoque virtutes...sic nec passiones Christi eius* (sc. *Marcionis*) *fidem merebuntur: nihil enim passus est qui non vere est passus, vere autem pati phantasma non potuit. eversum est igitur totum dei opus etc.* The subject is continued ibid. III. 10, and frequently recurs.

60 nec deum praeter hominem. Tertullian regularly uses *praeter* as a conjunction (=*nisi*), e.g. *De Res. Carn.* 22, *nec ulli praeter patri notum*: *Adv. Prax.* 13, *nemo alius praeter unus deus*. But I can find no parallel to the present case, where *praeter* is equivalent to *sine*.

CHAPTER VI

Some of Marcion's disciples (of whom Apelles is one) are prepared to admit the reality of Christ's flesh, while still denying that it was born. Apelles' informant is alleged to have been an angel who spoke in (or to) the woman Philumena: the apostle (at Galatians 1. 8) has provided us with a reply to this. Their statement is that Christ 'borrowed' flesh from the substances of the superior world, and they support it by pointing out that in the Scriptures angels are reported to have assumed human bodies without being born. But (1) since they have assigned the Old Testament to a god whose works they repudiate, they have no right to apply its precedents to their own god. However, we shall not press this objection, for our case is strong in itself. (2) The purposes in those cases were different from the purpose of Christ's incarnation. Christ came with the intention of dying (which the angels did not) and consequently must needs be born. And in fact, on the occasions referred to it was the Lord himself who appeared in flesh not yet born because not yet to die. (3) Yet since our adversaries do not admit that it was the Lord who thus appeared, we shall challenge them to prove their case as if it were angels. This they cannot do, for it is not so written: and we for our part are justified (in default of contrary evidence) in suggesting that the angels' bodies were created out of nothing for each occasion. (4) Neither are we told what happened to those bodies afterwards, and so may well be right in suggesting that they reverted to the non-existence from which they came. (5) Even if we should allow that those bodies were formed out of some material, it is more natural to suppose it to have been material from the earth than from heaven, for they fed on earthly food. And if it is objected that heavenly bodies could feed on earthly food no less than earthly bodies on the manna that came from heaven, we revert to our primary contention that the circumstances, like the purposes, of Christ's incarnation were different from these, and demanded a real birth as a precondition of a real death.

The question of the nature and origin of the corporal substance assumed by the angels who appeared to Abraham and to Lot (Genesis 18, 19) is discussed *Adv. Marc.* III. 9, under the following heads: (*a*) The Marcionite postulate of a superior and more perfect god demands that his methods also should be better than those of the Creator, his presumed inferior: and consequently *non admitteris ad eius dei exempla quem destruis*. (*b*) We do not admit that the flesh assumed by those angels was putative: for if it was easy for the Creator (as Marcion alleges) to have provided the semblance of putative flesh, it was even easier for him, being the creator of human flesh, to provide actual human flesh to act upon the perceptions of the observers. (*c*) Marcion's god (i.e. not the Creator), being incapable of creation, would necessarily have to produce a phantasm, being unable to provide the reality: whereas our God, who formed flesh in the beginning out of the dust of the ground, could equally well have formed flesh for the angels out of any material whatsoever. (*d*) As the Marcionite gospel (Luke 20. 36) records the promise that men will possess angelic substance, what is to prevent our God from making angels possess human substance *undeunde sumptam*? (*e*) As Marcion does not feel bound to explain from whence this angelic substance will be derived, neither are we bound to explain the origin of that human substance, but are at liberty to postulate its real impact upon the three senses of vision, touch, and hearing: *difficilius deo mentiri quam carnis veritatem undeunde producere, licet non natae*. (*f*) The flesh assumed by the two angels was true flesh, as also was that of the Lord who appeared with them: but in neither case would it have been proper for that flesh to be produced by process of birth. For birth is the antecedent of death, and the angels were not going to die, as neither was the Lord at that time. Afterwards, when the Lord came with intent to die for our redemption, he would obtain his flesh by birth: but the time for that was not yet. The angels, therefore, *neque ad moriendum pro nobis dispositi brevem carnis commeatum non debuerunt nascendo sumpsisse, sed undeunde sumptam et quoquo modo omnino dimissam, mentiti eam tamen non sunt.* (*g*) Since the Creator 'maketh his angels spirits and his ministers a flaming fire', he is equally capable of making them flesh. (*h*) And finally, the promise of reshaping men into angels (Luke 20. 36) is made by the same God who had in former time shaped angels into men: from which it appears that the same God is the God of both Testaments.

The argument of the present chapter covers only the section numbered (*f*) of the foregoing analysis. The suggestion that the bodies of the angels may have been created especially for the occasion seems to be Tertullian's own. The statement that one of the three who appeared to Abraham was the Lord himself appears in Justin Martyr and remains common form until the fourth century (cf. supra, p. 100): it undoubtedly provides the most reasonable account of the narrative. Cf. *Adv. Prax.* 14, and my note (page 269). Irenaeus, *Haer.* IV. 14, referring to Genesis 18. 1 says *deum...qui in figura locutus est humana ad Abraham*, without going more fully into the matter.

4 de calcaria in carbonariam. This ancient equivalent of 'out of the frying-pan into the fire' is not in the *Adagia* of Erasmus, and seems to be otherwise unknown.

7 solidum Christi corpus. *Solidus* is used by Tertullian in two senses: (*a*) 'Solid', as opposed to hollow, ethereal, or unstable: e.g. *Adv. Val.* 16, *exercitata vitia* (sc. of Achamoth) *et usu viriata confudit* (sc. Soter) *atque ita massaliter solidata defixit seorsum in materiae corporalem paraturam*: *Adv. Marc.* III. 9, *caro verae et solidae substantiae humanae*: so also *De Exhort. Cast.* 2, *solida fides*, and here, *solidum corpus*, 'a body in three dimensions'. (*b*) In a sense derived from testamentary usage, 100 per cent: e.g. *Ad Uxor.* I. 1, *tu modo ut solidum capere possis hoc meae admonitionis fideicommissum deus faciat*: *De Monog.* 16, *aliud est si apud Christum legibus Iuliis agi credunt, et existimant caelibes et orbos ex testamento dei solidum non posse capere* (= *haeredes ex asse fieri non posse*): hence *De Monog.* 3, *etiam si totam et solidam* (complete and entire) *virginitatem sive continentiam paracletus hodie determinasset, ut ne unis quidem nuptiis fervorem carnis despumare permitteret*: and *De Res. Carn.* 36, *solidam resurrectionem* (i.e., as appears from the context, *utriusque substantiae humanae*).

8 suscepit ab ea carries an unobtrusive reference to the Roman father's act of lifting up his wife's child from the ground and thus acknowledging it as his own: the two preceding words make it an oxymoron.

8 et angelo quidem etc. Cf. *Adv. Marc.* III. 11, *nam et Philumene illa magis persuasit Apelli ceterisque desertoribus Marcionis ex fide quidem Christum circumtulisse carnem, nullius tamen nativitatis, utpote de elementis eam mutuatum*. The citation of Galatians 1. 8 is repeated from *De Praesc. Haer.* 6, where there is the comment, *providerat iam tunc spiritus sanctus futurum in virgine quadem Philumene angelum seductionis transfigurantem se in angelum lucis, cuius signis et praestigiis Apelles inductus novam haeresim induxit* (? *introduxit*): cf. ibid. 30, where the angel becomes an *energema*.

11 his vero quae insuper etc. The apostolic text being sufficient to rebut the claim to angelic inspiration, our own task is to controvert their supporting arguments. On *argumentantur* see a note on §17 (page 156).

12 seqq. Kroymann's reconstruction of this passage is rash and unnecessary: the traditional text makes perfectly good sense. Moreover he is wrong in his observation that *qualitas idem fere quod substantia*: Tertullian is too careful with his words for this kind of equivocation, and *ex ea qualitate in qua videbatur* stands, by a common enough ellipsis, for *ex eius qualitatis materia in qua videbatur*.

22 sed utantur etc. Here, as frequently elsewhere, Tertullian will not insist on his *praescriptio*, having a sound case on other and more general grounds. Cf. *Adv. Prax.* 2, *sed salva ista praescriptione ubique tamen...dandus est etiam retractatibus locus*, etc.

28 **comparent velim et causas** etc. *Causa*, except where it means an action at law, seems to be used by Tertullian almost always for the final cause or purpose, while *ratio* refers to the precedent cause or preliminary reasoning: these two aspects of the same matter are indicated below, *consequens erat, immo praecedens,* etc. So also § 10, *et hic itaque causas requiro*, where, once more, final causes alone are brought under review. Cf. *Adv. Marc.* II. 4, *videbimus causas quae hoc quoque a deo exegerunt...si legis imponendae ratio praecessit, sequebatur etiam observandae*: ibid. II. 11, *ita prior bonitas dei secundum naturam, severitas posterior secundum causam*: and especially ibid. II. 6, where the *causa* for which men have freedom of will is, *oportebat dignum aliquid esse quod deum cognosceret*, while *ratio* is the reasoning by which God thought out this plan.

36 **forma** is the architect's or surveyor's plan: therefore 'purpose' or 'intention'.

40 **pro quo,** by ellipsis for *pro eo pro quo.*

44 **qui iam tunc** etc. Cf. *Adv. Marc.* III. 9 (referred to above), *ideoque et ipse tunc apud Abraham in veritate quidem carnis apparuit, sed nondum natae quia nondum moriturae, sed et discentis iam inter homines conversari*, but with the caveat that the 'learning' was for our sake rather than his, so that we might the more easily believe that he had come for our salvation if we knew that he had done something of the kind already.

46 **nisi prius...annuntiarentur,** i.e. until the prophetic announcement of his birth and death (by Isaiah and others) had prepared for him and ensured his recognition.

47 **carnem de sideribus concepisse** (*A*), as the more difficult reading, should perhaps stand: the other may well have been a marginal paraphrase of this, avoiding the apparently inappropriate word *concepisse*.

50 **etsi corporis alicuius:** the angels, being of spiritual substance, have a body, for spirit is body, of its own kind—on the

Stoic principle that everything that exists is 'body' of some kind. Cf. *Adv. Prax.* 7, *quis enim negabit deum corpus esse?* and my notes on pages 232, 234.

52 ad tempus: cf. *Adv. Marc.* III. 9, *brevem carnis commeatum*. The text as printed, with this punctuation, seems to me best to account for the variants: but there is little to choose between them.

67 fuerit, omitted by the MSS. of the Cluny group, seems to be necessary as introducing the following sentence, which modifies the preceding: it admits a point scored by a supposed interruption in court from the opposite party. But, though we make this admission, *non tamen infringitur etc.*—the point scored, and in fact the whole question of the theophanies, has no bearing on the case: for at the Incarnation the circumstances (*condicio*) and purposes (*causa*) were entirely different, in that, as Christ was to die, he must of necessity be born, and his flesh must needs be veritable human flesh.

CHAPTER VII

Whenever this subject is discussed, a suggestion is advanced that our Lord's question, 'Who is my mother, and who are my brethren?' constitutes a repudiation of those relationships and (by implication) a denial of his human birth and his possession of human flesh. Our answer is:

(1) Evidently the person who made the announcement was convinced that the mother and brethren were really who he said they were.

(2) The suggestion that the announcement was made for the purpose of tempting cannot be sustained:

(*a*) because the text of the Gospel does not say so, although elsewhere when persons ask questions 'tempting him' the fact is remarked upon:

(*b*) this was not a suitable occasion for tempting him in respect of his nativity:

(α) because such a question had never been raised, and there is nothing in the context to lead up to it:

(β) because a denial of one's present possession of a mother and brethren is not necessarily a denial of nativity—the mother might be dead, and the brethren never have existed:

(c) they would have been more likely to be testing his divine knowledge by making a false statement—though even this will not serve, for apart from divine insight he might have had private information which assured him that they could not possibly be there.

(3) The true explanation of his answer is that he denies them because of their unbelief, giving preference to others who were interested in the work he was doing. For a denial of human relationships a different occasion would have been required. Moreover, he is here doing what he instructs his disciples to do, giving the kingdom of God preference over earthly ties.

(4) The episode is also an allegory of the rejection of the Synagogue and the acceptance of the Church.

(5) Our Lord's answer to the exclamation of a woman from among the multitude is to be interpreted on the same lines.

The reference is to Matthew 12. 46–50, Mark 3. 31–35: Luke 8. 19–21 omits the question, 'Who is my mother and my brethren?' but retains 'My mother and my brethren are these which hear the word of God, and keep it.' The passage is also discussed *Adv. Marc.* IV. 19, for which see a note below: at *Adv. Marc.* III. 11 the woman's exclamation (Luke 11. 27) and the announcement of our Lord's mother and brethren (Luke 8. 19) are cited by Tertullian himself as proof that *qui homo videbatur natus utique credebatur*, with a promise of further discussion, which is given at IV. 19 and 26.

3 negare esse se natum. I have ventured to insert *se*, which could easily have fallen out after *esse*. Kroymann, improving on *A*, has *negasse se*, which comes to the same thing, except that the present tense seems more natural: so *Adv. Marc.* IV. 19, *ipse, inquiunt, contestatur se non esse natum*. But in view of *Adv. Marc.* IV. 26 (quoted below) possibly we should read, with *T*, *negare natum*.

4 **audiat igitur** etc. The reference is to *Adv. Marc.* IV. 19, where the argument follows the same lines as here, with some verbal coincidences but with sufficient difference to indicate that Tertullian is not here transcribing his earlier work but rehearsing such of it as he carries in mind. This is, he says, the *constantissimum argumentum* of those who question our Lord's nativity. Heretics make a practice of either complicating the meaning of plain statements, or else of the overdue simplifying of statements conditioned by their context or by the thought behind them (*condicionales et rationales*). The latter is what they are doing here. Our answer is: (1) The announcement that his mother and brethren stood without could only have been made on the assumption that he had a mother and brethren, *quos utique norat qui annuntiarat vel retro notos vel tunc ibidem compertos dum eum videre desiderant vel dum ipsi nuntium mandant*. (2) The common response to this proposition is that the announcement was made *temptandi gratia*: but (*a*) the Scripture does not say this, though it is accustomed to remark on such occasions. This reply would have been sufficient, but (*b*) *ex abundanti causas temptationis expostulo*: if (α) for the purpose of ascertaining whether he had been born or not, I object that the question had never arisen: his human characteristics made it perfectly evident that he had been born, and they found it easier to see in him a man and a prophet than God and Son of God. Again (β) even supposing there were need for this enquiry *quodcumque aliud argumentum temptationi competisset quam per earum personarum mentionem quas potuit etiam natus non habere*. Moreover (γ) they could have settled that question by consulting the census roll. Consequently, the suggestion of temptation falls to the ground, and we conclude that his mother and brethren were really there. (3) Then what was in his mind when he asked the question? He asked it *non simpliciter*, but *ex causae necessitate et condicione rationali*, being rightly indignant that, while strangers were within intent upon his words, these close relations should stand without and even seek to divert him from his task: *non tam abnegavit quam abdicavit*, as he explains by adding *nisi qui audiunt verba mea et faciunt ea* (Luke 8. 21), thus transferring to others those terms of relationship. But there could have been no transference

if there had not been those from whom (as well as to whom) to transfer. The substitution of others then was *meritorum condicione, non ex proximorum negatione*, and he was giving an example in himself of what he said to others elsewhere, *qui patrem aut matrem aut fratres praeponeret verbo dei non esse dignum discipulum* (Luke 14. 26). Thus his denial of his mother and his brethren is itself an acknowledgement of their existence: *quod alios adoptabat, confirmabat quos ex offensa negavit, quibus non ut veriores substituit sed ut digniores*. Finally, there would be no significance in his preferring adherents to blood relations, if he had had no blood relations, *si fidem sanguini praeposuit quem non habebat*.[1]

6 materiam pronuntiationis. Below (twice) *materia temptationis* seems to mean the raw material out of which a temptation could be constructed. So here it seems likely that the meaning is 'the circumstances which gave ground for that remark'.

11 ista: Matthew 13. 55, 56: Mark 6. 3: John 6. 42. Luke has nothing parallel to this. *Creditum* is of course Tertullian's insertion, safeguarding the truth which was unknown to those whose words he is quoting.

18 quod nemo etc. The sentence is admittedly awkward. The easiest way out would be to punctuate after *significari*, omitting *temptandi gratia factum* as being a marginal explanation of *quod*. But this would leave the end of a hexameter, a clausula which Tertullian avoids. Kroymann's *eo quod*, with a comma after *factum*, makes the beginning of the sentence ugly and breaks the force of *non recipio* etc.

21 putaverint (*A*) seems the correct form: 'what can they have thought a fit subject of temptation in him?' I have marked the following sentence as the Apelleasts' supposed answer to this question: logically, of course, it is a *petitio principii*.

23 eius de quo stands for *eius rei de qua*: so *Adv. Prax.* 30, *de isto = hac de re*: and frequently.

32 adhuc potest quis etc. I have ventured to insert *quis*: though *possis* would have served, except that it is too far from the

---

[1] With this interpretation the alteration by Fr. Junius of *quem* to *quam* becomes unnecessary.

MSS. Kroymann's *potes* is too abrupt. Possibly female mortality was at such a high rate that a man was more likely to have his father living than his mother: but I can conceive of no reason why a man was more likely to have maternal uncles than brothers.

33 adeo stands for *ideo* or *quapropter*: so in §16, q.v.

41 nota ei iam, Kroymann's excellent correction of *AT*.

44 simplicitas here means 'honesty', or what our grandfathers called 'candour': the person meant what he said. So also *Adv. Val.* 2, *simplices notamur apud illos*, 'guileless', 'simpletons'. Frequently the adjective and its derivatives indicate the literal, as distinguished from the allegorical, sense of scripture: e.g. *Ad Uxor.* I. 2, *ut tamen simpliciter interpretemur*, as opposed to *figuraliter*.

44 nuntiatoris seems to have the better MS. testimony: the following subjunctive is of indirect narration dependent on it (as in *quia dixerit* above).

44 vere is not so much Tertullian's comment on this, as what he supposes to have been in the messenger's mind, that certainty which would have fortified his reaffirmation if challenged.

46 ad praesens seems to mean 'for that occasion only'.

48 mater aeque etc. This is apparently intended to suggest more than it says, namely, that there is no direct evidence in the Gospels that our Lord's mother was in sympathy with his work. It might be added that there is equally no evidence that she was not. The statement about the brethren is made at John 7. 5: at Acts 1. 14 they are shown to have changed their minds. *Martha et Mariae aliae* is my reading: the MSS. vary. There was in fact one Martha and several Marys.

52 tam proximi may conceivably be emphatic for *tam propinqui*: so *Adv. Marc.* IV. 19, *tam proximas personas...magis proximos*. But possibly Tertullian has forgotten that the word is a superlative.

57 si forte tabula ludens etc. This kind of ill-mannered innuendo is almost a commonplace of the rhetoric of the schools. It is imitated from Cicero (e.g. *Philippic* II. 17. 42 *seqq.*—the admitted model of all speeches), who however had the excuse that his strictures were true.

63 alius fuisset etc. Oehler (followed by Kroymann) is insistent that *alius* is a genitive, to be construed with *sermonis*. In view of *eius* following they may be right, though this makes a very awkward sentence. I should prefer to place a comma after *tempus* and remove that after *sermonis*: 'He could have found a different place and occasion, and a turn of phrase such as could not have been used even by one who had a mother and brethren.'

74 sed et alias etc. This reference to the synagogue is omitted *Adv. Marc.* IV. 19, no doubt because it might have led to further argument as to why this is not a point in Marcion's favour.

79 eodem sensu etc. Cf. Luke 11. 27, 28: *Adv. Marc.* IV. 26, *exclamat mulier de turba beatum uterum qui illum portasset et ubera quae illum educassent: et dominus, Immo beati qui sermonem dei audiunt et faciunt. quia et retro sic reiecerat matrem aut fratres dum auditores et obsecutores dei praefert...adeo nec retro negaverat natum.* I had thought perhaps we should insert *mulieris cuiusdam* after *illi*: but *illi exclamationi* means 'that much canvassed remark', and the addition is unnecessary.

CHAPTER VIII

A further suggestion they make is that as the created world was the result of the sinful act of an errant angel, it would have been unseemly for Christ to become contaminated with earthly flesh, which is the product of sin: and so he must be supposed to have taken to himself not earthly flesh, but a celestial substance from the stars. We answer that this leaves us where we were: for the sky itself is part of creation, and if creation was a sin the matter which composes the stars is no less sinful than earthly matter. Moreover the text, 'The second man is from heaven', when rightly interpreted, supports our case, not theirs. The subject the apostle has under discussion is not the creation nor the constitution of Christ's human nature, but the contrast between man's earthly origin and the celestial attributes he receives from Christ. Consequently, since redeemed man is in Christ at once terrestrial and celestial, it follows that Christ, with whom he is equated, was not only celestial in his godhead but also became truly terrestrial in his manhood.

5 quam volunt etc. Cf. *De Praesc. Haer.* 34, *facilius de filio quam de patre haesitabatur donec...Apelles creatorem angelum nescioquem gloriosum superioris dei faceret deum legis et Israelis, illum igneum affirmans*: also *De Res. Carn.* 5, *frivolum istud corpusculum... ignei alicuius exstructio angeli, ut Apelles docet*: and *De Anima* 23, *Apelles sollicitatas refert animas terrenis escis de supercaelestibus sedibus ab igneo angelo deo Israelis et nostro, qui exinde illis peccatricem circumfinxerit carnem*. Thus what Tertullian reports here is not that the seduced souls were transmuted into flesh, but that sinful flesh was constructed for them: the material of which it was constructed is left unspecified.

9 nominant. The name was actually mentioned, but is suppressed by Tertullian. Apparently it was the divine tetragrammaton in its triliteral Greek form ΙΑΩ, for which see *Adv. Val.* 14 (=Irenaeus, *Haer.* I. I. 7).

11 The **libellus** is not one of Tertullian's extant works. This seems to be the only reference to it.

13 de figura erraticae ovis. According to Irenaeus, *Haer.* I. I. 17, the Valentinians interpreted this of the transgression of Achamoth, and her recovery by Soter. Tertullian refers to the parable *Adv. Marc.* IV. 32, remarking that evidently the person who seeks for a sheep or a coin must be the one who has lost it, and consequently we must conclude that the world already belonged to God who sent his Christ to recover it.

20 de peccatorio censu, 'by reason of its sinful origin'—almost 'ancestry': cf. *Adv. Prax.* 5, *imago et similitudo censeris*, and my note.

22 Christo dedignantur inducere: so *AT*: the other, a much weaker, reading seems to be an attempt to smooth out the difficulties of this: strictly speaking it would require *dedignetur*. *Inducere* here means 'clothe', but with a secondary sense of 'veil' or 'becloud': at *De Praesc. Haer.* 6 (quoted above on §6), if the text is correct *inductus* means 'misled' and *induxit* means 'introduced' or 'imported'.

25 legimus plane indicates that the Apelleasts quoted 1 Corinthians 15. 47 in favour of their own views. At *De Res. Carn.* 49 Tertullian has *Primus, inquit, homo de terra choicus, id est limaceus, id est Adam, secundus homo de caelo, id est sermo dei, id est Christus, non alias tamen homo, licet de caelo, nisi quia et ipse caro atque anima, quod homo, quod Adam*: at *Adv. Marc.* v. 10 he reads *Primus, inquit, homo de humo terrenus, secundus dominus de caelo*. On this we observe (1) that it does not appear what was the origin of the form *de terrae limo*, as quoted here: (2) that whether or not Tertullian has the interpolation ὁ κύριος, he takes that to be the meaning of St Paul's words, and not (as some modern commentators suggest) some supposed 'resurrection body' of heavenly origin: and (3) that as he reads *dominus de caelo* only in controverting Marcion, there is a possibility that he is refuting Marcion from Marcion's own text—that is, that the interpolated word is due to Marcion. Both versions of the text were known to Origen: it appears not to be quoted by Irenaeus or by any earlier writer.

29 ad spiritum, i.e. Christ's divine substance, by virtue of which, even *in hac carne terrena* (meaning, apparently, both in this present life and after the resurrection), Christians are *caelestes*.

33 qualis et Christus. *Et* has stronger MS. authority than *est*. The sense really requires *est*, to contrast with *fiunt*, which is possibly why some copyists wrote it.

CHAPTER IX

A further argument against the celestial origin of Christ's flesh is that everything derived from some previously existent material retains traces of the quality of that from which it was drawn. Thus the human body has manifest affinities with the earth from which it was moulded. All these earthly and human attributes were plainly observable in the flesh of Christ, and it was these alone which gave rise to the short-sighted view that he was a man and nothing more. In no respect did his body show signs of celestial origin. It was in his words and works alone that men found anything to marvel at, though they would certainly have remarked upon it if they had observed anything unusual in his physical constitution. It was solely because his manhood was not miraculous that they were astonished at his doctrine and his miracles. Moreover his form was of even less than ordinary comeliness, as the prophets testify, and as the indignities to which he was subjected bear witness. There is thus no reason for regarding his flesh as celestial, and every reason for knowing it to be terrestrial. It was terrestrial for the express purpose that it might be the object of contumely and reproach.

1 **praetendimus adhuc,** a further argument to the same effect. Oehler, in a note on *De Pud.* 17, observes: '*praetendere* castrense verbum est, significans praesidio esse.' He gives a number of examples from late authors which serve to prove it a military term, but its meaning in all of them is not 'defend' but 'contend'. So also Tertullian, *De Pud.* 17, *apostoli...pro sanctitate praetendunt*: *Adv. Marc.* II. 6, *ut et contra malum homo fortior praetenderet*: ibid. III. 13, *et Iudas praetendet apud Hierusalem* (quoted from Zechariah 14. 14, παρατάξεται, נִלְחַם: R.V. 'fight'). So here, 'we assert'. *Ut* is concessive, and equivalent to *quamvis*.

4 **in novam proprietatem.** *Proprietas* rarely, or perhaps never, in Tertullian means property or quality, but the fact that a thing is what it is and not something else. See my notes on *Adv. Prax.* 7 and 11, and ibid. 27, *secundum utramque substantiam in sua proprietate distantem...salva est utriusque proprietas substantiae*. So here 'a new identity'.

5 **de limo figulatum:** Genesis 2. 7: LXX ἔπλασεν: Lat. vg. *formavit*. Tertullian regularly uses *figulare* in this connexion: e.g. *De Exhort. Cast.* 5, *cum hominem figulasset*. At *De Bapt.* 3 we have *hominis figurandi opus*, where apparently none of the editors has suggested *figulandi*. Tertullian could hardly have used *formare* here: it would have meant 'made into a pattern or rule': cf. *De Exhort. Cast.* 5, *contestans quid deus in primordio constituerit*

in formam posteritati recensendam, 'a rule (sc. of monogamy) which was to need to be re-enacted for future generations'.

5 ad fabulas nationum veritas transmisit. Ovid, *Metam.* 1. 80, has a kindred word to Tertullian's *figulare*, and something approaching 'in his own image': '... *sive recens tellus seductaque nuper ab alto | aethere cognati retinebat semina caeli, | quam satus Iapeto mixtam fluvialibus undis | finxit in effigiem moderantum cuncta deorum: | ... sic modo quae fuerat rudis et sine imagine tellus | induit ignotas hominum conversa figuras.*' *Veritas*, not truth in the abstract, but the Truth of divine revelation: so *Adv. Prax.* 8, *viderit haeresis si quid de veritate imitata est*. It was common form among the apologists to allege that any correspondences between Christian and pagan ideas were due to borrowing by the pagans: cf. Theophilus, *Ad Autol.* 1. 14, ὧν τιμωριῶν προειρημένων ὑπὸ τῶν προφητῶν μεταγενέστεροι γενόμενοι οἱ ποιηταὶ καὶ φιλόσοφοι ἔκλεψαν ἐκ τῶν ἁγίων γραφῶν, where Otto gives references to Justin, *Apol.* 1. 44, Tatian, *Orat.* 40, Athenagoras, *Suppl.* 9: so also Tertullian, *Apol.* 47, *quis poetarum, quis sophistarum, qui non omnino de prophetarum fonte potaverit? inde igitur philosophi sitim ingenii sui rigaverunt*: and (in greater detail) *Ad Nat.* II. 2.

6 utrumque originis elementum, now that it has the support of *T*, is the better attested reading: but the other is attractive, as being logically less accurate and thus more likely to have provoked the editorial hand.

7 nam licet alia etc. The punctuation of this and the following sentence is mine. If (as Oehler and Kroymann seem to think) *hoc est etc.* were a parenthetic explanation of the preceding clause, we should need to read *fiat*: with *fit*, these seven words must be its apodosis. In any case, *ceterum* introduces a further step in the argument, and the question it introduces cannot (by its subject-matter) be the apodosis of *nam licet etc.*

17 humana extantem substantia. So I have ventured to write, this arrangement of the words seeming best to account for *extantem* (*A* alone), and the position of the not very apposite *tantum* (*T* alone). But it is tempting to read, with the Cluny group, *ex humana substantia*: for though *exstare*, equivalent to *esse*, 'exist', is classical and sufficiently common, and may easily enough come to mean 'consist' (as here), in Tertullian's usage a thing does not 'consist' of substance, but rather it 'is' substance: so that possibly *extantem* is wrong, and *tantum* could have crept in from *tantummodo*, three words back.

26 despicientium formam eius. *Forma* here is a reminiscence of 'form or comeliness' (LXX εἶδος οὐδὲ δόξα) at Isaiah 53. 2, a text frequently quoted, but usually to make the contrast between human weakness and heavenly glory: so *Adv. Marc.* III. 7, where Isaiah 53. 2–14, 8. 14, Psalm 8. 6 and 22. 7 are brought into contrast with Daniel 2. 34, 7. 13 *seqq.* and other such texts: the same set of texts, on both sides, are rehearsed at *Adv. Iud.* 14. At *Adv. Marc.* III. 17 Isaiah 52. 14 is quoted in the form, *Quemadmodum expavescent multi super te, sic sine gloria erit ab hominibus forma tua*, and Tertullian proceeds, Certainly David says, Thou art fairer than the children of men, but that is in an allegoric sense: *ceterum habitu incorporabili* (i.e. eo habitu quem cum corpore induturus erat) *apud eundem prophetam vermis etiam et non homo, ignominia hominis et nullificamen populi* (Psalm 22. 7): cf. *De Idol.* 18, *vultu denique et aspectu inglorius, sicut et Esaias pronuntiaverat*. The present is apparently the only place in which Tertullian, led away by his argument, suggests definite ugliness: so below, *nisi merentem*. At *De Pat.* 3, *sed contumeliosus insuper sibi est*, Oehler has a long note, with citations from Tertullian (as above), Origen, Augustine, and some moderns, in the last four lines of which he gives his own, evidently correct, interpretation of that phrase.

28 apud vos quoque, i.e. Apelles and his followers, as well as Marcion, rejected the prophets. *Nos* (FB Oeh.) seems insufficiently attested: if it is accepted the meaning is 'even though we, like you, were to reject the prophets'.

30 probaverunt is not in *AT*: if it is rejected we shall need to extract *affirmant* out of the preceding *loquuntur*—which does not seem very natural.

37 opinor is evidently ironical: see the note on *maluit, credo, nasci* (§ 5).

37 inquam is evidently correct: *inquitis* would require an answer, and moreover the question is not one which the opponents would ask.

38 sicut et dixit: Matthew 16. 21 (=Mark 8. 31, Luke 9. 22), and elsewhere.

CHAPTER X

The suggestion of some others, that Christ's flesh was made out of soul, equally breaks down on examination. Christ's purpose in assuming to himself a human soul was to save human soul, which cannot be saved except in him: but there is no reason for supposing that soul only becomes capable of salvation if turned into flesh. Christ saves our souls while they not only remain souls, but even when (in death) they are disjoined from the flesh: even less did that soul which he took to himself need to become flesh so that it might obtain salvation. Further, since these people assume that Christ came to save the soul alone, and not the flesh, why should he be supposed to change that which he was saving into that which he was not saving? If it was his purpose to deliver our souls by the agency of his soul, then his soul must needs have been of the same fashion as ours—and whatever that fashion is, it is not a fleshly one. It follows that if his soul was a fleshly one it was none of ours, and as it did not save ours it is of no concern to us. Moreover, soul that was not ours stood in no need of salvation. But as it is common ground among us that soul was saved, it follows that it was our sort of soul that Christ had, and not one turned into flesh. So then, as Christ's soul was not turned into flesh, neither was his flesh made out of soul.

This is clever debating, but of more than dubious theological import. There seems to be an underlying suggestion that the soul and flesh assumed by Christ needed to be brought to a state of salvation so that ours could be saved through them. This is a form of adoptionism of which there are traces in Hermas (e.g. *Similitude* v. 6), who could not be expected to know any better, and it might have pleased Nestorius: but the suggestion is not one which Tertullian would really regard as tolerable. Elsewhere he affirms that Christ's soul and flesh, though of the stock of Adam (on which he insists most strongly), because they were not conceived by the ordinary process of human generation are exempt from the consequences of Adam's sin (see especially § 16). So we must surmise that in the present instance he has been carried away by the implications of his opponents' supposition, which he is content to controvert without sufficiently safeguarding his own view of the truth.

It is not clearly indicated who these opponents were. That they were gnostics of some sort seems probable, since it appears from § 12 that they introduced the concept of salvation by knowledge. If they were, it is likely enough that when they said 'soul' they did not mean soul in the ordinary sense, but some sort of semi-celestial 'matter', a kind of substantification of the 'passion' of Achamoth. Tertullian was no doubt aware of this equivocation, but preferred to argue on simpler grounds.

In this translation *animalis* is represented by 'composed of soul', *carnalis* by 'turned into flesh', *carneus* by 'fleshly'. Evidently the terms have taken on a special meaning from their context. *Carneus* appears to differ from *carnalis* as referring to attributes rather than constitution: so that *anima carnalis* will mean soul turned into flesh, while *anima carnea* will be soul which has acquired fleshly characteristics.

1 **convertor ad alios** etc. Cf. *Adv. Val.* 26, *in hoc* (= εἰς τοῦτο) *et Soterem in mundo repraesentatum, in salutem scilicet animalis* (sc. *substantiae*). *alia autem compositione monstruosum volunt illum* (i.e. that 'Christ' composed of four elements) *prosicias* (= *porricias*: Irenaeus τὰς ἀπαρχάς) *earum substantiarum induisse quarum summam saluti esset redacturus, ut spiritalem quidem susceperit ab Achamoth, animalem vero quem mox a Demiurgo induit Christum, ceterum corporalem ex animali substantia, sed miro et inenarrabili rationis ingenio constructam administrationis causa ideo tulisse* [*incontulisse*, A: quaero an legendum *circumtulisse*] *quo congressui et conspectui et contactui et defunctui ingratis* (= *frustra*) *subiaceret: materiale autem nihil in illo fuisse, utpote salutis alienum*. The exposition is continued ibid. 27. **Sibi prudentes**, Romans 11. 25, 12. 16 παρ' ἑαυτοῖς φρόνιμοι.

4 causas requiro. Evidently throughout this context *causa* means the final cause or purpose: see a note on §6.

8 animas...a carne disiunctas. Cf. *De Anima* 58, *omnes ergo animae penes inferos, inquis? velis ac nolis et supplicia iam illic et refrigeria*, which are anticipations of those which will follow the final judgement.

10 item cum praesumant. *Praesumere* and *praesumptio* invariably in Tertullian refer to opinions formed without any foundation of evidence or reasoning: 'assume' and 'assumption' usually give the proper sense. See a note by Heraldus (quoted by Oehler on *Apol.* 49) who observes that the same word is used by Appuleius, *Metam.* IX. 14, of Christian belief in one God: *spretis atque calcatis divinis numinibus, in vicem certae religionis mentita sacrilega praesumptione dei quem praedicaret unicum, confictis observationibus vacuis, fallens omnes homines et miserum maritum decipiens etc.* So *Apol.* 16, *atque ita inde praesumptum opinor nos quoque ut Iudaicae religionis propinquos eidem simulacro initiari*, where Souter has 'presumed' (a Scoticism for 'assumed'): ibid. 21, *quasi sub umbraculo insignissimae religionis...aliquid propriae praesumptionis abscondat* (Souter, 'some of its own arrogance'—better, 'some assumptions of its own'): ibid., *neque aliter de deo praesumimus* (Souter, correctly, 'nor is our idea of God different from that of the Jews'): ibid. 25, *illa praesumptio dicentium Romanos pro merito religiositatis diligentissimae in tantum sublimitatis elatos* (Souter, 'prejudiced assertion'—better, 'unfounded statement'): ibid. 49, *hae sunt quae in nobis solis praesumptiones vocantur* (Souter, 'vain assumptions'—'assumptions' would be enough): ibid., *quae expedit vera praesumi ...in vobis itaque praesumptio est haec ipsa quae damnat utilia* (Souter, 'presumed to be true', again meaning 'assumed': 'this very prejudice', better, 'is neither more nor less than an assumption'): ibid. 50, *nec praesumptio perdita nec persuasio desperata* (Souter, 'neither reckless prejudice nor desperate persuasion'—perhaps, 'reckless assumption', 'criminal conspiracy'). In the passage before us the point is that the gnostic and Marcionite doctrine that the flesh, being material, is incapable of salvation, is a mere assumption, based neither on scriptural evidence nor on natural reason or observed facts: it is mere guesswork or surmise, erected into a dogma. At *sed animae nostrae* Codex Agobardinus ends.

15 illam quoque etc. The reading of *T* (followed by Kroymann) makes a sentence which will just construe but has no apparent bearing on the words that follow. Kroymann's punctuation here is impossible. *Forma* in this context has its original meaning 'shape'. Evidently soul, being *corpus sui generis*, has some sort of shape, though this is *in occulto*, not visible to the eye. At *De Anima* 9 it is alleged that when God breathed soul into Adam the fluid 'set' like a jelly in a mould, taking its shape from the body, *omni intus linea expressum esse* (sc. *flatum vitae*) *quam densatus impleverat et velut in forma gelasse*.

22 non carnea is evidently equivalent to the preceding *nostra*, not to *non nostra*.

24 iam ergo etc. clinches the first part of Tertullian's reply to the postulate of an animal flesh. In it he assumes by simple conversion that animal flesh implies carnal soul, which, on the ground of the doctrine of the Atonement, he shows to be inconceivable. The adversaries are now supposed to accept this argument by conversion and to suggest the *causa* demanded earlier in the chapter, 'for the purpose of making soul visible'—a suggestion dealt with in the next chapter.

CHAPTER XI

When we point out that the supposition that Christ's flesh was made out of soul involves the consequence that his soul was changed into flesh, our opponents offer as a reason for this latter, that it was God's intention that soul, of whose existence and attributes the impediment of the flesh had caused some uncertainty, should now be made visible in Christ: and consequently, they allege, in Christ soul was turned into body so that we might see it being born and dying and rising again. This is as much as to say that soul was made dark so that it might have power to shine. Moreover, the statement that soul was invisible implies that it already possessed body, an invisible one: so that, supposing it to have been God's purpose to make it visible, he could with greater veracity have made it visible in its own body than in the body of something else. Also, to make soul visible in the guise of flesh is not to display it but to hide it. Even if (*per impossibile*) soul, as invisible, did exist without body of its own, it would have been more fitting, as well as less embarrassing, for God to make it visible in a new kind of body than in one which was already appropriated to something else. 'To be visible among men', they say, 'Christ had to be man': quite so, and so he must have had the same sort of soul as any other man.

1 **sed aliam argumentationem etc.** This sentence, in connexion with what follows, is somewhat difficult. The solution seems to lie in the meaning of *convenimus*. Oehler's index (*s.v.*) gives these meanings: *deprehendere, invenire, petere, iudicio aggredi*, between which no distinction is made. His note at *Apol.* 10, to which he makes frequent reference elsewhere, says that *convenire* is a juristic term. This is true: and the most natural meaning to expect is *iudicio oppetere*, 'join issue with', 'tackle', as the following citations show: *Apol.* 10, *maiestatis rei convenimur*: ibid. 31, *de quorum maiestate convenimur in crimen*: ibid. 35, *in hac quoque religione secundae maiestatis de qua in secundum sacrilegium convenimur*: *De Res. Carn.* 18, *resurrectio carnis, duo verba expedita decisa detersa: ipsa conveniam, ipsa discutiam, cui se substantiae addicant*: *Ad Nat.* I. 1, *scio plane qua responsione soletis redundantiae nostrae testimonium convenire*. But if this is the most natural, it is not the only meaning: cf. *De Res. Carn.* 12, *quodcunque conveneris, fuit*, 'whatever you come across, has already existed': *De Ieiunio* 13, *convenio vos et praeter pascha ieiunantes*, 'I find you keeping other fasts besides the Easter vigil': *De Cor.* 10, *illorum deputatur* (sc. *habitus iste*) *in quorum et antiquitatibus et sollemnitatibus et officiis convenitur*, 'is found in use': *Adv. Hermog.* 45, *atquin magis apparere coepit et ubique conveniri deus ex quo factus est mundus*. Transitional between this meaning and the other is *Adv. Marc.* I. 6, *conveniens enim et quodammodo iniecta manu detinens adversarii sensum*. At *Adv. Marc.* IV. 6 the meaning seems to be 'welcome' (unless perchance the sentence is chiastic): *haec conveniemus, haec amplectemur, si nobiscum*

magis fuerint, si Marcionis praesumptionem percusserint. Our suggestion then is that in the passage before us the meaning is not 'we join issue with' but 'we meet with another argument of theirs in answer to our inquiry why etc.'

1 **exigentes cur etc.** This also is difficult, through excessive brevity. The argument of the preceding chapter is compressed into one sentence and made the ground of a further interrogation. The original suggestion was *Christum animalem carnem subisse*, that Christ assumed flesh made out of soul. Tertullian has shown that this involves the admission *Christum animam carnalem habuisse*, that Christ had a soul that was turned into flesh. Assuming that his adversaries acquiesce in this deduction by simple inversion, he asks what reason they can suggest for Christ having had a soul of that sort. Their answer follows, that it was for the purpose of making evident certain facts about soul which until then had been concealed through the hindrance of the flesh. The suggestion has a Platonic sound, and it was no doubt from Platonic sources (though not apparently immediately from Plato) that the Valentinians derived it: indeed the whole gnostic theory of salvation by knowledge has a Platonic background, though the knowledge on which Plato would have made salvation contingent would not have been of particular facts such as the true nature of the soul, but of the ideal and transcendent Good. That the suggestion is ridiculous is summarily shown in the sentence *et hoc autem quale erit etc.*, after which the argument becomes more detailed.

11 **dum id fit cui latebat.** The sentence as punctuated gives a perfectly good sense. Kroymann's *cur latebat* might perhaps be right if *cur* could mean *ob quod*, and if *ob quod* could mean *per quod*: the former seems unlikely, the latter is of no concern here.

12 **denique ad hoc etc.** This sentence also is difficult, and the text must be regarded as doubtful. If *prius* and *dehinc* are correct, Tertullian outlines a course of argument which he does not proceed to follow. Also we must either read *an in totum* as equivalent to *si in totum*, or else take *utrum...an* as meaning *sive...sive*, either of which is difficult, though neither is quite impossible. Kroymann, besides several other quite unnecessary alterations of the

text, reads *adhuc pressius* for *ad hoc prius*, and *dicant qui* for *dehinc an*. This simplifies the sentence, and may conceivably (though not, I think, probably) be what Tertullian wrote: *adhuc* is certainly not impossible. Kroymann further suggests that *et hoc autem* (above, line 9) has begun the second part of the refutation, the first part having got displaced and now appearing as §13 and its appendix §14. In this he seems to be mistaken, for the order of the refutation is (1) that if it were necessary to make soul visible, that would be better done by making it visible as itself and not as something else (§11): (2) soul is of its own nature competent to be cognisant of itself, so that it was unnecessary for it to be made visible either as flesh or as itself (§12): (3) soul is one thing and flesh is another, and the terms cannot be interchanged: moreover our Lord himself speaks of his soul and his flesh as two distinct things and not as one thing confused (§13). This concludes the argument, in Tertullian's usual style, with an appeal to scriptural facts: §14, an appendix to the main theme, treats of a suggestion advanced in answer to a further consequence of Tertullian's argument, that on the theory just criticized Christ would be left without an effective human soul at all.

20 omne quod est corpus est. See a previous note, on §6 line 50: and on the corporeal nature of soul see the curious narrative at *De Anima* 9.

23 quia nec hic etc., a back reference to §3, *plane interest illud ut falsum non patiatur quod vere non est*.

27 in carne conversa: whether or not it is worth while to read *carnem*, the accusative is certainly to be understood. *Conversa* (*TR*³) is evidently correct.

33 alterius iam notitiae, 'already known as something else'. Kroymann's *notae* in this context could only mean 'brand', and has no particular point. *Sine causa* here means *frustra*, 'to no effective purpose'.

34 istis scilicet quaestionibus etc. Kroymann, at first sight plausibly, reads *iustis*. But there is a reference back to the 'rackings' suggested in §1. The last clause of the present sentence means 'so as to establish the case of human flesh against it', and racking of some sort might be supposed to be necessary for the extraction of evidence.

35 sed non poterat etc. This I regard as a supposed objection by the adversaries, whose 'Christ', being of 'animal' nature, needed to become 'carnal' so as to be visible to men. Tertullian here disregards their supposition of a semi-divine 'Christ' and concentrates on the matter in hand. See previous notes.

CHAPTER XII

We might admit that soul was revealed through flesh, if we first agreed that it stood in need of revelation, either to itself or to us—though soul is not distinguishable from us, our whole existence being soul: for without soul we are not men but corpses. Was soul then in need of knowing itself? Soul is by nature perceptive, and perception is so to speak the soul of soul. Since then soul gives perception to things perceptive, is it reasonable to suppose it was ever without perception of itself? Rather is it characteristic of soul to be cognisant of itself: without such cognisance it could not function as itself. And especially is this the case in man, who is rational because he possesses a rational (and not merely a vegetative) soul: if soul were ignorant of itself, it could not make man rational. And the facts show that it was not ignorant: even apart from revelation it is conscious of its maker, its judge, and its own permanence. Further, if it had been true that soul was ignorant of itself, we might have expected Christ to give it instruction about itself. But the instruction we do find him giving is not of the soul's attributes but of its salvation: for the purpose of his coming was not that soul should know itself ⟨by seeing itself visible⟩ in Christ, but that it should know Christ ⟨by being conscious of his grace⟩ in itself: and its salvation was in danger through ignorance not of itself but of the Word of God. It was the Life that was made manifest, not the soul: and Christ came to save the soul, not to reveal it. We were in no ignorance of the soul's birth and death, but only of its rising again. This Christ did reveal, in himself as in Lazarus and others; and it follows that, as their flesh was not composed of soul, neither was his. Is there anything else about itself that soul needed to learn?

4 cum totum quod sumus anima sit is a deliberately one-sided statement or exaggeration for the purpose of the present argument, and not necessarily in contradiction with *De Res. Carn.* 40, *porro nec anima per semetipsam homo, quae figmento iam homini appellato postea inserta est, nec caro sine anima homo, quae post exilium animae cadaver inscribitur*: cf. ibid. 17, *habet enim de suo solummodo cogitare, velle, cupere, disponere: ad perficiendum autem operam carnis expectat.*

7 fieret evidently stands for *fieri deberet.*

8 sensualis. *Sensus* can mean either perception of things without, or consciousness of thoughts within: here the emphasis is on the latter. Cf. *De Anima* 38, where the natural attributes of the soul are enumerated as *immortalitas, rationalitas, sensualitas, intellectualitas, arbitrii libertas.*

13 ex naturalium necessitate, 'from the necessity imposed by, or arising from, its natural attributes and relationships'. Cf. *De Anima* 38: *auferenda est enim argumentatoris occasio, qui quod anima desiderare videatur alimenta, hinc quoque mortalem eam intelligi cupit, quae cibis sustineatur, denique derogatis eis evigescat, postremo subtractis intercidat. porro non solum proponendum est quisnam ea desideret, sed et cui: et si propter se, sed et cur et quando et quonam usque: tum quod aliud natura desideret, aliud necessitate, aliud secundum proprietatem, aliud in causam. desiderabit igitur cibos anima sibi quidem ex causa necessitatis, carni vero ex natura proprietatis. certe enim domus animae caro est, et inquilinus carnis anima. desiderabit itaque inquilinus ex causa et necessitate huius nominis profutura domui toto inquilinatus sui tempore, non ut ipse substruendus nec ut ipse loricandus nec ut ipse tibicinandus sed tantummodo continendus, quia non aliter contineri possit quam domo fulta.*

16 se ministrare: 'cause itself to function': so almost, *Apol.* 2, *ne qua vis lateat in occulto* (i.e. some diabolic power) *quae vos... contra ipsas quoque leges ministret.*

17 **compotem et animam etc.** will just construe with the following relative clause. Should *compotem* require a dependent genitive, this would be *rationis*, which could easily have fallen out after *rationale*.

21 **statum suum** must have the meaning required by the explanatory clause *nihil magis audiens etc.*, i.e. 'its own permanence', though not excluding the other four natural attributes enumerated at *De Anima* 38 (quoted above): so, perhaps, as a more inclusive phrase, 'its own estate'.

21 **nihil adhuc etc.** These observations first appear at *Apol.* 17, *cum tamen ⟨anima⟩ resipiscit, ut ex crapula, ut ex somno, ut ex aliqua valetudine, et sanitatem suam patitur, 'deum' nominat, hoc solo, quia proprie verus hic unus. 'deus bonus et magnus' et 'quod deus dederit' omnium vox est. iudicem quoque contestatur illum: 'deus videt' et 'deo commendo' et 'deus mihi reddet'. o testimonium animae naturaliter Christianae!* They are expanded *De Test. Anim.* 2 (of the one God, the judge), 3 (of the existence of the devil), 4 (of the immortality of the soul, and the resurrection of the flesh). The object of *deo commendare*, as appears from *Apol.* 17 (above), is either 'itself' or 'its cause', i.e. not *amicum peregrinaturum* or anything of that nature.

25 **imprecari** in a good sense is uncommon: so Lewis and Short, who quote Appuleius, *Metam.* 9. 25, *salutem ei fuerat imprecatus* (after sneezing): Petronius, *Sat.* 78, *ut totus mihi populus bene imprecetur*, is hardly in point, for Trimalchio was not an authority on Latin usage. Here the verb takes its tone from both adverbs.

27 **nihil...nisi** seems to stand for *nihil...potius quam*.

28 **effigiem.** This instance should be noted as an exception to my general statement (*Adv. Prax.*, pages 234, 236) that Tertullian commonly uses *effigies* for what is appearance and not fact.

29 **non ut ipsa etc.** Gnostics and others, both ancient and modern, are prone to regard the gospel not as a gospel but as a system of information, which if not given to their satisfaction

leaves them complaining of its uselessness. Tertullian may condescend to argue with such on their own ground: but he cannot in the long run forget that Christianity is a gospel of salvation and not a source of occult knowledge, and that salvation depends not on knowledge of facts but on the knowledge of Christ.

33 ignorabamus nimirum etc. The text must be regarded as doubtful, the authorities differing among themselves. That given here is the reading of the Cluny group, and makes a satisfactory sense, provided it is observed that *nimirum* marks the sentence as not Tertullian's own view but that imputed by him to his adversaries: otherwise *et mori* will be wrong. Failure to observe this may account for the editorial variations of the other authorities. *Ignoravimus plane* marks Tertullian's own comment on his adversaries' supposed view. A little lower, *erit* must be correct: 'this it must be that Christ did make evident', the future tense (as frequently) marking a necessary deduction.

38 dispositione refers to the same set of facts as *status, natura, qualitas,* and possibly also *condicio*, but from the point of view not of what they are in themselves but of God who ordained that so they should be.

CHAPTER XIII

It is inconceivable that soul should have been revealed as soul by being turned into flesh, for the two things, if they are the same thing, are neither the one nor the other. All understanding and all discourse become impossible if names do not remain attached to the things to which they belong. Even when one thing is turned into another, as clay into pottery, it loses its old name and assumes another. So the soul of Christ, if turned into flesh, will be flesh and not soul, and must be so named, and there will result one uniform substance in which the two elements cannot be discerned. But in fact we find Christ himself referring in set terms to his soul and to his flesh, not as one indiscrete thing but as two distinct things: and that being so, neither has he a soul turned into flesh nor flesh composed of soul. For no one will suggest that the texts quoted refer to another soul and other flesh besides that which, being both, is neither. Thus he himself safeguards the duality of the two substances each in its own species, excluding the idea of both together appearing under one single form.

1 **caro facta est etc.** The sentence is a summary and interpretation of the adversaries' answer to the question at the beginning of §11. Such *lemmata* are a common enough rhetorical device, and there is no need for Kroymann's observation that there is no formula of transition: the repetition itself is such a formula.

2 **si caro anima est etc.** The variations of *T* (see critical note) are a misguided attempt to clarify the structure of the clauses, the copyist (or his authority) being unaware that the most natural Latin order is predicate before subject, as below, line 28, *porro si anima caro fuisset*. Kroymann follows *T*.

4 **ubi ergo caro etc.** The text of this sentence here printed is that of *T*. That of the other authorities, given by Oehler, is neither grammatical nor comprehensible. Even so, this use of *alterutro alterutrum*, 'each made into the other out of the other', is difficult to defend. The word usually means 'one or the other, no matter which': but Lewis and Short quote it from Columella in the sense of *utrumque*, and that may be the meaning here, in which case *alterutro* in both cases will be due to scribal attempts at correction, and should be omitted.

9 **fides nominum etc.** Cf. *Adv. Marc.* I. 7, where Tertullian admits that names, such as 'god', are sometimes equivocal, and contends that what we must discuss is not the names or terms but the *substantiae* represented by them.

11 **vocabulorum possessiones.** Kroymann marks a lacuna and suggests that *aliorum* has fallen out. If any alteration were needed we should perhaps insert *novas* before *accipiunt*. But in fact *possessiones* in Latin are 'new possessions', obtained by squatter's right.

18 **quod autem etc.** I have ventured to insert *nomen*, which could easily have dropped out through confusion with *non*:

in that case *quod autem* must be construed as equivalent to *eius autem quod*—a kind of ellipsis of which there are several examples.

19 ergo et anima etc. On *soliditas* see a note on §6: here the meaning seems to be 'completeness', though 'solidity' is not impossible. *Singularitas* occurs at *De Exhort. Cast.* 1 meaning bachelordom or widowhood: here it is 'singleness' as opposed to duality: cf. §14, *hominem a solo et singulari serpente deiectum*.

23 animam-carnem etc. The hyphens here are mine. I imagine previous editors have seen the point, but I have preferred to make it plain.

25 duarum qualitatum. *Qualitas* is not 'a quality' in the sense of one among many attributes, but the whole set of attributes which constitute the *natura* of each object.

26 quid is evidently no part of the text *Anxia est etc.*, and it is surprising that the editors, including Oehler and Kroymann, have printed it so. Matthew 26. 38 (=Mark 14. 34) περίλυπός ἐστιν ἡ ψυχή μου ἕως θανάτου.

36 in suo genere...unicam speciem. *Genus* and *species* are here apparently not used in any technical sense: 'each in its own kind'...'one single form': so also above, *dividit species*, 'distinguishes the two forms'. At *De Bapt.* 4, water (the whole of the earth's water) is *genus unum*, but there are *species complures: quod autem generi attributum est etiam in species redundat*, i.e. the possibility of its becoming a vehicle of the Spirit, indicated in the narrative of the creation, becomes true of all or any water, whether sea or pond, river or spring, lake or river bed: so that *genus* means species, and *species* the individual instances.

CHAPTER XIV

We have proved that to suggest that Christ's body was made out of soul is tantamount to saying that in his case soul was changed into flesh. When we point out that this would leave him without an effective soul, our adversaries reply that in addition to soul he had also assumed to himself an angel who discharged the soul's functions. Here again we ask for what purpose. (1) Certainly not for the purpose of saving angels in the same way as his assumption of humanity was for the purpose of saving man: for though there are angels for whom the fire of damnation is prepared, it is nowhere on record that restoration has been promised to them or that Christ has received from the Father any mandate concerning their salvation. (2) Could it be then that he assumed an angel as an attendant or assistant in the work of man's salvation? Certainly not: for (*a*) the Son of God was by himself competent without assistance to deliver those whom the devil without assistance had enslaved: and (*b*) such a view would suggest that there is not one God and one Saviour, but two saviours each ineffective without the other. Or (3) could it be that the angel was not his assistant but his agent? In that case why did he need to come himself? (4) Certainly he is described as the angel of great counsel: but in this case 'angel' means messenger, being a term of office, not of nature, for the Son is the angel or messenger of the Father, and yet is not on that account reduced to equal terms with other messengers. (5) The Psalm says that as man Christ is not the equal of the angels, but is a little lower than they—though as spirit of God and power of the Most High he is far above them: but if he were possessed of an angel he would not be lower, and the Psalm would be falsified. (6) This theory about an angel is Ebionite in principle, for it makes Christ a mere man, inspired as the prophets were inspired, as Zechariah ascribes his inspiration to 'the angel that spake in me'. But Christ, who speaks of himself in higher terms than the prophets, never uses this expression, nor even the common prophetic formula 'Thus saith the Lord', but 'I say unto you.' Finally (7) scripture explicitly rules out the suggestion, when Isaiah says, 'Neither an angel nor a deputy, but the Lord himself hath saved us.'

In this chapter codex *T* presents an unusually large number of variations from the traditional text, most of which are at least interesting and not to be rejected without careful consideration. In general they seem to give the impression of being due to editing, not indeed by the actual writer of the codex but by someone farther back who was no mean Latinist. A possibility, but not (I think) a probability, is that the editor or reviser was Tertullian himself, as Hoppe has suggested was the case with the *Apology*. In the event, I have produced an eclectic text, which I submit with much deference to the judgement of the learned.

1–4 sed et angelum etc. The punctuation of these sentences is that which I wrote in my copy of Oehler thirty years ago: in placing a period after *causa* it agrees with Kroymann's.

Qua ratione could mean 'on what principle', *ratio* referring to the antecedent or formal cause, as below §17 *ratio quae praefuit*: cf. *De Cor.* 4, *rationem traditioni et consuetudini et fidei patrocinaturam aut ipse perspicies etc.*, and *consuetudo autem etiam in civilibus rebus pro lege suscipitur cum deficit lex, nec differt scriptura an ratione consistat, quando et legem ratio commendet*, and the whole chapter: or the meaning may be 'in what manner', as at *Scorp.* 1, The scorpion's tail *hamatile spiculum in summo tormenti ratione stringit*, 'after the manner of a catapulted javelin'. In either case *qua et hominem*, the adversaries' supposed answer, must mean *qua et hominem vos eum profitemini gestasse*, for the adversaries did not admit the manhood.

2 eadem ergo etc. Between *est* and *sit* there is not much to choose: but *ergo* as a rule introduces a deduction of fact, rather than of requirement, and it seems more likely that Tertullian wrote *est*, meaning, 'In that case there is the same purpose and intention.' *Causa* once more refers to the final cause: see a note on §10, to which add *De Anima* 24, *si tempus in causa est oblivionis*, where the efficient cause is indicated: and *Adv. Marc.* v. 20, where *causatio* (twice) is a translation of πρόφασις at Philippians 1. 18, 'pretence'. Below, *nihil tale de causa est* is perfectly good Latin, and (in spite of Kroymann's rejection) the last three words should be retained.

7 nullum mandatum etc. A reminiscence of John 10. 18, ταύτην τὴν ἐντολὴν ἔλαβον παρὰ τοῦ πατρός μου, and Hebrews 2. 16, οὐ γὰρ δήπου ἀγγέλων ἐπιλαμβάνεται, which latter might (if its authority had been acknowledged on all hands) have settled the question under discussion.

10 **cui igitur rei** etc. Here, for the reason suggested above, *igitur* seems the right word. Both *forte* (T) and *fortem* (XRB) make good sense and it is difficult to choose between them: the sentence naturally requires *gestaverit*, and possibly *forte* supplies the suggestion of contingency which the indicative verb lacks. *Cum quo* is in some slight contrast with *per angelum*, below: first Tertullian rejects the idea of the angel as a partner or attendant, then that of an agent for an absent principal.

13 **salutificator.** Oehler's index gives these references: in every case there is a scriptural text in the background, and in each case a variant reading: *De Res. Carn.* 47 = Philippians 3. 20 (σωτήρ): *Adv. Marc.* II. 19 = Psalm 24 (23). 4 (παρὰ θεοῦ σωτῆρος αὐτοῦ): *De Ieiunio* 6 = Deuteronomy 32. 15 (ἀπὸ θεοῦ σωτῆρος αὐτοῦ): *De Pud.* 2 = 1 Timothy 4. 10 (σωτὴρ πάντων ἀνθρώπων). The last reference, with ἐπὶ θεῷ ζῶντι in the context, suggests that here *deus* is right and *dominus* (T) due to editing.

15 **cur ergo descendit.** *ipse* is in T alone; without it the emphasis of the sentence is on *descendit*, where it ought to be, for this word (and concept) here appears for the first time.

17 **magni consilii angelus.** T has *angelus magni cogitatus*, here as below. Kroymann suggests that *magni consilii angelus* is an editorial alteration based on μεγάλης βουλῆς ἄγγελος (Isaiah 9. 5 LXX). It seems equally possible that (certainly with that text in mind) Tertullian wrote *magni consilii angelus*, and in the next half-sentence proceeded to interpret this as *magnum cogitatum*, equating βουλή with βούλευμα. In that case it is T which has the edited text. Also, the explanation *id est nuntius* comes more naturally if *angelus* has just preceded: as below. Irenaeus, *Haer.* III. 17. 3, has *magni consilii patris nuntius*. LXX makes heavy weather of the whole verse, so that the 'Prince of the Five Names' does not appear. Tertullian quotes the earlier part of the verse *Adv. Marc.* III. 19.

21 **nam et filius** etc. Luke 20. 9–18. *Deo vineae* (T) is manifestly wrong. *Vinitores* (T) is attractive, though the word means 'vine-dressers' (Virgil, *Ecl.* x. 36), not 'vine-growers': and why

should *XRB* have altered it to *cultores*? If Tertullian wrote *viticultores* both readings are accounted for.

27 quomodo videbitur angelum induisse seems to give the required sense. The contestants did not say that the Son became an angel, or was an angel, but that an angel occupied the place of the soul which had ceased to be soul by turning into flesh: *angelum induisse* is the way that would be expressed. If we read with *T* we must remove the comma which Kroymann puts after *angelus*, and translate, 'How shall it have come about that an angel has been, in the manner indicated, made lower than angels by becoming man etc.?' It is possible that Tertullian wrote *angelum*, leaving *induisse* or *gestasse*, or some such word, to be understood, and that *T*'s prototype short-sightedly altered this to the nominative.

29 qua autem spiritus dei etc. Luke 1. 35: cf. *Adv. Prax.* 26, 27, and my Introduction, pp. 65–70. Kroymann suggests the deletion of this sentence on the ground that it has nothing to do with the present argument, and that the required safeguard against the misunderstanding of the previous sentence comes a few lines lower in the remarks on the Ebionites. This is misconceived, it being quite in Tertullian's style to interrupt his argument with a passing caution (as an orator would interject an 'aside' in making a speech): and in fact there is no anticipation of the remarks on the Ebionites.

31 tanto non, dum etc. All the authorities are at fault here: *tanto* (*TB*) is evidently right: *non, dum* is from Gelenius. It does not appear that, for the second *gestat*, any editor has suggested *gestet*, though that is the mood required: for in fact the Son did not take to himself an angel—a mere supposition of Tertullian's opponent.

32 poterit haec opinio etc. If sequence of tenses is of any account, *poterit* is the correct form, with *edicat* following: *poterat* could be the correction of one who recollected that Ebion (if there ever was such a person) had long been dead when Tertullian wrote. According to Irenaeus, from whom our other authorities copy the information, the Ebionite doctrine of Christ was in agreement with that of Cerinthus and Carpocrates, namely, that Jesus was *nudus homo* (=ψιλὸς ἄνθρωπος), the son of Joseph and Mary, and that Christ (apparently a kind of semi-divine personage) came upon him at his baptism and left him before his crucifixion. Tertullian's other references to the Ebionites mention only their observance of the Mosaic law, and say nothing about their doctrine of Christ. In the present passage we seem to have indications of a doctrine somewhat different from that described by Irenaeus, namely that Jesus was a mere man, not exactly possessed by any semi-divine 'power', but inspired in the same manner as the prophets were inspired. *Prophetis aliquo gloriosiorem* must be taken as one of Tertullian's ironical interjections, meaning that if it were the case that Jesus was a mere man, then he was somewhat less reticent about his own importance and greatness than the prophets were about theirs: which of course is true, as Tertullian shows in the following sentence, and as is evident from the Gospels in which our Lord is recorded as having from the beginning made himself the subject of his own preaching and as having represented himself as the indispensable and only Mediator and way of access to the Father. *Gloriosior* is an intentionally offensive word, indicating that if the Ebionite doctrine of Christ were true, then we should have to regard him as having said too much about himself: but the odium of the offensive term is thrown back upon the heretics who provoke it. Whether we read *aliquo* or *aliquid*, it makes no difference to the meaning: Kroymann's *aliquot* could only mean 'more boastful than a certain number of prophets'—though it is unlikely that that was the meaning intended.

34 ut ita in illo angelum fuisse dicat (or *edicat*, or even *dicatur*) is apparently the right reading. *Ut* introduces a consecutive clause dependent on *constituit* (*plane...gloriosiorem* being parenthetic): *ita* is balanced by *quemadmodum*, below. This is in some slight contradiction with *angelum gestavit, angelum induisse,* above: but Tertullian is not now concerned with the main theme of this chapter, his answer to *sed et angelum gestavit*, but with a supposed parallel with the inspiration of Zechariah which he suggests that the Ebionite doctrine amounts to. *In nonnullis* (*TB*

Kroymann) will not do: Zechariah is the only prophet of whom such a statement is made, and moreover the sentence in this form is pointless. Between *dicatur* (*TB*) and *edicat* (*XR*) there is not much to choose, though the latter seems too strong a word and I suspect the prefix has been borrowed from *fuisse*: the passive of *dicere* commonly introduces scriptural references, which is not the case here.

39 quid ultra etc. It is difficult to imagine how *audi* got into the text unless it (and the accusatives) were original. *Quid ultra etc.* seems to expect something new, which the text from Isaiah in fact provides, returning from the digression about the Ebionites and summarizing the argument of the whole chapter (as often) in a scriptural quotation. If the preliminary *et* (*T*) has any authority at all, perhaps we should read *ecquid*: certainly not *sed* (Kroymann).

CHAPTER XV

The Valentinian theory that Christ's flesh was spiritual is, no less than the theories we have examined, discountenanced by the express statements of our Lord himself, as of the prophets and apostles, that he is truly Man. One of the Valentinians objects (*a*) that if Christ did possess earthly and human substance, that would make him inferior to the angels: and (*b*) that truly human flesh would need to be born, as we are, of the will of a man. He quotes texts which he thinks prove his case, and asks (*c*) why, if our flesh is like his, we do not rise again the third day, or alternatively, why his flesh did not see corruption. These are the sort of questions the heathen raise, though with better excuse. We answer (*a*) that there is good scriptural authority for saying that in some sense Christ was made inferior to the angels: (*b*) that the heretics are inconsistent, professing a sort of incarnation while denying Christ's humanity: and (*c*) that the time for our resurrection has not come, and will not, until Christ has put all his enemies (including these heretics) beneath his feet.

1 licuit etc. It is surprising that someone with an itch for correcting Latin prose has not suggested *libuit*: but cf. §3, *hoc putas* *arbitrio tuo licuisse.* On *ex privilegio haeretico* cf. §1, *licentia haeretica*, and the note there: it appears that the presumption which has assumed a permission which has not been granted has now become so inveterate as to be the basis of a claim for *privilegium*, the right to take the initiative on any subject of discussion.

1 carnem Christi spiritalem comminisci. Again, why has not someone suggested *Christo*? *Caro spiritalis* is evidently, in this context, flesh constructed of, or condensed from, spirit. But 'spirit' to the Valentinians had a special meaning. The lower Wisdom, Achamoth, despite her fall, retained some traces of the divine or spiritual essence of her mother Sophia. These, without being conscious of it, she in part communicated to her son Craftsman, the non-divine creator of the world: he in turn, himself unknowing, passed on, in part, this *semen spiritale* to his creation. It is this seed, breathed with the breath into Adam, which when ripened (*adultum*) becomes competent to receive (*suscipere*, i.e. physically assimilate) the *sermo perfectus*. Cf. *Adv. Val.* 25, and *passim*. Spirit, in this context of thought, does not mean (as elsewhere in Tertullian) the divine Word, but a kind of rather less than divine substance, which (presumably) the divine Christ collected from Achamoth on his way down to earth, and converted into the semblance of flesh.

4 ex qua substantia could conceivably mean 'with what confidence or assurance': cf. *Adv. Prax.* 31, and my note. But, if this seems too far-fetched, it may be better to take it as 'in view of what substance', seeing that the Valentinians held Christ to be divine and his flesh 'spiritual', and so left him with nothing in any sense human. *Se*, supplied by Ursinus after *ipse*, now appears in *T* in a less suitable place: its omission altogether is not unparalleled.

8 et homo est etc. At Jeremiah 17. 9 LXX has βαθεῖα ἡ καρδία παρὰ πάντα καὶ ἄνθρωπός ἐστιν καὶ τίς γνώσεται αὐτόν; misreading אָנֻשׁ (weak or sickly) as אֱנוֹשׁ (man, or mankind): English R.V. 'The heart is deceitful above all things and desperately wicked: who can know it?' Lat. vg. *Pravum est cor omnium et inscrutabile: quis cognoscet illud?* The text is quoted (also from

LXX) by Irenaeus, *Haer.* III. 18. 2, *quis est autem qui communicavit nobis de escis* (1 Cor. 10. 16)? *utrum is qui ab illis affigitur sursum Christus superextensus Horo, id est fini, et formavit eorum Matrem: an vero qui ex virgine est Immanuel qui butyrum et mel manducavit, de quo ait propheta, Et homo est et quis cognoscet eum?* Cf. also ibid. III. 20. 2 where the text is quoted against those who allege that Joseph was his father: and ibid. IV. 55. 2 among a long series of prophetic testimonies to Christ. Tertullian, *Adv. Marc.* III. 7 in reference to the day of judgement, and in illustration of Zechariah 12. 12, *cognoscent eum qui compugerunt*: so also *Adv. Jud.* 14.

12 virum vobis a deo destinatum: so *De Pud.* 21. At Acts 2. 22 ἀποδεδειγμένον appears to mean 'shown to be what we claim him to be', or 'approved' (in the older sense of that word): Tertullian seems to take it to mean 'appointed' or 'predestined', which will not suit its original context. Lat. vg. *approbatum.*

13 vice does not mean 'instead of' but 'as equivalent to': cf. *Apol.* 17, the demons *vice rebellantium ergastulorum sive carcerum vel metallorum vel hoc genus poenalis servitutis*, 'after the manner of rebellious slaves etc.': ibid. 48, *mundi species temporalis, quae illi dispositioni aeternitatis aulaei vice oppansa est*, 'after the manner of a drop-curtain'. The texts quoted ought to serve as a *praescriptio* and preclude all further argument, and would do so if it were possible for heretics to be unprejudiced, and so forth.

15 imaginariae, XRB: the double reading of T, *putative imaginarie*, only means that the copyist wrote down the wrong word out of his head and immediately referred to his copy and wrote the right one as well.

15 sine studio etc. *Studium* is prejudice in favour of a person or opinion: so Tacitus, *Ann.* I. 1 *sine ira et studio*, 'without rancour or partiality'. *Artificium contentionis* hints that the discussion or conflict was by far-fetched devices kept alive long after the question ought to have been settled: at *Adv. Marc.* V. 20 *per invidiam et contentionem* translates Philippians 1. 15 διὰ φθόνον καὶ ἔριν, to which there is also a veiled reference here.

16 quendam ex Valentini factiuncula will be the Alexander dismissed briefly in §17. *Factiuncula* comes from $B^{mg}\cdot T$: the difficulty is that the Valentinianism was not a small faction, but a wide-spread and influential movement. There is just a possibility that *ratione* (*XRB*) may be right: if *via* can mean the Christian religion, it is conceivable that *ratio* may mean a school of thought.

18 informatam can hardly mean *indutam*, as Oehler's index suggests, but more probably 'was brought into shape', 'was given organic form', namely, by the *spiritus dei* (in Tertullian's sense of that term), which (or who) formed and brought into organic shape that which was conceived in the virgin's womb.

20 similem nostri carnem is only intelligible if *nostri* stands for *nostrae*, the feminine dative singular: if not, we should read *nostrae*, as below, *par nostrae*.

21–24 et cur…dissoluta est? I assign these three sentences to a supposed objector. The last two, which form a dilemma, are perfectly clear. The first seems to have troubled the editors, including Kroymann, who has altered the text into something quite unintelligible. The objector is supposed to say, 'If Christ had true human flesh, how do you account for the text, "Not of corruption but of incorruption"?' The fact that 1 Peter 1. 23, ἀναγεγεννημένοι οὐκ ἐκ σπορᾶς φθαρτῆς ἀλλὰ ἀφθάρτου, has no bearing on the subject, would not trouble a controversialist, any more than Jeremiah 17. 9 (above) troubled Tertullian.

25 exhaustus is evidently correct, as a reference to Philippians 2. 7 *exhausit semetipsum accepta effigie servi* (so quoted *Adv. Marc.* v. 20). *Exhibitus* (*T*) is meaningless in this context: its true sense is to be observed *De Pat.* 1, *uti pudor non exhibendi quod aliis suggestum imus exhibendi fiat magisterium* ('exemplifying' or 'displaying'): *Adv. Marc.* II. 23, *exhibe bonum semper* ('put in evidence a man who is always good'—if you can): *De Res. Carn.* 17, *haec erit ratio in ultimum finem destinati iudicii, ut exhibitione carnis omnis divina censura perfici possit* (what is elsewhere called *repraesentatio*, almost 'bringing into court').

28 non credendo credunt seems to mean that the heathen, though they do not assent to the faith, at least know what it is that Christians believe, whereas heretics *credendo non credunt*, profess to believe, while refusing to accept the faith as we know it.

29 minorasti etc. Psalm 8. 5 is often quoted, as is Psalm 22. 6, always in conjunction with these texts from Isaiah 52, 53: e.g. *Adv. Marc.* III. 7, 17; IV. 21.

34 hominem deo mixtum: see the Introduction, page viii.

CHAPTER XVI

Alexander argues that since, as he supposes, our belief is that Christ's purpose in taking flesh of human origin was to bring to nought sinful flesh, the implication is that Christ's flesh was sinful —a conclusion abhorrent both to him and to us. 'Bring to nought in himself the flesh of sin' is not precisely the expression we use, and even if it were, his conclusion would not follow: for evidently Christ's flesh, since it is now in heaven and is to come again in glory, has not been brought to nought: and as in it there was no guile it was not sinful. Our position in fact is, not that sinful flesh was brought to nought in Christ, but that the sin of the flesh was—the guilt of it, not the substance. When the apostle says that Christ was in the likeness of sinful flesh he does not mean the mere likeness of flesh and not its reality, but that Christ's flesh, itself sinless, was in the likeness of ours which is sinful, being like ours in natural kind but not like ours in defect. Thus sin was brought to nought in Christ's flesh in that it, being sinless, was the same flesh as in us is sinful. Moreover there would have been nothing noteworthy in his bringing to nought the sin of the flesh in flesh of a different kind from that which in us is sinful: nor would it have been feasible for him to do it. So then, it was our flesh he assumed; though in assuming it he made it his own, that is, sinless. As for the suggestion (§ 15) that Christ's flesh cannot have been our sort of flesh, because it was conceived without male seed, the case of Adam is our answer: for his flesh was constructed out of earth, also without the usual act of procreation.

This chapter completes Tertullian's answer to the cavils noted in the previous chapter, mentioning first a further objection raised by Alexander, based on the Pauline phrase, 'in the likeness of sinful flesh', and 'condemned sin in the flesh', and then reverting to a previous allegation that there could have been no truly human flesh apart from the act of a human father.

That Tertullian has given the correct interpretation of 'likeness of flesh of sin' will no doubt be generally admitted. What he says here is summarized from what he had already written *Adv. Marc.* v. 14:

Though it is true that the Father sent Christ into the likeness of flesh of sin, it will not follow that the flesh which was visible in him was a phantasm. St Paul has already (Romans 7. 18, 23) attributed sin to the flesh, and has described the flesh as the law of sin dwelling in our members, hostile to the law of the mind (*legi sensus*). So he means that the Son was sent into the likeness of sinful flesh for the purpose of redeeming sin with a like substance, a fleshly substance, which was like sinful flesh while itself not sinful. *Nam et haec erit dei virtus, in substantia pari perficere salutem.* It would have been nothing noteworthy for the Spirit of God (i.e. the divine Word) to bring remedy to the flesh: the great thing was for flesh like sinful flesh to do this, while it was indeed flesh but not flesh of sin. Thus 'likeness' will apply only to 'of sin' (*similitudo ad titulum peccati pertinebit*), but will not extend to denial of the substance. He would not have added 'of sin' if his intention had been to indicate only likeness of substance while denying its verity: he would have said merely 'likeness of flesh'. But the form he has used, 'of the flesh of sin', involves an affirmation of the substance, the flesh, while it relates the similitude to the defect (*vitium*) of the substance, the sin. But even supposing he had said 'likeness of the substance' there would still have been no denial of the verity of the substance. If you ask in what sense flesh which is 'like' is also 'true', this is because it is indeed veritable, though not conceived of seed of like status, yet veritable in descent and quality.[1] There is no likeness or similitude in the case of opposites: spirit could not be referred to as 'the likeness of flesh', nor could flesh be in the likeness of spirit. If a thing were not what it was visible as, the right word for it would be

---

[1] This sentence is difficult, as editorial attempts at emendation show: what is written above is a paraphrase.

'phantasm'. 'Likeness' is the word used when a thing is what it is visible as: and it 'is' when it is equal to or like that other thing. A phantasm, if only a phantasm, is not a 'likeness'.

At *De Res. Carn.* 46, for a different purpose, the same method is employed: *misso deus filio suo in simulacro carnis delinquentiae et per delinquentiam damnavit delinquentiam in carne, non carnem in delinquentia: neque enim domus cum habitatore damnabitur. habitare enim peccatum dixit in corpore nostro. damnata autem delinquentia caro absoluta est, sicut indemnatā eā legi mortis et delinquentiae obstricta est.* Something of the same kind had already appeared in Irenaeus, *Haer.* III, 21. 2, *quoniam et ipse in similitudine carnis peccati factus est, uti condemnaret peccatum et iam quasi condemnatum proiceret illud extra carnem*: but Irenaeus, as a good pastor, proceeds, *provocaret autem in similitudinem suam hominem, imitatorem eum assignans deo*, and more to the same effect.

2 Alexander ille. Oehler observes, 'non constat de eo'. But *ille* identifies him with the individual *ex Valentini factiuncula* who wrote the book referred to in §15. *Locum sibi fecit* may mean 'has made himself conspicuous', though his theory seems hardly significant enough for that: so possibly the meaning is 'has broached the topic', or something of that nature.

3 ut evacuaret etc. is inaccurately adapted (by Alexander, not by Tertullian) from Romans 6. 6, ὁ παλαιὸς ἡμῶν ἄνθρωπος συνεσταυρώθη, ἵνα καταργηθῇ τὸ σῶμα τῆς ἁμαρτίας. Καταργεῖν, regularly represented by *evacuare*, need mean no more than 'bring into desuetude', though frequently it appears from its context to mean 'destroy'. Later in this chapter *evacuavit peccatum in carne* is an inaccurate rendering of Romans 8. 3, κατέκρινε τὴν ἁμαρτίαν ἐν τῇ σαρκί. The substitution of *evacuavit* for *condemnavit* is accounted for by quotation from memory: apparently Tertullian thought this text belonged to the Romans 6 context, for immediately afterwards, quoting the other half of Romans 8. 3 ἐν ὁμοιώματι σαρκὸς ἁμαρτίας, he says *et alibi inquit*—which causes Kroymann needless concern.

8 in suggestu. Oehler's index says the word means *apparatus, ornatus*, which appears to be the case in many of the places referred to. Here however it has its original meaning of the raised seat of a judge or king.

9 adeo, ut evacuatam etc. This is the punctuation I wrote in my copy of Oehler long ago: Kroymann agrees. *Adeo* once more stands for *ideo*: see a note on §7 and *Adv. Marc.* v. 14, *adeo et carnis resurrectionem confirmavit*. The MSS. here are in some confusion. After *non possumus dicere* a relative clause is needed, to balance *in qua dolus non fuit* at the end of the sentence. Kroymann's *quia non est evacuata*, despite the partial support of *T*, is mere tautology. I long ago thought the lost words were *quae in caelis est*.

12 non materiam sed naturam. If, as previously suggested, *natura* indicates the essential attributes of an object, and since in this context *natura* is balanced by *culpa*, we must suppose that the *vitium* shortly to be referred to has taken such hold upon humanity as to be no fortuitous accident but to have become a factor in what St Augustine calls *natura secunda*: that is, Tertullian, with his usual sense of realities, is prepared to face the fact of original sin (*vitium*), and original guilt (*culpa*).

18 Adae aequanda was my own correction of Oehler's text. *Adaequanda* is now restored by Kroymann from *T*: but I still think the reference to Adam is necessary, (1) because *aequare* seems to require a secondary object in the dative, and (2) because the reference to Adam at the end of the chapter (an anticipation of what is to come later), along with *ipsum*, seems to have been suggested by the mention of his name here.

22 neque ad propositum etc. Christ's *propositum*, purpose, was to cleanse human nature from within itself, and not by some external act of divine power: his glory is to have done this in human weakness, by the hiding of his power.

25 naevum peccati peremit is a conflation of the MS. readings. *T* has *vim peccati peremit*, which is easy: the others either have or attest *naevum peccati redemit*. It is difficult to account for the unusual word *naevus* unless Tertullian wrote it, though *redemit* is hardly a suitable verb. *Naevus* is a birth-mark, a fault or disfiguration with which one is born, and is thus a fair enough metaphor for original sin: the way to remove it is not by paying a price but by submitting to a surgical operation, for which *perimere* is a more appropriate word than *redimere*.

30 quia non fuit. *Fuerit* (T) would be syntactically correct if the statement implied in the subordinate clause were merely a supposition or allegation of those who denied that Christ's flesh was human flesh: but in Tertullian's view it was no supposition of his adversaries but a fact drawn from Scripture and affirmed by himself—for which reason he would write *fuit* (so, for that matter, would Cicero).

31 sicut terra etc. See the passages from Irenaeus quoted on the following chapter.

CHAPTER XVII

Leaving these *a priori* arguments, we restate the crucial question as one of fact: Was the flesh that was Christ's derived from his mother, or not? If it was, then it was human flesh by virtue of its human origin—and this apart from further proofs, which also are matters of fact, namely, his being habitually described as man, as well as such human characteristics as that he could be touched and handled, and that his passion issued in death. But the first question of all is why it was requisite that he should be born of a virgin. It was because, as the author of the new birth, he must himself be born in a new manner, thus constituting the 'sign' of which Isaiah spoke. This new birth, by which man is born in God, begins at the point at which God was born in man, taking human flesh without the agency of human seed, so that having first cleansed it of its guilt he might reshape it of new and spiritual seed. This newness, in all its aspects, was prefigured in the old. It was virgin soil which brought forth the first Adam, a virgin mother who brought forth the second or last Adam: and observe in passing that the apostle's use of the term 'second Adam' is a proof of Christ's humanity. Moreover the Incarnation is a reversal of the Fall: so that, as the word of temptation entering into

Eve engendered death, so the Word of God entering into Mary engendered life: the evil effect of Eve's credulity is set right by Mary's faith: the offspring of Eve was the wicked brother, his brother's slayer, while the offspring of Mary was the good Brother, his brother's Saviour. Christ must needs be born of woman, so as to undo the evil wrought before the first woman conceived.

The subject of this chapter is also discussed *Adv. Marc.* IV. 10, where the argument takes a different form; briefly as follows:

We begin with two postulates, (1) that when Christ called himself the Son of Man he cannot have been lying, and (2) that no one can be a man without at least one human parent: consequently we must ask, in his case, whether this parent was father or mother. It is admitted that God is his father, and (since God is not a man) it follows that the human parent was his mother. Since God and not man is his father, it follows that his mother is a virgin: otherwise he will have two fathers, which is like the heathen stories of Castor and of Hercules. Since then he is Son of Man by descent from his mother, and since, because he has no human father, his mother is a virgin, we have the fulfilment of Isaiah's prophecy. If Marcion says a man was his father, he denies the divine sonship: if he says that God is the father of his manhood, the idea is heathenish: if that his manhood is from his mother, he agrees with me: if that it is from neither father nor mother, he makes Christ a liar. From this last result only one thing can save him, namely, to affirm that Marcion's god, the father of Marcion's Christ, is a man (as Valentinus did by putting Anthropos in the pleroma), or to allege that the Virgin is not human (which even Valentinus did not presume to do).

[What Tertullian means by this last alternative is not very clear: I suspect we should perhaps read *et* for *aut* both times—'to affirm that Marcion's god is a man, while denying that the Virgin is human'. See a note on page 109.]

Much of what Tertullian says in this and the following chapters seems to have been borrowed from Irenaeus, as the following citations show: though perhaps by this time many things that Irenaeus had written had become the standard Christian expositions of the texts referred to.

Iren. *Haer.* III. 31. Si igitur primus Adam habuit patrem hominem et ex semine viri natus est, merito dicerent et secundum Adam ex Ioseph esse generatum. si autem ille de terra quidem sumptus est et verbo dei plasmatus est, oportebat id ipsum verbum recapitulationem Adae in semetipsum faciens eiusdem generationis habere similitudinem. quare igitur non iterum sumpsit limum deus, sed ex Maria operatus est plasmationem fieri? ut non alia plasmatio fieret neque alia esset plasmatio quae salvaretur sed eadem ipsa recapitularetur, servata similitudine. errant igitur qui dicunt eum nihil ex virgine accepisse, ut abiciant carnis haereditatem, abiciant autem et similitudinem. si enim ille quidem de terra et manu et artificio dei plasmationem et substantiam habuit, hic autem non manu et artificio dei, iam non servavit similitudinem hominis qui factus est secundum imaginem ipsius et similitudinem, et inconstans artificium videbitur, non habens circa quod ostendat sapientiam suam. hoc autem dicere est et putative apparuisse eum, et tanquam hominem cum non esset homo, et factum eum hominem nihil assumentem de homine. si enim non accepit ab homine substantiam carnis, neque homo factus est, neque filius hominis: et si hoc non factus est quod nos eramus, non magnum faciebat quod passus est et sustinuit. nos autem quoniam corpus sumus de terra acceptum et anima accipiens a deo spiritum omnis quicunque confitebitur. hoc itaque factum est verbum dei, suum plasma in semetipsum recapitulans. et propter hoc filium hominis se confitetur et beatificat mites quoniam ipsi haereditabunt terram: et apostolus Paulus in epistula quae est ad Galatas manifeste ait, Misit deus filium suum factum de muliere [et Rom. I. 3, 4].

Iren. *Haer.* v. 21. Misit deus filium suum, factum de muliere. Neque enim iuste victus fuisset inimicus nisi ex muliere homo esset qui vicit eum. per mulierem enim homini dominatus est ab initio, semetipsum contrarium statuens homini. propter hoc et dominus semetipsum filium hominis confitetur, principalem hominem illum, ex quo ea quae secundum mulierem est plasmatio facta est, in semetipsum recapitulans: uti quemadmodum per hominem victum descendit in mortem genus nostrum, sic iterum per hominem victorem ascendamus in vitam: et quemadmodum accepit palmam mors per hominem adversus nos, sic iterum nos adversus mortem per hominem accipiamus palmam.

On St Matt. I. 20, the following observation is worth recording:

[Justin] *Quaestt. et Responss. ad Orthod.* [acc. to Bardenhewer, by an unknown author of the 5th century or later]: resp. 133, Ἰωσήφ, φησίν, υἱὸς Δαυίδ, μὴ φοβηθῇς παραλαβεῖν Μαριὰμ τὴν γυναῖκά σου. τὸ γὰρ ἐκ γυναικός τινος χωρὶς πορνείας τικτόμενον υἱός ἐστιν ἐξ ἀνάγκης τοῦ ἀνδρὸς καὶ τῆς γυναικός, ᾧ τρόπῳ βούλεται ὁ θεὸς δοῦναι υἱὸν τῷ ἀνδρί, ἢ διὰ συναφείας ἢ χωρὶς συναφείας. That is, 'pater est quem nuptiae demonstrant'.

1 **remisso Alexandro etc.** I suspect that *Syllogismi* was the title of the book written by Alexander. Tertullian's dislike of syllogisms stems from his general dislike of argumentation, for he seems never to use *argumentari* for argument of which he approves. He disapproved, in fact, of deductive argument altogether, for he regarded theology not as a deductive science deriving its conclusions by syllogistic reasoning from one transcendental first principle or major premiss, but as bound to work by induction from the recorded facts of Scripture or from what was implied in the faith and practice of the Church. The *Psalms of Valentinus* are referred to again in §20, and not (apparently) elsewhere: Irenaeus, *Haer.* III. 11. 12, says that the later Valentinians had compiled a 'Gospel of Truth', and, ibid. 1 *praef.*, that they possessed certain ὑπομνήματα, 'Commentaries', which he had read. The subject of *interserit* is Alexander.

4 **linea** (like *gradus*) is used for a position taken up in discussion. The primary reference would be to the line marked in the ring at a wrestling-match, *congressio*.

4 **an carnem Christus ex virgine etc.** There are two questions involved: (1) whether it was, or was not, human flesh which Christ derived from his virgin mother: (2) whether it was from his mother herself that he derived what he did derive, or whether what appeared to be his human flesh was not derived from her but merely passed through her without her contributing anything to it. The present chapter deals with the former question: the other is discussed in §18. What was not in question by either party was the truth of the scriptural statement that Christ was conceived (or at least, appeared to be conceived) without the normal process of human procreation. The virginity of Mary was admitted (or even insisted on) by both parties: arguments may be drawn from it or

explanations given of its reasonableness (as here), but, except in the presence of Ebionites, it was never necessary to argue to it.

6 licuit is from *liquere*, not from *licere*: *liquuit* (introduced by Mesnart) has no MS. authority, and is not Latin. It is already clear from the four considerations mentioned, without need of further discussion, that Christ's *substantia* is human: he was referred to as 'Son of man', he 'was found in fashion as a man', he was touched and handled (Luke 24. 39, 1 John 1. 1), and he died a human death.

8 commendanda, 'must be recommended for consideration': Kroymann, with greater felicity than usual, prints *commentanda*, 'must be discussed' or 'considered'. *Ratio*, once more, is the precedent cause, the thought in the mind of God which saw that this form of birth was necessary.

10 novae nativitatis dedicator. The meaning of *nova nativitas*, both here and below, depends on the correct reading in the latter context. If *T* is correct, with *ex quo in homine*, the new birth is that which is the beginning of the Christian life, or of the eternal life of which all Christians are heirs. If *in quo homine* is correct, the new birth, in the second mention of it, is the birth of Christ: the earlier reference (with *dedicator*) will still be to Christian regeneration: the sign (Isaiah 7. 14) is a sign concerning this precisely because it is itself the birth of Emmanuel, and it was his act which was to make this regeneration possible.

13 Emmanuelem, nobiscum deum. The reading of *T* looks like an editorial accommodation to the text of Matthew 1. 23.

14 ex quo in homine (*T*) seems to give the more satisfactory sense. It would hardly be true to imply, with the other authorities, that Christ was born in man already regenerate. But I wonder if Tertullian did not write *quo in homine*, using *quo* for *quoniam* as e.g. *De Orat.* 1 (several times).

15 ut illam novo semine etc. This clause states the purpose (not the manner) of the Incarnation, *illam* referring to *caro antiqui seminis* in general, and not to *caro a Christo suscepta*. It comprises three statements: (1) of the fact of regeneration through Christ, and of the new constitution built up from that new birth by the operation of spiritual seed (i.e. the divine Word): (2) of Christ's redemptive sacrifice by which previous guilt is removed: and (3), by the tense of the participle *expiatam*, of the logical precedence of the latter. With some hesitation I have accepted *spiritali* from *T*: *semine spiritali*, if it is the true reading, will be a reminiscence of 1 Peter 1. 23, οὐκ ἐκ σπορᾶς φθαρτῆς ἀλλὰ ἀφθάρτου διὰ λόγου ζῶντος θεοῦ καὶ μένοντος, in the line of Tertullian's practice of using 'spirit' of all or any of the divine Persons.

17 sed tota novitas ista etc. The general meaning of this sentence is that there is a parallel, both in the fact itself and in various subsidiary respects (which are indicated in the sentences which follow) between the virginal birth of Christ and the virginal birth of man as he was first born to the Lord (*homine domino nascente*) when God formed him of the dust of the earth. *Rationali dispositione* seems to mean, 'by an ordinance or act of God the reasons for which were pre-existent in God's mind'.

19 virgo erat etc. I wonder if Tertullian did not write *nondum vomere compressa*, in the sense familiar to readers of Terence. There follows a reference to 1 Corinthians 15. 45, εἰς ψυχὴν ζῶσαν... εἰς πνεῦμα ζωοποιοῦν, which is St Paul's commentary on Genesis 2. 7.

26 sed et hic etc. *Ratio defendit*, 'God's intention supplies the answer'—as an advocate answers a question raised in court. This sentence refers only to the main question, why the apostle calls Christ the second Adam, not to the qualification of that question, 'if his manhood was not of terrestrial origin'. *Aemulus* in Tertullian invariably means 'opposite' or 'hostile'.

29 Kroymann's insertion of *diaboli* before *verbum* is unnecessary: Tertullian's readers did not need to have every point driven home with a sledge-hammer: and, if we must be precise, the word required is *serpentis*. The parallel and contrast here indicated between Eve and Mary is abbreviated somewhat from Irenaeus, *Haer*. III. 32. 1.

33 haec credendo delevit. Between the two readings there is not much to choose, and it is not easy to see how the variation arose. *Correxit* gives a better balance with *deliquit*, but *delevit* makes a sort of assonance which is attractive.

34–35 ut abiecta pārēret. Genesis 3. 16, 'Thy desire shall be to thine husband, and he shall rule over thee': *et in doloribus păreret*, 'in sorrow shalt thou bring forth children'. Cf. *Adv. Marc.* II. II, *statim mulier in doloribus parere et viro servire damnatur, sed quae ante sine ulla contristatione per benedictionem incrementum generis audierat, Crescite tantum et multiplicamini, sed quae in adiutorium masculo, non in servitium, fuerat destinata.*

40 quo homo iam damnatus intraverat. This seems to mean that Scripture does not make the statement *Adam cognovit uxorem suam* (Genesis 4. 1) until after their condemnation and expulsion from Paradise. See my Latin note at the end of the introduction to §23, page 179.

CHAPTER XVIII

If Christ had been conceived of human seed there would have been no room for divine sonship. Being already the Son of God, of the Father's seed (which is spirit), he needed only to take to himself human flesh, without the agency of man's seed. Before the Incarnation God was his Father and he had no mother: at the Incarnation the blessed virgin became his mother and no man was his father. From God he derived his divinity ⟨and his personality⟩, from his mother his humanity ⟨without personality⟩. Consequently the body born of the virgin was of her substance. When it says that the Word was made flesh it certainly does not mean that the Word transmuted part of himself into flesh. As it only says 'what' the Word was made, and not 'out of what', it leaves us to understand that it means 'out of something else' and not out of himself: and 'out of what' more likely than out of that flesh within which he was made flesh? In the statement *That which is born in the flesh is flesh and that which is born of the spirit is spirit*, both clauses alike apply both to him and to those who believe in him: for it cannot be supposed that the first part applies only to other men (for this would be a denial of Christ's manhood) and the second part both to him and to believers. So it does state that of the Spirit he was born of God, while of the flesh and within flesh he was conceived as man.

In this chapter Tertullian proposes (or assumes) a thesis which he cannot express clearly in the terminology at his disposal. This is that, whatever may be the contribution of the mother to the corporal constitution of her offspring, and whatever may be the joint contribution of father and mother to the constitution of the soul (these being questions he discusses elsewhere, e.g. *De Anima* 36), the origin of the personality is in the father alone. What he needed was some means of differentiating (no real distinction is possible) between 'personality' and 'person'. This the Greek theologians possessed, at least from the late fourth century onward, in the two terms ὑπόστασις and πρόσωπον, in the sense conventionally imposed upon them: for which the Latins had to be content with *persona* alone. Tertullian, having no term for 'personality', is forced back to its point of origin, the paternal *semen*: a term which, suitable or not in the case of human generation, needs a great deal of interpretation when transferred by analogy to the divine. This interpretation he supplies by his explanation *ex patris dei semine, id est spiritu*. But the explanation, if pressed, is itself misleading. It appears, however, that it is not intended to be pressed, but rather that wherever *semen* appears in divine connexion it is immediately to be interpreted as *spiritus*: for (as he explains frequently elsewhere) the text *deus est spiritus* indicates that 'spirit' (in this conventionally defined sense of the word) is the kind of 'substance' God is. His meaning then is, if we may express it in later terminology, that as in 'substance' (i.e. *what* he is) the Son is identical with the Father, so in ὑπόστασις (i.e. 'personality', *who* he is) the Son, not being identical with the Father, is begotten by him *spiritu*, by the divine fact (into which we forbear to enquire) of eternal generation. So then, as the Son from all eternity is a Person, possessing a divine ὑπόστασις, there is no room at the Incarnation for human paternity: for this would have brought into being a second ὑπόστασις—which is impossible, since Christ is one Person and not two. And as he was to be the same Person incarnate as he was from all eternity (*habentem dei semen*), human paternity was not only impracticable (*non competebat*) but otiose (*vacabat*).

By parity of reasoning it is maintained that as the Son possesses his divine nature and his ὑπόστασις by spiritual generation from the Father, so that which he is as man and Son of Man must be derived from his mother, and consequently is flesh as real as that within which it was formed. There is of course no suggestion that at the Annunciation there took place any divine act analogous to the process of human generation: in fact, in connexion with the Incarnation the question of paternity does not arise in any form whatever (as St Augustine explains at some length, *Enchiridion* 38). That such a misunderstanding could arise is shown by Justin's care to deny it (*Apol.* 1. 33), and (without expressly mentioning it) Tertullian here tacitly excludes it by the phrase *caro sine semine ex homine*.

There is some doubt about certain details of the text and its punctuation, and it seems impossible to follow either group of authorities consistently throughout. I have in a few places corrected (as I hope) the punctuation, and have at least succeeded in making a text which will construe. The best contribution of *T* is its confirmation (in three places) of Mesnart's *in semetipso* for *in semine ipso*.

1 **simplicius,** 'more literally': by contrast with the allegories of §17, we now proceed to deal with texts which directly bear on the subject.

3 **ut de Hebionis opinione etc.** See a note on §14, line 32. Oehler's suggestion of *ut* should probably be accepted: *et* would require *esset* for *erat*.

12 **igitur si fuit etc.** *Dispositio rationis* refers back to *dispositio rationalis* in §17. Kroymann's objection to *super filium...proferendum* is hard to understand: it is equally possible (if we are going to use Greek illustrations) to say ὑπὲρ τοῦ υἱοῦ or περὶ τοῦ υἱοῦ, and what Luke 24. 49 and Hebrews 1. 3 have to do with it (or with each other) is not apparent. *Cur non ex virgine etc.*: it being admitted (by both parties, as it seems) that there was at least the apparent birth of a human body from the blessed Virgin, what

reason can there be for supposing that this birth was no more than apparent? There is in fact every reason for acknowledging it to have been real: and in that case the body that was born took its substance from that body of which it was born, and must be presumed to be of the same nature with it. *Quia aliud est etc.*, must go with what precedes, however awkward it makes the end of the sentence: if attached to what follows it makes nonsense, and throws *inquiunt* too far from the beginning. The point is, that we know what it was that Christ received from God: and it follows (as already observed) that he must have received the rest from his human mother.

14 quoniam, inquiunt etc. suggests the opponents' presumed answer: *vox ista etc.* is Tertullian's further reply—if we affirm that it was from human flesh that the Word took the flesh in which he 'was made flesh', it does not follow that it was not the Word, but something unspecified, that was made flesh.

18 cum scriptura non dicat etc. Here we may disagree with our author. Unless we had reasons both scriptural and rational for knowing better, at least a possible interpretation of *verbum caro factum est* might have been that the Word *conversum est in carnem*, i.e., *ex semetipso*. But such an explanation would be quite contrary to the whole of the rest of our data, and would reduce the Incarnation to unreality and thereby stultify the doctrine of the Atonement.

22 vel quia etc., 'for other reasons, and especially because etc.' *Sententialiter et definitive*, like a judge or a jurisconsult making an authoritative and determinative statement.

23 quod in carne etc. The text is incorrectly quoted, both here and *Adv. Prax.* 27: John 3. 6, τὸ γεγεννημένον ἐκ τῆς σαρκὸς σάρξ ἐστι. Once again we disagree: the text undoubtedly refers, in both its contrasting clauses, to ordinary human generation and regeneration, and has no immediate bearing on the Incarnation. But Tertullian is right in his claim that if the second clause (*quod de spiritu etc.*) refers to Christ, so does the first: and he is right also in his further suggestion that the whole sentence can only be true of believers because it is already true of Christ.

26 atquin subicit...credentes ipsius. The whole of this should apparently be assigned to an objector, who (1) finishes the sentence half quoted (John 3. 6), and (2) adds two more of like character (John 4. 24 and 1. 13) with a comment on all three. The awkward use of the participle *credentes* as a substantive apparently arose from the collecting together of several applications of the verb πιστεύειν in this context: and cf. John 7. 39, περὶ τοῦ πνεύματος οὗ ἔμελλον λαμβάνειν οἱ πιστεύσαντες εἰς αὐτόν.

31 utramque substantiam...non negas. Tertullian's adversaries did not flatly deny the flesh of Christ: they merely cast doubts upon its origin, and consequently upon its nature. His claim here is that if they quote the second half of John 3. 6 in their own favour, they must be consistent and quote the first half in his: in which case the whole text is on his side.

33 conditione here apparently means both 'origin' and attributes or quality as determined by origin. *In semetipso* is my own alteration, for *in semet ipse*.

35 I have revised the punctuation of the concluding sentence, giving an eclectic text, which seems to make sense—as that of the MSS. and editors does not. There seems to be no important difference intended between *natus* and *generatus*, but only a stylistic variation: otherwise *generatus* (if it means more than 'conceived') would imply paternity at the Incarnation—which has just been denied.

CHAPTER XIX

The text John 1. 13 (already referred to in passing), when read in the singular number, which is its only authentic form, refers not (as the Valentinians claim) to 'those who believe on his name' but to Christ himself: with the result that 'born of God' refers to his divinity, while 'not of blood, etc.' is a denial of human paternity. This, however, does not constitute a denial of human substance: for it does not say 'not of the flesh' but 'not of the will of the flesh', which is precisely what we mean by a denial of human paternity. A consideration of the physiology of conception shows this to be a valid interpretation of the text: and moreover the piling up of the three negative phrases indicates that Christ's flesh was of such reality that, apart from these denials, one might have supposed it to have been naturally, not supernaturally, conceived. And, besides this, there would have been no use in his being conceived in the womb unless it was his intention to receive from his mother something which he did not yet possess: and this can only have been human flesh, of the same quality as hers.

1 quid est ergo etc. This sentence must be ascribed to the same supposed interlocutor who quoted part of it in the preceding chapter: Tertullian gives him the credit of quoting (as he thinks) the correct form of the text: he is not one of the *adulteratores* mentioned below.

2 ex deo natus est. The text in this form seems to be quoted only by 'western' authorities, and by these only infrequently. (Souter's *apparatus criticus* to John 1. 13 says it is found in Ambrose and Augustine: the Benedictine indexes to these fathers make no mention of it.) It occurs in one fragmentary MS. of the Old Latin. Its first appearance (but no earlier appearance would have been possible) is by implication in Justin, *Dial.* 63, commenting on Isaiah 53. 8: τὴν γενεὰν αὐτοῦ τίς διηγήσεται;—οὐ δοκεῖ σοι λελέχθαι ὡς οὐκ ἐξ ἀνθρώπων ἔχοντος τὸ γένος τοῦ διὰ τὰς ἀνομίας τοῦ λαοῦ εἰς θάνατον παραδεδόσθαι εἰρημένου ὑπὸ τοῦ θεοῦ; περὶ οὗ καὶ Μωυσῆς τοῦ αἵματος... αἵματι σταφυλῆς... τὴν στολὴν αὐτοῦ πλυνεῖν ἔφη, ὡς τοῦ αἵματος αὐτοῦ οὐκ ἐξ ἀνθρωπείου σπέρματος γεγεννημένου ἀλλ' ἐκ θελήματος θεοῦ. This differs somewhat from Tertullian's explanation, for Justin, paraphrasing 'but of God' as 'but by the will of God' makes the whole text refer to the Incarnation. Irenaeus had this passage of Justin in mind (*Adv. Haer.* III. 20. 2): *propter hoc generationem eius quis enarrabit? quoniam homo est et quis agnoscet eum? cognoscit autem illum is cui pater qui est in caelis revelavit, ut intellegat quoniam is qui non ex voluntate carnis neque ex voluntate viri natus est filius hominis, hic est Christus filius dei vivi*. Irenaeus also agrees with Justin as to the bearing of the concluding phrase: *ibid.* v. 1. 3: *et propter hoc in fine non ex voluntate carnis neque ex voluntate viri* *sed ex placito patris manus eius vivum perfecerunt hominem uti fiat Adam secundum imaginem et similitudinem dei.* Apparently both Justin and Irenaeus thought that ἀλλ' ἐκ θεοῦ stood for ἀλλ' ἐκ θελήματος θεοῦ. In a note on Irenaeus, *Haer.* III. 17. 1, W. W. Harvey explains how the variant could most easily have arisen in a Syriac version by the omission of one letter: but we should still have to account for ܐܝܬܘ (or οσι) at the beginning of the sentence.

3 obduxero: cf. *Apol.* 50, *sed obducimur, certe, cum obtinuimus. ergo vicimus cum occidimur, denique evadimus cum obducimur,* where Souter translates 'are convicted', and Mayor's note suggests that this meaning arose from the practice of blindfolding criminals led to execution.

6 ut ostendant etc. I suspect that Kroymann may be mistaken in his suggestion that *esse* means 'really exist': it seems more natural for the words to mean 'that these (sc. believers in his name) are that mystic seed'. *Semen illud arcanum*: cf. *Adv. Val.* 25: Achamoth, they said, had unwittingly derived from her mother, the errant Wisdom, a certain portion of spiritual seed, which (no less unwittingly) she communicated to her son Demiurge (the gnostic creator). He in his turn, also unwittingly, when he breathed into Adam's nostrils and gave him a soul, gave him with it a portion of this spiritual seed. This it is which alone is capable of receiving and welcoming the 'perfect Word', and this alone is capable of salvation. This spiritual seed is the church, the reflexion or antitype (*speculum*) of the syzygy Man and Church within the Pleroma. So man consists of four elements: the spiritual derived through Achamoth, the 'animal' (i.e. soul) contributed by Demiurge, the choic (a sort of semi-material matter), and the flesh (which is matter as we know it). 'Saviour' also, when he made his appearance, had the counterparts of each of these four elements—spiritual from Achamoth, animal (psychic, soul) from Demiurge, but a corporal substance constructed of soul, so that he might be visible, and so forth, but might not have contact with matter, which is of necessity incapable of salvation—*et totum hoc* (says Tertullian) *ut carnis nostrae habitum alienando a Christo a spe etiam salutis expellant. Quod sibi imbuunt* would naturally mean 'which they baptize for themselves', and perhaps it does: but cf. *Adv. Iud.* 3, *circumcisio carnalis, quae temporalis erat, imbuta est in signum populo contumaci*, where the meaning seems to be 'was instituted': so perhaps here, 'which they invent for themselves'.

7 quomodo autem etc. Tertullian will not admit that, even in a secondary sense, the text *Non ex sanguine etc.* applies to the faithful. He has already (§ 18) stated his preference for the interpretation of John 3. 6 as applicable to the Incarnation, and not to believers only. For it appears from *De Baptismo* 5–8 that he had no strong conception of baptismal regeneration. He describes the ceremonies of baptism in three stages, as follows:

(1) There is a washing with water, which conveys forgiveness of sins and restitution to God, *ad similitudinem eius qui retro ad imaginem dei fuerat*.[1] This, according to Tertullian, is a preparatory ceremony, and its effectiveness derives not from any direct action of the divine Spirit, but from an angel who descends upon the water: *non quod in aqua spiritum sanctum consequamur, sed in aqua emendati [?emundati] sub angelo spiritui sancto praeparamur*. This remission or cleansing is obtained in response to faith sealed with the threefold Name of God: *angelus baptismi arbiter spiritui sancto vias dirigit abolitione delictorum quam fides impetrat obsignata in patre et filio et spiritu sancto*.[2]

(2) The unction follows. This had its ancient precedent in the anointing of priests. On account of it we are called Christians, just as Christ receives his title because of his anointing by the Father. Also, as baptism (sc. the washing already described) is a *carnalis actus* with a *spiritalis effectus*, so the unction *carnaliter currit sed spiritaliter proficit*.[3]

---

[1] It seems more likely that *eius* in this sentence means Adam, perhaps with no sharp distinction between the second Adam and the first Adam in that state in which he was created. Borleffs (wrongly, I suspect) thinks *eius* means *dei*.
[2] This probably refers not to the baptismal formula as such, but to the Creed, apparently a four-clause creed, adding to the divine names the mention of the Church, *quae trium corpus est*. There are several points of doctrine here which later teachers thought it more prudent tacitly to drop.
[3] *Unctio* seems to mean the oil, not the act of anointing: and *currit* stands for *manat*.

(3) There follows an imposition of the hand *per benedictionem, advocans et invitans spiritum sanctum*. At this point the most holy Spirit descends from the Father upon bodies which have been cleansed and blessed. A parallel is suggested with the descent of the Holy Spirit in the form of a dove at our Lord's baptism, and reference is made to the presence of the dove of peace at the cessation of the waters of the Flood.

In all this there is no reference to any regeneration or new birth unto everlasting life. The original sacramental act is limited in its effect to the remission of sins, and that only as preparatory to what Tertullian regards as the more spiritually effective acts of unction (the grace of which is not precisely defined) and benediction (which ensures the descent of the Holy Spirit). Further, it seems to be Tertullian's view that this conveyance of the supreme spiritual gift or presence is not the conveyance of a gift already corporately held by the Church (for there is no reference at this point to Pentecost) but is a repetition in each individual case of what was done at our Lord's own baptism. Tertullian appears nowhere to make any direct quotation of 1 Peter 1. 23 or of John 3. 7.

11 quia verbum dei etc. As already observed, Tertullian equates Luke 1. 35 (where he read *spiritus dei* and *virtus altissimi*) with John 1. 14 (*verbum dei*). See my notes *Adv. Prax.* 26. His meaning here is that at John 1. 13 only the negatives apply to the Incarnation: *ex deo natus est* applies to the eternal generation. The Incarnation, he suggests, was not an act of generation but of creation (*factum est*), and that creation took place *ex dei voluntate*.

15 formalis apparently construes with *nativitatis*: 'a nativity after our fashion' or 'according to our precedent'.

16 negans autem etc. I assign this sentence to the interlocutor, and suggest that we should read *negarit* for *negavit*: 'But when he denies, among other things, that he was born of the will of the flesh, why should we not take him to have denied also that he was born of the substance of the flesh?' Kroymann can only make sense by omitting *quoque* and *cur*, an entirely illegitimate treatment of the authorities.

18 neque enim etc. The general meaning of the sentence is perfectly clear, and the statement is near enough to the physiological truth to be acceptable. Kroymann's suggestion of *colatum humorem* for *calorem* is attractive, though the parallels he cites in support of it prove nothing: what is needed is some quotation from the medical writers to justify *constat*, failing which, *collatum humorem* would be better. The second half of the sentence, as it stands, is a simile drawn from the dairy: Kroymann's *incaseatio* (which he admits he invented) would turn the simile into a metaphor, and thus demand the removal of *id est lactis*. *Vis* (restored by Gelenius) could easily have fallen out through confusion with *eius*: though (if we could account for its omission) *materies* would be better.

22 intellegimus ergo etc. Kroymann here, amending the text of *T*, reads: *intellegimus ergo ex concubitu nativitatem domini negatam, quod sapit et ⟨'non⟩ ex voluntate viri et carnis', ⟨id est⟩ non ex vulvae participatione*. This could only be right if the precise distinction between *uterus* and *vulva*, noted on page 179, applied here also and were unduly emphasized. But it appears from what follows that in the present chapter, as Kroymann himself prints it, the words are synonymous.

28 quia non perinde etc.: i.e. the text of the Gospel does not say *non ex carne* but *non ex voluntate carnis*, denying the existence of a father but not of a mother.

30 cur descendit in vulvam?, omitted by *T* (Kroymann) is necessary to complete the sense: *oro vos* introduces a peremptory question, not a statement interrupted by a parenthesis, as Kroymann reconstructs these sentences. Tertullian supposed that the divine Word *descendit in vulvam* to effect his own incarnation: which is true, though not perhaps in the sense he intended.

30 potuit enim etc. The text is in some disorder, and probably *extra vulvam* (at the end) must be removed: it could have crept in as a marginal note on *extra eam*. Possibly also *fieret* should go, unless we read *ut intra vulvam* (*T*), which is awkward. But the meaning of the sentence is quite clear: flesh of spiritual origin or constitution, if there were such a thing, could have been formed with much less to-do without any pretence of a nativity at all. Cf.

Irenaeus, *Haer.* III. 31. 2, ἐπεὶ περισσὴ καὶ ἡ εἰς τὴν Μαρίαν αὐτοῦ κάθοδος. τί γὰρ καὶ εἰς αὐτὴν κατῄει εἰ μηδὲν ἔμελλε λήψεσθαι παρ' αὐτῆς;

32 sed non etc. In Kroymann's critical note read 37 for 38. The text as given by Oehler is that of the authorities (except *T*) and makes good sense. *Maxime...futurus* can only mean *praesertim si...futurus esset.*

CHAPTER XX

The attempt of our opponents to substitute 'by the virgin' for 'of the virgin' must fail, as must their suggestion that 'conceived in her' (Matthew 1. 20) excludes 'born of her'. The two statements are not inconsistent: and our interpretation of them is confirmed by St Paul, who says 'made of a woman'—where by using the word 'made' he brings himself into verbal conformity with 'the Word was made flesh'. Also the twenty-second psalm is in our favour, where it says 'thou didst rend me out of my mother's womb', for evidently that which is rent away carries with it something of that from which it is rent—which as a physiological fact does happen at childbirth. Also the psalm says 'I hanged yet upon my mother's breasts', and it is well known that the milk does not flow unless there has been a veritable birth —a fact for which there are obvious physical reasons. So we conclude this discussion with the observation that the reason for Christ's being born of a virgin was not that this was to be less than a true birth, but that our regeneration in Christ was to be of virgin purity.

The expression *natum ex Maria virgine* may be supposed to be derived from Luke 1. 35 τὸ γεννώμενον ἐκ σοῦ ἅγιον. It is however not quite certain that ἐκ σοῦ is part of the text: it is absent from most Greek MSS., but occurs in 'western' authorities from the second century onwards. Tertullian himself has *ex te* (*Adv. Prax.* 26), *in te* (*Adv. Marc.* IV. 7, in a conflate quotation), but at *Adv. Prax.* 27 (in a secondary quotation) omits the phrase entirely: Souter's *apparatus criticus* should be corrected on this point. By their substitution of *per virginem* Tertullian's adversaries meant that Christ was not born 'of' the Virgin in such a manner as to be in any real sense her son, but merely passed 'through' her: certain Apollinarians in the fourth century are reported to have added, more explicitly, 'as through a pipe'. In that case his apparently human body was not really human and was not real flesh, but was supposed to be some 'psychical' or 'spiritual' substance transformed into the appearance of flesh. Tertullian insists that the word is *ex*, and not *per*, and that the preposition must be understood in all its full implications, which he proceeds to elucidate in detail. See also Irenaeus, *Haer.* III. 31 (quoted above on §17), and v. 21. 1: here also Rom. 1. 3, 4 and Gal. 4. 4 are referred to. Justin, *Dial.* 100, quotes Luke 1. 35 obliquely, διὸ καὶ τὸ γεννώμενον ἐξ αὐτῆς ἅγιόν ἐστιν [probably read ἅγιον ἔσται] υἱὸς θεοῦ, and immediately, without any special emphasis on the change of preposition, comments, καὶ διὰ ταύτης γεγέννηται οὗτος. It seems unlikely that Tertullian's adversaries claimed Justin as their authority.

3 in hac specie: cf. infr. *ad hanc speciem*. *Species* being the particular application of a *forma* or rule of law, the phrase here will mean 'in this case' or 'on this particular subject'.

5 The punctuation given in the text seems the best way of treating what otherwise would be an awkward sentence. There is at least a pretence, throughout this and several other of Tertullian's works, that they are speeches addressed to a court: in such a case, asides are quite in order. See also below, *sine dubio quae hausit*.

6 nempe tamen etc. This and the following sentence together mean that for the sake of our present argument the difference between *in ea* and *ex ea* is of no great significance: the phrases could be used indiscriminately without affecting our main contention. But the sentences are awkwardly expressed: their meaning would be clearer if the author had written *diceret... dixisset...fuerat...erat*, and again, *quod in ea fuerat*. *Consonare* as a transitive verb is unusual: its subject here is perhaps the evangelist, or the angel of God, who 'when he says "in her", at the same time gives expression to "of her"': or possibly the subject is the phrase *ex ea*—'When it says *in ea, ex ea* sounds along with it.'

11 nascitur must be retained: the fact that the Greek has ἐγεννήθη and the Latin vulgate *natus est* will have prompted *T* and *N* to make this alteration.

12 misit etc. Gal. 4. 4 is quoted *De Virg. Vel.* 6, with the remark that in this text, as in some others, *mulier* includes *virgo*. Strictly speaking, Tertullian says, a woman ceases to be *virgo* as soon as she is betrothed, but that in his instructions regarding the dress of women (1 Cor. 11. 5) St Paul is using the generic term to include the particular. See also *De Orat.* 23.

14 potius is only in *TB*; its omission would be almost but not quite in Tertullian's style.

20 se cecinit ipse Christus. Certain of the Messianic psalms (e.g. Ps. 2. 7–12) represent Christ as speaking of himself. Psalm 22. 9 and 10 does not seem to be quoted by Tertullian elsewhere. Justin quotes and comments on the whole psalm, *Dial.* 98–105, but with nothing bearing on the present subject. *Colloquentem* ($TB^{mg.}$) may be what Tertullian wrote: actually the psalm is a monologue, not a colloquy between the Son and the Father.

28 si adhaesit etc. The general meaning of the sentence is clear, but its construction is difficult, and is not really improved by Kroymann's transference of *ex utero* to the end of the conditional clause. If the mood and tense of *adhaesisset* have any significance, it can only be 'how should we be aware of its adherence?' In the latter part of the sentence *est* is too far from *avulsus* to be naturally construed with it. At the risk of correcting the author himself, I should be disposed to write, *quomodo adhaesisset nisi, dum ex utero exit, per illum nervum umbilicarem quasi folliculi sui traducem adnexus adhaeret origini vulvae. Folliculus* is a skin or bag: here it apparently means the caul: *tradux* is the horticultural term for a 'layer' or shoot.

30 etiam cum quid etc. The omission of *aliquid* and *quasi*, with some MSS., makes no difference to the meaning of this sentence, but greatly improves its form. Kroymann's alterations are no improvement. *Produx* apparently occurs only here: its natural meaning is 'aftermath', which suits the present theme: *traducem*, of some MSS., is obviously due to confusion with the previous sentence. *Mutui coitus* probably means nothing more recondite than 'interconnexion'. The point of the illustration is that if things originally unconnected cannot, after being cemented together, be taken apart again without force, and without one taking something away from the other, even more, in the case of those so closely connected as mother and child, must the child at birth take something from his mother, and that by force. Hence *avulsisti* in the psalm. But possibly *avellere* is too strong for the Hebrew: Driver translates 'caused me to burst forth': LXX, ὁ ἐκσπάσας.

37 suspendentibus seems here to mean 'paying over', *subministrantibus*, but I know of no parallel case. At *Scorp.* 6, *suspendere votum* means 'attach one's hopes': at *De Anima* 18, *suspendendae veritatis*, 'holding back the truth'. The rest of this clause, as printed, is what Gelenius made of the various MS. readings: *in mamillam*, omitted by TB$^{mg.}$, may have originated as a marginal note, or its omission may be due to confusion with *illam*.

41 communicatione has an active sense: 'of that which the womb provided' or 'imparted to him': not 'of that which he borrowed from the womb'. *Operata vulva*, with the other two participles, is evidently nominative, not ablative. *Quae nisi pariendo*: I have presumed to write *pariendo* for the MS. *habendo*, which is meaningless, and could have been a copyist's anticipation of *habere* in the next sentence. Kroymann retains *habendo*, and writes *quem* for *quae*, leaving the sentence still meaningless.

45 quid fuerit etc. The meaning of the sentence is perfectly clear, though it would be difficult to explain the syntax of *nascendi*, except perhaps as a Graecism: ὅτι μὲν οὖν ἂν εἴη τὸ καινὸν ἐν Χριστῷ τοῦ ἐκ παρθένου γεννηθῆναι πρόχειρόν ἐστιν. Kroymann's punctuation makes nonsense of the sentence, and his suggested alterations of the text are not Latin. If any alteration were needed it would be the insertion of *et* after *esset*. *Novitatis* looks back to §17, the beginning of this part of the discussion. *Etiam carnaliter* means 'even in physical origin and constitution, and apart from any suggestion (which God forbid!) of actual sin': for 'the flesh', that is, the animate body, is for the rest of mankind the breeding ground of sin, inheriting the corrupt nature of fallen humanity.

CHAPTER XXI

The 'newness' of Christ's birth admittedly consists in his having been conceived without the agency of a human father: but there is nothing in our authorities to suggest that his mother also was totally inactive in the matter—indeed there is very good evidence to the contrary. The prophecy of Isaiah certainly contemplates conception without human paternity: but this conception is stated to be for the purpose of child-bearing, and as the conception is the mother's act, so the child to be born is his mother's son. The alternative (an impossible one) is that the Word should conceive and bear himself, that is, should convert himself into flesh: in which case the mother's part is otiose, and the prophecy loses its point. So also do the words of the Annunciation to Mary, along with every other Scripture which refers to the mother of Christ: among which is the salutation of Elisabeth who addresses Mary as 'the mother of my Lord' and says 'Blessed is the fruit of thy womb'. Moreover (reverting to Isaiah) how can Christ be the flower of the stem which comes forth from the stock of Jesse unless he is in true physical descent from Jesse through David? He is the fruit of David's loins, which again postulates physical descent from David: and this can only be a fact if he is veritably the son of Mary, herself descended from David.

Of the scriptural texts quoted in this chapter, Luke 1. 42, 43 appears not to be used elsewhere by Tertullian.

Isaiah 7. 14 has already been referred to in §17 and will appear again in §23. At *Adv. Marc.* III. 13 Tertullian writes: *Sed et virginem, inquit* (sc. Marcion), *parere natura non patitur, et tamen creditur prophetae. et merito. praestruxit enim fidem incredibili rei, rationem edendo, quod in signo esset futura. Propterea, inquit, dabit vobis dominus signum: Ecce virgo concipiet in utero et pariet filium. signum autem a deo, nisi novitas aliqua monstruosa, tam dignum* [*iam signum*, Latinius] *non fuisset*. The Jews wish to read *iuvenculam* for *virginem*: but such an event would not constitute a sign. *sed signo nativitatis novae adscripto exinde post signum alius ordo infantis edicitur* etc. At *Adv. Iud.* 9 this is repeated, at greater length, and in a more controversial manner. At *Adv. Marc.* IV. 10, he says, *si ex deo patre est, utique non est ex homine: si non et ex homine, superest ut ex homine sit matre: si ex homine, iam apparet quia ex virgine....ceterum duo iam patres habebuntur, deus et homo, si non virgo sit mater....si ex matre filius est hominis quia ex patre non est, ex matre autem virgine quia non ex patre homine, hic erit Christus Esaiae quem concepturam virginem praedicat*. All this is consistent with what is said in the present chapter, though it belongs to a previous stage of the argument, and is designed to prove that the Christ of the New Testament is identical with the Christ promised in the Old. Our present purpose is the further one of proving that Christ belongs to our humanity in full reality and in no docetic sense.

Isaiah 11. 1 is referred to, *Adv. Marc.* IV. 1: *eundem ex genere David secundum Mariae censum etiam in virga ex radice Iesse processura figurate praedicabat*. The text is quoted *Adv. Marc.* V. 8, and the seven gifts of the Spirit enumerated, the claim being made (a theme derived from Justin) *quoniam exinde quo floruisset in carne sumpta ex stirpe David, requiescere in illo omnis haberet operatio gratiae spiritalis et concessare et finem facere quantum ad Iudaeos: sicut et res ipsa testatur* etc. This also is repeated *Adv. Iud.* 9. The text is referred to, *De Cor.* 15: *quid tibi cum flore morituro? habes florem ex virga Iesse, super quem tota divini spiritus gratia requievit, florem incorruptum immarcescibilem sempiternum*. Here apparently *requievit* is taken in its more natural sense.

Through this chapter Kroymann's alterations seem not to need particular consideration.

1 si ergo contendunt etc. This sentence summarizes the preceding discussion concerning *novitas*: with the next sentence the argument takes a new turn, suggested by the concluding words of this. *Competisse* usually means 'be appropriate' or 'be pertinent':

here it seems to mean 'be essential'. I suspect that at the end of the sentence Tertullian wrote *ut caro non ex semine nata ex carne semine nata processerit.*

7 ergo ut ipsius etc. The text given is that of *T*. All the other authorities have *Ergo ut ipsius fuit concepisse, ita ipsius est etc.*

9 si verbum ex se etc.: that is, if the Word converted himself into flesh, a suggestion not yet discussed. But it was put forward in the fourth century by the second generation of Apollinarians, against whom is directed the sentence in *Quicunque vult, Unus autem non conversione divinitatis in carnem, sed adsumptione humanitatis in deum.*

14 quomodo enim etc. Kroymann's alterations of this sentence are not convincing. There does however seem to be something wrong, and I should suggest reading, ...*nisi quia in utero eius fuit?* ⟨*ut quid in utero*⟩ *si nihil ex utero etc.*

19–28 tacebit igitur etc. The punctuation of these sentences, down to *ipse erit et fructus?*, is mine.

25 If **et qui** is right, *qui* is an adverb, standing for *quomodo* or *qua ratione*, and this seems to be the sense required. *Ut quid*, adopted by Kroymann from *T*, can only mean *quem ad finem*, which is not in keeping with the answer given in the next sentence.

31 suam (before *radix*) evidently construes with *proprietatem*: 'and thus make it impossible for the root, with the stem as intermediary, to establish its claim that that which grows from the stem, namely the flower and the fruit, are its own inalienable possession'. Whether this sentence is punctuated as a statement or as a question seems to make little difference: in the latter case we might have expected an answer, which in fact is not given.

33 Before **siquidem** it is necessary to supply, at least in thought, something like *non recte* (*Adv. Prax.* 3). Perhaps some such words have fallen out: in which case the preceding sentence was a question.

35 adhaerere is perhaps too 'close' a word for the present context: it is carried over from the previous part of the discussion. *Pertinere* would have been sufficient.

35 **adeo**: so *T* Kroy. The MSS. and early editions had *deo*, which is meaningless. Pamelius wrote *ideo*, which gives the sense required. But Tertullian regularly says *adeo* for *ideo*: see notes on §§ 7, 16.

38 **in lumbis** (at the end of the chapter): cf. Heb. 7. 10. There was no need for *T* to change *in* to *ex*: even on stylistic grounds, complete uniformity is inadvisable.

CHAPTER XXII

If the witness which devils bore to Christ as the Son of David is not acceptable, there remain various testimonies of St Matthew and of St Paul that he is the son of David, and through David also of Abraham. All these link up with the fact that he is the son of Mary, through whom he is descended from these, and through these from Adam. Thus he is the Second Adam, and his flesh can no more have been of spiritual origin and constitution than was that of his forefathers.

The genealogies are not discussed by Tertullian elsewhere. Romans 1. 3, 4 is adduced *Adv. Prax.* 27: *sic et apostolus de utraque eius substantia docet. Qui factus est, inquit, ex semine David: hic erit homo et filius hominis. Qui definitus est filius dei secundum spiritum: hic erit deus, et sermo dei filius. videmus duplicem statum, non confusum sed coniunctum in una persona, deum et hominem Iesum.* Galatians 3. 8, 16 is referred to *Adv. Marc.* v. 4, but with no observations that bear on our present subject: the same is true of the reference at *De Pat.* 6.

1 **deleant** is concessive: the ellipsis of *quamvis* is sufficiently frequent to need no illustration. The testimonies that Jesus is the Son of David were in fact not given by devils, but by afflicted men asking for healing—Matthew 20. 30, Mark 10. 47, Luke 18. 38. Tertullian's memory has slipped, and confused these passages with such as Matt. 8. 29: Mark 1. 24, 3. 11, 5. 7: Luke 4. 34, 41, where the testimony of devils is that he is Christ, the Son of God.

1 **proclamantia.** The genitive plural (*T* alone) may safely be disregarded: it is an alteration even in *T*. *Ad Iesum*, in the majority of MSS., is more difficult—*ad* being grammatically

impossible: I suspect we should read *dominum Iesum*, for κύριε υἱὸς Δαβίδ occurs at Matt. 20. 30, and again, after Ἰησοῦ υἱὲ Δαβίδ at Luke 18. 38, we have κύριε ἵνα ἀναβλέψω at verse 42.

4 commentator a rare word, quoted by Lewis and Short from Appuleius in the sense of inventor (*omnium falsorum*), which is obviously not the meaning here: and from the jurists in the sense of interpreter, which would serve here if by 'the gospel' Tertullian means not the written record but the whole act of God which the Gospel is. Or conceivably he means 'writer', with the title of Caesar's work at the back of his mind.

5 compotes evidently means 'acquainted with': cf. *De Pall.* 2, *qui vero divinas lectitamus* (sc. *historias*) *ab ipsius mundi natalibus compotes sumus*, 'are well informed': *Adv. Hermog.* 22, *si tantam curam instructionis nostrae insumpsit spiritus sanctus ut sciremus quid unde processerit, nonne proinde nos et de caelo et de terra compotes reddidisset significando unde ea esset operatus, si de aliqua materia origo constaret illorum?* At *De Anima* 45, *si compotes somniaremus*, there seems to be a recollection of the standing phrase *compotes mentis*, 'in full possession of our faculties'.

8 ad Christi nativitatem is what Tertullian ought to have written, and for that reason may perhaps be an editorial correction. *A Christi nativitate* (all MSS. except *T*) would be true of St Luke's genealogy, but not of St Matthew's.

10 inferens Christum, the reading of all the MSS., must evidently stand: it should be construed closely with *de virgine*, the intervening words being a partial correction. The reason for the correction is that of course the flesh itself was not an active agent either during the line of descent or at the Incarnation itself, as the less than accurately expressed beginning of the sentence might have suggested: at the Incarnation at least the divine Word, who is Christ, was the agent of his own incarnation. For the views of Tertullian and others on this subject see my edition of *Adv. Prax.*, Introduction, pages 63–74. *Proditur*, the reading of all MSS. except *T*, would be grammatically tolerable: *producitur* ($TB^{mg.}$) is an obvious correction of some copyist who thought that *proditur* could only mean 'is betrayed'. For all that, *proditur* can hardly stand: an active verb is required, as Kroymann saw, though his *proditurus* is in the wrong tense and is out of syntax. If we could read *prodit*, 'comes forth', all would be well: the passive termination may have slipped in by confusion with *describitur* in the line above.

13 utique ipsius: i.e., when St Paul says 'according to the flesh', he means Christ's flesh, not David's.

14 sed secundum etc. We gain nothing, and lose nothing, by following Kroymann in assigning this sentence to a supposed objector.

16 quod (*bis*) appears to be the relative pronoun.

21 semine ($TB^{mg.}$) should almost certainly be restored: there is nothing in Galatians 3. 8 *seqq.* to suggest *nomine*.

24 nihilominus (*T* alone) accentuates the fact (which would be clear in any case) that whereas Galatians 3. 15, 16 was cut out of the Marcionite Bible (cf. *Adv. Marc.* v. 14), we have retained it in ours.

32 eadem conditio substantiae here almost means 'the same created substance', for substance is not the same as *materia*, and the substance of Christ's flesh is the substance of the flesh of Adam, and of all humanity, and that flesh is a created thing. But probably Tertullian meant something more: 'the same substance, with all those characteristics which essentially constitute that nature in which it was created'.

CHAPTER XXIII

The prophecy of Simeon, that the Child would be 'for a sign that shall be spoken against', is come to effect in these persons who deny the truth of the sign. For the sign is that prophesied by Isaiah, of the virginal conception and child-bearing. These people have seized upon the expression 'She bare and bare not', alleging that it signifies the appearance of child-bearing without its reality. Even if the text meant what they think it means, our statement of the truth would be more in accordance with it, viz. that 'she bare' in that she really was a mother, and 'bare not' in that she was never a wife. Actually however she did become a wife, not at the conception but at her delivery: that which remained closed at the conception was opened at the nativity. Hence the expression 'every male that openeth the womb'—an event which, in the sense really intended, actually took place only on this single occasion. Hence also St Paul's expression, 'born of a woman'. Thus it appears that the text from Ezekiel was not a prophecy of what actually was to happen, but was a warning against these people and the quibble they were going to invent. For the Holy Spirit does not indulge in that kind of ambiguity, but speaks clearly and directly, as in Isaiah, 'shall conceive and bear'.

The alleged quotation from Ezekiel is not from Ezekiel but apparently from some lost apocryphal writing. It was known to Clement of Alexandria, who writes as follows (*Strom.* VII. 93, 94):

It seems likely that the majority of people even now think that Mary is a puerpera, having become so through the birth of the Child: though she is not a puerpera, for there is a report current that after her confinement she was examined by a midwife and found to be a virgin. Now the divine Scriptures we find are like that. They give birth to the truth while conserving their virginity, while they also conserve the mysteries of the truth under a veil. The scripture says, 'She bare and bare not', meaning that she conceived of her own initiative and not in consequence of marital intercourse. This is why, for those who are gnostics, the scriptures are pregnant, whereas the heresies through lack of intelligence consider them barren and hold them of no account.

[It is to be observed that by 'gnostics' Clement does not mean Gnostics, but orthodox Christians of rather more than ordinary spiritual intelligence.]

The expression is also quoted by Epiphanius, *Haer.* xxx. 30, where it appears that it was a heifer which bare and bare not: but in later Greek δάμαλις can mean a girl. Apparently only Tertullian ascribes the phrase to Ezekiel.

Ex eis quae sub hoc capitulo permisit sibi Septimius, vulvam constabit haud ipsum uterum esse sed os eius externum: qua de re, si ita curiosus sis, conferas quae scripserunt Iuvenalis, Martialis, et alii profani.

4 contradicitur. *Contradicibile* (*T*) seems to be an anticipation of what is written below. The Greek of Luke 2. 34 has the present tense (ἀντιλεγόμενον), Lat. vg. the future, *cui contradicetur*.

8 Philosophers of the Academic school made a profession of the uncertainty of all knowledge, and affected to avoid any direct affirmation or negation. Tertullian suggests that a statement in the form 'is and is not', 'did and did not', would be quite in their line. His opponents were not in fact adherents of that school: they would have repudiated any such connexion.

12 pepererit was a marginal suggestion in the first edition of Rhenanus, and has been adopted by all editors until Kroymann. It must almost certainly be retained. Kroymann attempts to escape the difficulty by writing *non tamen, ut apud illos, ideo non peperit quae peperit quia etc*. This removes the grammatical difficulty from the first part of the sentence, but introduces a new difficulty of meaning, as well as making *sed apud nos* syntactically impossible.

16 peperit quae peperit…resignavit. The meaning of the sentence is perfectly clear, and Kroymann's alterations are uncalled for. No alterations can obliterate the appalling bad taste of Tertullian's observation *in quo nihil interfuit etc*. *Illud* evidently means *corpus*, and *idem* is masculine.

32 dubitative. Kroymann's *dubitativam* hardly improves the sentence, and his explanatory note explains nothing. The point is that the Holy Spirit is not accustomed to speak in ambiguous terms, so that if (through Ezekiel) he did say *peperit quae non peperit* he was referring beforehand not to a fact which was to be doubtful, but to these quibblers who were to doubt it.

CHAPTER XXIV

All these various forms of heresy were foreseen and censured by the Holy Spirit in the Scriptures, who condemns, first, the common practice by which heretics refuse to employ or understand scriptural language in its natural sense: then, the Marcionite postulate of another god besides God, and the Valentinian invention of the genealogies of Æons anterior to God, as well as the Ebionite denial of Christ's divinity, and the claim made by Apelles that his particular theories were revealed by an angel. Likewise St John strikes at these persons who deny that Christ came in the flesh, as well as all those who divide Christ into two persons of opposite or complementary characteristics. The intention of these last, when they allege that Christ who rose again is not the same as Christ who died, is to find support for their further assumption that their own resurrection will be in a different flesh from this present. But, in fact, Christ who will come again is the same Christ that suffered, as they will find, to their cost, when he does come: and thus there is no truth in the idea that at the present time Christ's body, with or without the soul, is set aside like an empty scabbard with Christ himself withdrawn.

1 Kroymann is no doubt right in his suggestion that the subject of this sentence (and indeed of those that follow) is *spiritus sanctus*. So read *et alias*, with *T*. [Kroymann's apparatus is ambiguous regarding *F*.] *Suggillatio* is bruising: cf. Petronius 128, *noli suggillare miserias*, 'don't hit a man when he's down'. Whether we read the ablative or the accusative, it seems to be the accusative that is intended. The metaphors are slightly mixed: *iaculari* suggests a shooting match, *suggillatio* a boxing match. The quotation of Isaiah 5. 20 was suggested by the reference to it above, §23: cf. *Scorp*. 1, *vae autem qui dulce in amarum et lumen in tenebras convertunt*.

3 **qui nec vocabula etc:** *ista* could mean *anima, caro, deus*; *ipsa* (*T*) is probably right. On heretical methods in general, cf. §1, *licentia haeretica*.

7 **alio idipsum modo.** This is what I make of the somewhat confused MS. testimony. It has at least the advantage of being good Latin and of being true.

10 The subject of *respondit* is still *spiritus sanctus*: the quotation is the direct object of the verb. So in the following sentence, with *dirigit*.

13 filium probably got into the MSS. by confusion with Philumena, and is better away. Cf. *De Praesc. Haer.* 30 Apelles *in alteram feminam impegit, illam virginem Philumenen...cuius energemate circumventus quae ab ea didicit Phaneroses scripsit.* At Diodorus IV. 51, ἐνεργήματα are the effects of Medea's magic: Philumena's *energema* seems to be not the effect of her possession, but the evil spirit (reputed to be an angel) which possessed her.

13 Before **qui negat** we must supply in thought *cum dicit* or some such phrase, to balance *sicut et definiens*, below: but it may not be necessary (with Kroymann) to write it in the text. *Disceptatores* appears to mean here those who dispute or deny its existence: for the true sense of the word see Cicero *De Part. Orat.* 3. 10 *quid habes igitur de causa dicere? auditorum eam genere distingui: nam aut auscultator est modo qui audit aut disceptator, id est rei sententiaeque moderator, ita ut aut delectetur aut statuat aliquid.* In legal language a *disceptator* was a judge in a private suit.

16 ipsum Christum unum, a reference to 1 Corinthians 8. 6, and perhaps to the variant reading at 1 John 4. 3.

16 multiformis Christi argumentatores could be the Valentinians who conjectured a fourfold Christ. But the rest of the sentence describes opinions or interpretations which more properly belong to other forms of gnosticism, from Cerinthus onwards. All of them began, or ended, by despising the flesh and denying its resurrection.

20 ignobilem lacks anything to balance it: probably read *alium nobilem alium ignobilem*.

26 nec ipse esse etc., 'he can neither be, nor be seen to be, himself'.

28 Kroymann's insertion of *inanem* after *vaginam* is uncalled for. The note of Franciscus Junius, printed by Oehler, explains this sentence perfectly: and there is probably no need to ask precisely who were the persons responsible for the several suggestions, which are in any case outside the particular subject of the treatise, assuming as they do that the flesh of Christ exists, and that it is real. Junius wrote: There are three possible opinions regarding the flesh of Christ. The first, that it did not rise again, and consequently is not in heaven: which is the Valentinian view. The second, that Christ's flesh rose again, and is where Christ is, continuing in unity of person with his deity: which is the doctrine of the Church. The third, that Christ's flesh rose again, but with Christ abstracted from it—that is, out of union with the Word and his divine nature. Of this last view there are three possible ramifications, some imagining that the flesh abides alone in heaven without personal union, others that this is the case with flesh and soul together, and others again that the soul alone is in heaven.

CHAPTER XXV

Thus we dispose of the present subject. To have proved what Christ's flesh is, ought to have been enough to prove also what it is not: in spite of which, we have done more than was strictly necessary, controverting various erroneous opinions. Also, as we observed at the beginning, the present work will serve as preliminary matter for the discussion of our own resurrection, which is to follow: for as it was Christ's flesh that rose again, so also will it be ours.

3 **citra...abundanti:** I have marked this as parenthetic, so that *ut cum eo etc.* completes the sense of *sufficere*.

8 **commonefaciat** is Kroymann's excellent correction of the MS. text.

10 **resurrexerit** is on Ciceronian principles syntactically correct, and has better MS. support: *resurrexit* is what Tertullian would be more likely to have written.

INDEX OF SCRIPTURAL REFERENCES

According to the pages of this edition.

Genesis		53. 2		39
2. 7	124, 158	53. 3		53, 55
3. 1	61	53. 8		164
3. 16	61, 159	63. 9 LXX		53
4. 1	61			
18. 1	113	Jeremiah		
18. 19	11, 25, 100	17. 9 LXX		53, 146, 148
19. 1	23	31. 15		92
22. 18	75			
		Daniel		
Exodus		2. 34		126
13. 2	77	7. 13		53
Deuteronomy		Zechariah		
32. 15	142	1. 14		53
		12. 10		81
Psalms		14. 14		124
2. 7–12	171			
8. 6	51, 55, 126, 149	Matthew		
		1. 16		67
8. 8	55	1. 20		67, 71, 169
22. 7	55, 126, 149	1. 23		71, 157
22. 9	69, 171	2. 1–18		7
22. 10	69	2. 17		92
23. 4 LXX	142	4. 2–4		39
78. 25	27	5. 20		53
132. 11	73, 75	5. 37		77
		7. 17		35
Isaiah		8. 29		176
5. 20	77, 79, 181	10. 32		19, 108
7. 14	7, 59, 71, 77, 79, 157, 173	12. 8		53
		12. 33		35
		12. 46–50		117
8. 14	126	12. 48		27
9. 5 LXX	51, 142	13. 54		37
11. 1	73, 75, 174	13. 55, 56		29
40. 18–25	100	16. 21		39, 127
43. 10	79	16. 27		57
45. 5, 6	79	19. 3		29
53. 2–14	126	20. 30		176, 177

INDEX OF SCRIPTURAL REFERENCES

Matthew (cont.)		14. 26	119
21. 33	51	18. 38	176, 177
25. 41	49	20. 36	113
26. 38	49	22. 64	39
26. 41	39	24. 39	21, 157
27. 30	39		
27. 56	31	John	
		1. 12	65
Mark		1. 13	63, 65, 163, 164
1. 24	176		
3. 11	176	1. 14	61, 63, 67, 79, 167
3. 31–35	117		
3. 33	27	1. 32–34	13
5. 7	176	3. 6	63, 162, 163
6. 2–4	29	3. 7	167
8. 31	39, 127	4. 3	79
8. 38	19, 57, 108	4. 24	63, 163
10. 47	176	6. 51	49
14. 30	49	7. 5	31, 120
14. 38	39	7. 39	163
15. 19	39	8. 40	53
16. 1	31	10. 18	141
16. 19	57	11. 5, 19, 24, 39	31
		19. 37	81
Luke			
1. 26–30	7	Acts	
1. 31	71	1. 11	79
1. 35	61, 143, 167, 169, 170	1. 14	120
		2	xviii
1. 41–44	71	2. 22	53
1. 42, 43	73, 173	2. 30	73
2. 1–14	7, 91, 92	3. 19	xix
2. 21–38	7	23. 8	5, 83
2. 22–24	92		
2. 34	180	Romans	
3. 22	13	1. 3	75
3. 23	29	1. 3, 4	170, 176
4. 31	xxix	6. 6	55, 151
4. 34	176	8. 3	57, 151
4. 41	176		
6. 43	35	1 Corinthians	
8. 20, 21	27, 117	1. 27	15
9. 22	39, 127	2. 2	17
9. 26	19, 104, 108	4. 4	98
9. 56	47	6. 20	15, 105
10. 25	29	7. 23	105
10. 27, 28	33	8. 6	79, 182
11. 27	117, 121	10. 16	147

1 Corinthians (cont.)
- 11. 5 — 171
- 15. 4 — 17
- 15. 17–19 — 17
- 15. 27, 28 — 55
- 15. 45 — 59, 75, 158
- 15. 47 — 35
- 15. 50 — xix

Galatians
- 1. 8 — 23, 79
- 3. 8 — 176
- 3. 16 — 75, 176
- 4. 4 — 67, 77, 170

Philippians
- 2. 8 — 15
- 3. 13 — 94
- 3. 20 — 142

1 Thessalonians
- 5. 13 — xix

1 Timothy
- 2. 5 — 53
- 4. 10 — 142

2 Timothy
- 2. 8 — 75

Hebrews
- 2. 16 — 141
- 9. 11 — 21

1 Peter
- 1. 23 — 55, 148, 158, 167
- 2. 22 — 57

1 John
- 1. 1 — 157
- 1. 2 — 47
- 4. 3 — 182

INDEX LOCORUM

Tertullianus [secundum ordinem librorum ab Oehlero dispositorum].

De Idololatria
18   126

Apologeticum
       vii
1   97
2   135
4   108
9   86, 97
10   131
16   129
17   105, 136, 147
18   92
19   94, 97
21   vii, viii, 93, 129 (*bis*)
25   129
31   131
35   97, 131
39   98
47   125
48   147
49   129 (*bis*)
50   129, 165

Ad Nationes
       vii
i. 1   131
ii. 2   125

De Testimonio Animae
       vii
2–4   136

De Corona Militis
4   141
10   131
11   86, 92
13   107
15   174

Scorpiace
1   141, 181
6   172

De Oratione
1   157
23   171

De Patientia
1   148
3   126
4   83
6   176

De Baptismo
3   124
4   139
5–8   166 *sq.*

Ad Uxorem
i. 1   113
i. 2   86, 120

De Exhortatione Castitatis
1   139
2   113
5   124 (*bis*)
8   86

De Monogamia
3   114
6   92
7   92
10   107
16   114

De Pudicitia
2   142
9   89
17   124
21   94, 147

INDEX LOCORUM

De Ieiunio
6	142
13	131

De Virginibus Velandis
6	171
15	92

De Pallio
2	177

De Praescriptione Haereticorum
	ix
6	114, 122
7	xxvi, 105
21	92
30	xxv, xxxi, 87, 93, 94, 95, 114, 182
32	93, 95
33	93
34	xxvi, 122
38	94

Adversus Marcionem
	ix
i	91
i. 1	xxv, 94, 95, 97
i. 2	xxvi
i. 3	xxxix, xli, 87, 99
i. 4	100
i. 6	xxvi, 87, 99, 131
i. 7	xli, 138
i. 11	98, 102
i. 14	104
i. 15	xxxix, 91
i. 16	95
i. 19	xxviii, xxix, 90, 91
i. 21	93, 94
i. 22	xxxvii
i. 24	xli
i. 29	xxix, 86, 105
ii. 1	84, 102
ii. 4	115
ii. 5	xl, xlii
ii. 6	xxxvii, xxxix, 124
ii. 9	xlii (*bis*), 85, 93, 113
ii. 11	115, 117, 159
ii. 19	142
ii. 22	xl
ii. 23	148
ii. 27	102
ii. 29	98
iii. 6	xxxix (*bis*)
iii. 7	126, 147, 149
iii. 8	88, 110
iii. 9	101, 112 *sq.*, 115
iii. 11	xxxi, 104 (*bis*), 114
iii. 13	124, 173
iii. 17	126, 149
iii. 19	142
iv. 1	174
iv. 4	94, 95
iv. 6	131
iv. 7	89, 91 (*bis*), 169
iv. 10	154, 174
iv. 15	83
iv. 19	xl, 117 (*bis*), 118 *sq.*, 120
iv. 20	104
iv. 21	89, 149
iv. 26	117, 121
iv. 32	122
iv. 40–42	107
v. 2	94
v. 4	xxx, 176
v. 5	105
v. 6	90
v. 8	174
v. 10	123
v. 14	150, 152
v. 20	84, 89, 141, 147, 148

Adversus Hermogenem

	ix, xxi
19	93
22	177
43	xxxv
45	131

Adversus Valentinianos

	ix, 88
2	120
14	122
16	113
17	107
25	146, 165
26	128
27	107, 128

De Carne Christi

	xxi
1	xxix, xxxi, 146
2	xxv
3	viii, 133, 145
4	83
5	xxvii
6	84
7	ix, 152
8	xxxii
14	139
15	viii, 151
17	83, 141

De Resurrectione Carnis

	vii, xi, xxi
4	84, 85
5	122
12	131
17	135, 148
18	131
22	111
36	114
40	135
46	151
47	142
49	123

De Anima

3	93
9	xiii, 130
14	105
18	172
23	xxxii, 122
24	141
33	83
38	135 (bis), 136
45	177
58	129

Adversus Praxean

	viii, 177
2	115
3	175
7	116, 124
8	125
11	110, 124
13	98, 111
14	113
26	167
26, 27	143, 169
27	viii, 99, 109, 124, 162, 176
30	99, 119
31	146

Adversus Iudaeos

3	166
9	174 (bis)
14	126, 147

Appuleius
Metamorphoses

ix. 4	129
ix. 25	136

Athenagoras
Supplicatio

9	125

De Resurrectione

	xxi

Cicero
De Partibus Orationis

3. 10	182

INDEX LOCORUM 191

Cicero (cont.)
  De Inventione
    i. 4. 19   x
    i. 15. 20   xi
    i. 31. 143   x
    ii. 19. 79   x
  Topica
    97   x
  De Oratore
    ii. 19. 77 *sqq.*   x
  Pro Flacco
    32. 78   93
  De Lege Agraria
    ii. 17. 46   109
    iii. 2. 5   109
    iii. 2. 8   109
  Pro Milone
    21. 57   84
  Pro Murena
    8. 18   86
  Philippica
    ii. 17. 42   121
    x. 7. 15   110
    x. 9. 18   110
  Pro Roscio Comoedo
    4. 10   97
  De Natura Deorum
    i. 19. 49   103

Clemens Alexandrinus
  Stromata
    vii. 93, 94   179

Demosthenes
  Philippica
    i. 40   109

Diodorus Siculus
  Bibliotheca
    iv. 51   182

Epiphanius
  Haereses
    xxx. 30   179

Hippolytus
  Philosophumena
    vi   88
    vii. 38   87

Horatius
  Carmina
    iii. 29. 46   94

Irenaeus
  Adversus Haereses
         ix. 88
    i *praef.*   156
    i. 1. 7   122
    i. 1. 17   122
    iii. 11. 12   156
    iii. 17. 1   165
    iii. 17. 3   142
    iii. 18. 2   147
    iii. 20. 2   147, 164
    iii. 21. 2   151
    iii. 31. 1   155, 170
    iii. 31. 2   169
    iv. 14   113
    iv. 55. 2   147
    v. 1. 3   164
    v. 21   155

Iustinus Martyr
  Apologia
    i. 26   xxv
    i. 33   161
    i. 44   125
    i. 58   xxv
  Dialogus
    35   xxv
    63   164

Iuvenalis
  Satira
    vi. 1   83

Novatianus
  De Trinitate
    10   83, 91

Ovidius
  Metamorphoses
    i. 80 *sqq.*   125

Petronius Arbiter
  Satirae
    78   136
    128   181

Quintilianus
  Institutio Oratoria
    iv. 5. 15   96
    v. 6. 2   96
    xii. 3. 6   85

Stobaeus
  Eclogae
    i. *pag.* 730   103

Tacitus
  Annales
    i. 1   147
    vi. 51   97
    xvi. 1   89

  Historiae
    i. 26   89
    ii. 27   110
    ii. 39   110
    ii. 97   110

Tatianus
  Oratio ad Graecos
    40   125

Theophilus
  Ad Autolycum
    i. 14   125

Virgilius
  Ecloga
    x. 36   142

Pseudo-Iustinus
  Quaestiones, etc.
    133   155

INDEX VERBORUM LATINORUM

Secundum capitula et lineas huius editionis.

ex abundanti ii. 29; xxv. 6
accusare iv. 3
adaequare viii. 36; xvi. 18 (*v.l.*)
adamare iv. 22
adeo (=ideo) vii. 33; xvi. 9
admittere i. 16; viii. 10
adulterator xix. 3
aedificatorius xvii. 29
aemulatio iv. 44
aemulus xvii. 27
aeonum genealogiae xxiv. 9
aliqui (=aliquis) ix. 31
aliter ii. 24, 25; iv. 16; vi. 22
alteruter xiii. 4, 5
anceps defensio xxiii. 15
animalis x, xi *passim*; xii. 37; xiii. 31; xv. 15
apostolicus ii. 15
arbiter xii. 21; xxiv. 19
arbitrium iii. 1
arcanum semen xix. 6
argumentari vi. 12; vii. 26; xvi. 1
argumentatio vi. 21; xi. 1; xvii. 1; xxv. 5
argumentator xxiv. 17
auctoritas ii. 14
audientia vii. 67
avocator v. 62

de calcaria in carbonariam vi. 4
calor xix. 19
capitulum viii. 1; xix. 2
carnalis vii. 78; x. xi *passim*; xii. 37; xiii. 31; xvii. 37; xxii. 5
carneus iv. 42; v. 39; x, xi *passim*
causa vi. 28 *sqq.*; x. 4; xiv. 2 *sqq.*; xix. 33 *sq.*; xxi. 20; xxii. 5
censura iv. 33
census ii. 5; v. 38; viii. 21; xvi. 3; xvii. 26

circulatorius coetus v. 60
circumferre xiii. 33
circumvenire v. 57
coagulare iv. 17
coagulum iv. 5; xvi. 33; xix. 20 *sq.*
cogere vii. 25
cogitatus xiv. 19
commentator xxii. 4
commercium vii. 49
comminius (*adv.*) xxi. 4
commonefacere (*conj.*) xxv. 8
communicare xiii. 12
comparare viii. 30, 32
compendium iii. 4
competere iii. 24; vi. 40; vii. 33; viii. 8; xi. 31; xviii. 26, 28; xix. 5
concarnare xx. 31
conceptus (*subs.*) i. 21; ii. 2; xxi. 11, 13; xxiii. 7
concipere vi. 47
condesertor i. 18
condicio vi. 72; vii. 68; ix. 24; xi. 38
condiscipulus i. 18
conditio iii. 28; v. 41; xviii. 33; xxii. 32
configere xxiv. 25
confiteri i. 18
confundi v. 20 *sqq.*
confusio v. 22
congressio xvii. 4; xxv. 4
congruere xviii. 21
congruentius (*adv.*) xi. 31
conluctari iii. 37
conscientia iii. 11, 15, 16
consequens est xxii. 31
consonare xx. 8
constantius (*adv.*) iii. 13
constare vii. 35; viii. 20; xvii. 5
contendere vii. 1, 58
contradicibilis xxiii. 7

contristare ii. 11
contumelia iv. 43; v. 1
convenire xi. 1; xiv. 32
conversio iii. 24, 34; iv. 37
convertere iii. 21, 23 sqq.; vi. 62 sq.;
   ix. 9; xvi. 31
convertibilis iii. 25
corporalis i. 8
corporaliter xii. 34
corporare iii. 22; vi. 31
corporatio iv. 2
corpulentia iii. 39
credens (subs.) xviii. 28; xix. 5

decurrere iii. 5
dedicator xvii. 10
defectus (adj.) xv. 32
defendere xvii. 26
defensio viii. 4
definitive xviii. 23
deicere iv. 19
deliniare vii. 77
demutare vi. 64; ix. 4
deputare xi. 29; xiv. 23
desertor i. 17
desidēre iii. 48
despumatio xix. 20
destinare xv. 12
destruere i. 7; v. 18
deus inferior iii. 39
dimidiare v. 46
discentes (subs.) vi. 1
disceptator xxiv. 15
disciplina vi. 6
dispositio vi. 72; xii. 38; xviii. 12
dispungere v. 42
distrahere i. 4
diversitas iii. 30; vi. 43
divinitas vii. 36
dubitative xxiii. 32

effigies iii. 34; xii. 28
electus xix. 6
elementum iv. 4
eludere i. 23
emendicare ix. 19
energema xxiv. 12
erraticus viii. 11

ethnicus xv. 24 sqq.
evacuare xvi passim; xxi. 12
exaggeranter xix. 24
examinare i. 8
excīdere ii. 20
excludere xvii. 16
excutere vii. 62
exhibere ii. 14; iii. 18; iv. 24; v. 38;
   vi. 57; xi. 4; xii. 34
existimatio iii. 13 sq.
exitus iii. 34; xviii. 8
expedire xiv. 16
expiare xvii. 17
explicabilis xvi. 27
exstructorius xvii. 30
extare xv. 19

fascinare ii. 12
fatigare ii. 7
fiducia iii. 15
figere (=crucifigere) v. 25
figulare ix. 5
figura vii. 74; viii. 13; ix. 9
figurare xvii. 18
filia uteri caro xxi. 18
forma vi. 36; x. 16; xvi. 1
formalis xix. 15
fraternitas vii. 73, 78
frequentari vii. 49

genus vi. 51, 66; vii. 78; xiii. 13, 36;
   xvi. 8
gestare carnem v. 4, 48; vi. 50; viii.
   34; x. 14 sqq.
   animam xiii. 33
   angelum xiv. 1 sqq.
gestire xi. 34
gloriosus xiv. 34
grammaticus xx. 12

habere (=debere) vi. 34, 39
habitus (subs.) vi. 45
homo iii. 19; xvii. 26; xviii. 9 sqq.
honorare iv. 9

imaginarius v. 10; xv. 15
imago v. 51; xvi. 15
imbuere xix. 8

INDEX VERBORUM LATINORUM 195

impossibilis iii. 2 *sq.*; iv. 1; v. 26
imprecari xii. 25
impressius (*adv.*) xx. 14
inconveniens iii. 2
inconvertibilis iii. 23
incorporalis xi. 14, 21, 28
inculcare v. 15
incursus xvii. 24
inducere viii. 22; xi. 27
induere iii. 19, 42; iv. 32; xi. 38; xiv. 27; xvi. 3
indignius (*adj.*) v. 3
inferre v. 57; vii. 2, 25; xxii. 10
informare xv. 18
infringere vi. 71
ingenium vii. 39
ingerere v. 14
iniuria iii. 15
inquietare i. 2
insolescere iv. 6
instruere vi. 25
instrumentum vi. 20
intercipere iii. 52
interfector v. 11
interficere iii. 50
introducere i. 19
invehi iv. 8

licentia haeretica i. 15
licere iii. 1; vi. 18; vii. 34; xv. 1
linea xvii. 4
liquere xvii. 6
ludibria (*pl.*) iv. 18

manna vi. 70
materia vi. 13, 55 *sqq.*; vii. 6, 20, 43; viii. 23, 26; ix. 3; xvi. 12; xxv. 1
cum maxime vii. 55
medicare xix. 21
merito i. 3; ii. 17; iv. 21
meritum vii. 67
minorare xv. 29
ministrare xii. 16
miscere (hominem deo mixtum) xv. 34
morari i. 2
mortalitas vi. 36, 46
multiformis xxiv. 16

naevus xvi. 25
natura iii. 27; iv. 9, 12, 42; vi. 50, 58; xiv. 18; xvi. 12, 19, 22
naturalia (*pl.*) xii. 13
necessarius (*comp.*) vii. 55
noctibus (=noctu) ii. 6
notitia xi. 33; xii. 15
nudus homo xiv. 32

obducere xix. 3
oblatio (*v.l.* obligatio) ii. 10
obtinere iii. 31; vi. 26
opinio iii. 8, 45
ordo i. 22
originalia instrumenta ii. 12

par iii. 27, 32
paratura viii. 8
părēre, părĕre xvii. 35
passio v. 2, 8, 43 *sqq.*; ix. 29
peccatrix (*adj. fem.*) xvi *passim*
penes iv. 46
percutere vii. 61
perinde v. 44 *et saepius*
perseverare iii. 31, 42
persona vii. 30; xi. 27
phantasma i. 20; iii. 43; v. 9, 15, 51 *sq.*
possessio xiii. 11
praecedens erat vi. 38
praecinere vi. 10
praefortis v. 40
praeiudicare i. 6; vii. 2; xxv. 7
praeiudicium vi. 2
praelatio vii. 67
praenuntiare ii. 14
praescribere iv. 33; vi. 26
praescriptio ii. 28; xv. 13
praesentia vii. 38
in praesentia vii. 38
praeses mali viii. 6
praestare (*trans.*) iii. 6; iv. 25 *et saepius*
praestructio xxv. 9
praestruere i. 8
praesumere iii. 10; iv. 40; x. 11
praetendere viii. 5; ix. 1
praeter (=sine) v. 60

INDEX VERBORUM LATINORUM

privilegium xv. 1
procedere vi. 18, 29; vii. 24; x. 12
prodire xxii. 10
produx xx. 33
proferre iii. 53; iv. 17
pronuntiatio vii. 7
propheticus xxiii. 1
proprietas v. 41; ix. 4; xiii. 10; xxi. 32; xxiv. 4
provocare vii. 6
tam proximi vii. 52
pulsare xxiv. 9
putativus i. 19

quaerere i. 9
quaestio vii. 25, 28
quaestiones i. 4; xi. 34
qualitas i. 10; vi. 13, 67; ix. 8, 10; xii. 11; xiii. 10, 25; xvii. 7; xix. 34
quo (=quanto) iii. 13
quotidianus xiv. 37

ratio ii. 30; vii. 45; xi. 29; xii. 20; xiv. 1; xvi. 4; xvii. 9, 26; xviii. 12; xx. 47
rationalis xii. 17 sq.
recensere xxi. 33
receptissimus xx. 19
reformare iv. 27; xvii. 16
regeneratio iv. 28
regula vi. 20
religiosus iv. 9
reluminare iv. 29
renuntiatio i. 11
repercutere viii. 8
reprobare iii. 8
reputare iii. 15
rescindere ii *passim*; v. 8
resistere iii. 46
testimonium respondere i. 14
respuere vii. 1
retexere xii. 20
retractare i. 10; xxiii. 26
retro ii. 20 *et saepius*

saecularis iv. 44
saeculum v. 7
salutificator xiv. 13

satelles xiv. 11
scriptura vii. 15, 20; xviii. 18; xxi. 14
sementis xvii. 20
sensualis xii. 8 *sq.*
sensus iv. 35; v. 58; vii. 79; xii. 8 *sqq.*; xvi. 27; xvii. 7; xix. 25
sententialiter xviii. 23
sequens (=secundus) xvii. 22
sidereus vi. 68; xv. 15
simplex v. 56; xiii. 21; xviii. 1
simplicitas vii. 44; xxiii. 31
simpliciter xix. 31; xx. 15
singularis xiv. 12
singularitas xiii. 20
singulariter xix. 10
soliditas iii. 55; xiii. 20
solidus v. 49; vi. 7
sollicitare viii. 6
sortiri xii. 12, 17
species iii. 47; ix. 7; xi. 31; xiii. 30, 37; xx. 3
spiritalis i. 9; v. 39; vi. 50; xv. 2; xvii. 16; xix. 7, 35
spiritus [dei] v. 37, 42 *sqq.*; viii. 11, 28 *sqq.*; xiv. 29; xv. 20; xvii. 23; xviii, xix *passim*
spiritus [hominis] vi. 7
spiritus sanctus xxiii. 30
status iii. 20; xii. 21; xvii. 7
subducere iii. 54
subire xi. 2; xii. 29
substantia i. 8; iii. 50; v. 38; vi. 16, 50, 58, 66; viii. 7, 21, 27 *sqq.*; ix. 17; xiii. 20, 24, 36; xv. 4, 14, 30; xvi. 12; xvii. 6; xviii. 31 *sqq.*; xix. 17 *sqq.*
suffigere v. 5
suffundere v. 29
suggestus xvi. 8
suggillatio xxiv. 1
superficies xi. 28
suscitatio xxiii. 3
suspendere xx. 37
sustinere iii. 13, 17; vii. 54
syllogismus xvii. 1

tantum ii. 16
ad tempus vi. 52

torquere xvii. 2
tortuositas xx. 1
tradux ix. 12; xx. 30; xxii. 9
transfigurabilis vi. 52

uterus vi. 18; vii. 80; xx, xxi *saepius*
utique iii. 33

vacare v. 9; vii. 39; xvii. 24; xviii. 6; xxi. 10

vacua ludibria v. 10
veneratio iv. 12
veritas vi. 25; vii. 2; viii. 2; ix. 6
vinitor xiv. 22
virtutes v. 43
vivificare xvii. 23
volutare iv. 43; vii. 26
vulva xvii. 38; xix. 24 *sqq.*; xx *passim*; xxiii

www.ingramcontent.com/pod-product-compliance
Lightning Source LLC
Chambersburg PA
CBHW051639230426
43669CB00013B/2366